SLAVE NARRATIVES

A Folk History of Slavery in the United States.
From Interviews with Former Slaves

**UNITED STATES.
WORK PROJECTS ADMINISTRATION**

TYPEWRITTEN RECORDS PREPARED BY
THE FEDERAL WRITERS' PROJECT
1936-1938
ASSEMBLED BY
THE LIBRARY OF CONGRESS PROJECT
WORK PROJECTS ADMINISTRATION
FOR THE DISTRICT OF COLUMBIA
SPONSORED BY THE LIBRARY OF
CONGRESS

WASHINGTON 1941

VOLUME XIV
SOUTH CAROLINA NARRATIVES
PART 2

Prepared by
The Federal Writers' Project of
The Works Progress Administration
For the State of South Carolina

CONTENTS

Harriet Eddington 1
Mary Edwards 3
John B. Elliott 5
Emanuel Elmore 9
Ryer Emmanuel 15
Ryer Emmanuel 21
Ryer Emmanuel 25
Eubanks Pen 31
Lewis Evans 35
Phillip Evans 39
Phillip Evans 45
Caroline Farrow 47
Caroline Farrow 51
Gus Feaster 53
Gus Feaster 59
Gus Feaster 65
Ann Ferguson 83
Aaron Ford 85
Charlotte Foster 91
John Franklin 95
Emma Fraser 99
Adele Frost 101
Amos Gadsden 105

Janie Gallman	111
Lucy Gallman	115
Simon Gallman	119
Simon Gallman	121
Laurence Gary	125
Louisa Gause	127
Gracie Gibson	133
Charlie Giles	137
Willis Gillison	141
Brawley Gilmore	145
Pick Gladdeny	149
Henry Gladney	153
Emoline Glasgow	159
Silas Glenn	163
John Glover	167
Hector Godbold	173
Daniel Goddard	179
Ellen Godfrey	185
Ellen Godfrey	191
Ellen Godfrey	193
Ellen Godfrey	197
Thomas Goodwater	199
Charlie Grant	205
Grant Rebeccajane	211
Rebecca Janegrant	217
John Graves	221
Sim Greeley	225

Elijah Green	231
W. M. Green	237
Adeline Grey	241
Fannie Griffin	247
Madison Griffin	251
Peggy Grigsby	255
Violet Guntharpe	257
John Hamilton	263
Susan Hamlin	265
Susan Hamlin	269
Susan Hamilton	275
Anson Harp	281
Thomas Harper	285
Abe Harris	289
Eli Harrison	293
Charlie Jeffharvey	297
Eliza Hasty	303
Dolly Haynes	311
Liney Henderson	313
Jim Henry	317
Zack Herndon	323
Lavinia Heyward	329
Lucretia Heyward	333
Mariah Heywood	337
Jerry Hill	343
Jane Hollins	347
Cornelius Holmes	351

Uncle Ben Horry	357
Uncle Ben Horry	367
Ben Horry	377
Uncle Ben Horry	385
Margaret Hughes	389
Hester Hunter	393
Mom Hester Hunter	397
Hester Hunter	403

Project 1885-1
FOLKLORE
Spartanburg Dist. 4
May 25, 1937

Edited by:
Elmer Turnage

HARRIET EDDINGTON

"I was born in the town of Newberry, and was a servant of Major John P. Kinard. I married Sam Eddington. I was a Baker, daughter of Mike and Patience Baker. My mother was a free woman. She had her freedom before the war started; so I was not a slave. I worked on the farm with my mother when she moved back from town. Mama worked in town at hotels; then went back to the country and died. In war time and slavery time, we didn't go to school, 'cause there was no schools for the negroes. After the war was over and everything was settled, negro schools was started. We had a church after the war. I used to go to the white folks' Lutheran church and set in the gallery. On Saturday afternoons we was off, and could do anything we wanted to do, but some of the negroes had to work on Saturdays. In the country, my mother would card, spin, and weave, and I learned it. I could do lots of it."

Source: Harriet Eddington (86), Newberry, S.C.
Interviewer: G.L. Summer, Newberry, S.C. May 20, 1937.

United States. Work Projects Administration

Project 1885-1
FOLKLORE
Spartanburg Dist. 4
June 16, 1937

Edited by:
Elmer Turnage

MARY EDWARDS

"I was born in the section of Greenwood County called 'the promised land'. My parents were Henry and Julis Watkins. I married Frank Edwards when I was young. Our master, Marshall Jordon, was not so mean. He had lots o' slaves and he give 'em good quarters and plenty to eat. He had big gardens, lots of hogs and cattle and a big farm. My master had two children.

"Sometimes dey hunted rabbits, squirrels, possums and doves.

"De master had two overseers, but we never worked at night. We made our own clothes which we done sometimes late in evening.

"We had no school, and didn't learn to read and write, not 'till freedom come when a school started there by a Yankee named Backinstore. Later, our church and Sunday school was in de yard.

"We had cotton pickings, cornshuckings and big suppers. We didn't have to work on Christmas.

"One of de old-time cures was boiling fever-grass and drinking de tea. Pokeberry salad was cooked, too. A cure for rheumatism was to carry a raw potato in the pocket until it dried up.

"I had 11 children and 8 grandchildren.

"I think Abe Lincoln was a great man. Don't know much about Jeff Davis. Booker Washington is all right.

"I joined church in Flordia, the Methodist church. I was 50 years old. I joined because they had meetings and my daughter had already joined. I think all ought to join de church."

Source: Mary Edwards (79), Greenwood, S.C.
Interviewed by: G.L. Summer, Newberry, S.C. (6/10/37)

Project #1655
Stiles M. Scruggs
Columbia, S.C.

A SON OF SLAVES CLIMBS UP.

JOHN B. ELLIOTT

The Rev. John B. Elliott, A.B.A. A.M., D.D., 1315 Liberty Hill Avenue, Columbia, S.C., is the son of slaves. He was born at Mount Olive, N.C., in 1869, and missed being a slave by only four years. His college degrees were won at Shaw University, Raleigh, N.C., and the degree of Doctor of Divinity was conferred on him by Allen University of Columbia, S.C.

Sitting on the parsonage piazza recently, the Rector of St. Anna's Episcopal Church talked about his struggle for education, and his labors up from slavery.

"I was born at Mount Olive, N.C., the son of Soloman Elliott and Alice (Roberts) Elliott. They were slaves when they married, and I escaped bondage by only four years, since slaves were not freed in the South, until 1865.

"My father was owned by Robert W. Williams, of Mount Olive, and he was the most highly prized Negro in the vicinity. He was a natural carpenter and builder. Often he would go to the woods and pick out trees for the job in hand. Some of the houses he built there are standing today. Mother was equally trained and well equipped to make a home and keep it neat and clean. When they were free in 1865, half the community was eager to employ them and pay them well for their services. And, when I came along, they were living in their own house and prospering.

"I chose a religious career when quite a boy, and, when I was ready for college, I was much pleased. I finished at Shaw University at Raleigh, took a year's study at Columbia University in New York and then finished a religious course at the Bishop Payne Divinity School at Petersburg, Virginia, where most of the colored clergymen of the Episcopal Church are finished. After I felt that I was fairly well fitted to begin my clerical work, I chose South Carolina as my field.

"My first assignment was at Waccamaw Neck, a little below Georgetown, S.C., and a big industrial center. There the Negro population is keen for wine and whiskey. One of the men whom I was interested in, was pretty tipsy when I called, and, as I sat and talked with him, he said: 'You're drunk, too.' This surprised me, and I asked him why he thought so. 'Well, you got your vest and collar on backwards, so you must be drunk!'

"Since, I have had pastorates at Aiken, Peak, Rock Hill, and Walterboro. From Walterboro I came to Columbia as pastor of St. Anna's Episcopal Church and the missions of Ann's at New Brookland and St. Thomas at Eastover. I presume I have done pretty well in this field, since the Rt. Rev. Bishop Kirkman G. Finlay, D.D., appointed me arch-deacon for Negro work in upper South Carolina.

"As I was coming away from the Bishop's office, I was accompanied by another colored rector, who had very short legs. I am six feet, four inches in height, and he looked up at me as we walked along and asked quizzically: 'How long should a man's legs be?' I smiled and told him I thought, perhaps, every man should have legs long enough to reach to the ground. Yes, of course, we laughed at each other, but my argument won, because Bishop Finlay is about six feet, three inches, and I told my short friend: 'When Bishop Finlay and I talk, we are able to look each other in the eye on the level.'

"I married Susan McMahan, a colored school teacher, and the Lord has blessed us with a son, John B. Jr., a fine wood-worker, like his grandfather was, and two sweet daughters. Alice, the older one, is a teacher in the public schools of Columbia and Annie is a student. Our home life has always been pleasant and unusually sunny.

"I had one very humorous experience three years ago when I was invited to deliver an address near Mount Olive, N.C., to a convention of young people. Arriving about 10 o'clock that day, I was met by a citizen who told me he was assigned to introduce me that evening. As we rode along, I cautioned him not to boost me too highly. He said little.

"When the big, and, I may say, expectant audience was seated that night, he arose and seemed much embarrassed, ultimately saying: 'Ladies and gentlemen, I have an unpleasant duty to perform this evening.' Then, pointing at me, he went on: 'I don't know this man, much. Fact is, I only know two things about him. One is, he has never been in jail; and the other is, I never could figure why.'

"No, I am not related to the late Robert Bruce Elliott

by ties of consanguinity. He was successively twice a member of Congress from South Carolina, and a member and Speaker of the South Carolina House of Representatives in 1876. Perhaps these honors came to him because he had a good education before he met the opportunity for service.

"When I think of the '60's-'70's period, I am surprised that recent slaves, suddenly placed in administrative positions of honor and trust, did as well as they did.

"In the seventy-two years since slavery, I have noted much improvement along the road, and I am sure that our nation has far less discord now, than it had when I was a small lad. And, when one can note progress in our march toward the light, I guess that ought to be sufficient for my optimism."

Project 1885-1
Folklore
Spartanburg, Dist. 4
Dec. 23, 1937

Edited by:
Elmer Turnage

EX-SLAVE STORIES

EMANUEL ELMORE

"I was born on June 20th and I remember when the war broke out, for I was about five years old. We lived in Spartanburg County not far from old Cherokee ford. My father was Emanuel Elmore, and he lived to be about 90 years old.

"My marster was called by everybody, Col. Elmore, and that is all that I can remember about his name. When he went to the war I wanted to go with him, but I was too little. He joined the Spartanburg Sharp Shooters. They had a drill ground near the Falls. My pa took me to see them drill, and they were calling him Col. Elmore then. When I got home I tried to do like him and everybody laughed at me. That is about all that I remember about the war. In those days, children did not know things like thay do now, and grown folks did not know as much either.

"I used to go and watch my father work. He was a moulder in the Cherokee Iron Works, way back there when everything was done by hand. He moulded everything from knives and forks to skillets and wash pots. If you could have seen pa's hammer, you would have seen something worth looking at. It was so big that it jarred the whole earth when it struck a lick. Of course it was a forge hammer, driven by water power. They called the hammer 'Big Henry'. The butt end was as big as an ordinary telephone pole.

"The water wheel had fifteen or twenty spokes in it, but when it was running it looked like it was solid. I used to like to sit and watch that old wheel. The water ran over it and the more water came over, the more power the wheel gave out.

"At the Iron Works they made everything by hand that was used in a hardware store, like nails, horse shoes and rims for all kinds of wheels, like wagon and buggy wheels. There were moulds for everything no matter how large or small the thing to be made was. Pa could almost pick up the right mould in the dark, he was so used to doing it. The patterns for the pots and kettles of different sizes were all in rows, each row being a different size. In my mind I can still see them.

"Hot molten iron from the vats was dipped with spoons which were handled by two men. Both spoons had long handles, with a man at each handle. The spoons would hold from four to five gallons of hot iron that poured just like water does. As quick as the men poured the hot iron in the mould, another man came along behind them and closed the mould. The large moulds had doors and the small moulds had lids. They had small pans and small spoons for little things, like nails, knives and forks, When the mould had set until cold, the piece was prized out.

"Pa had a turn for making covered skillets and fire dogs. He made them so pretty that white ladies would come and give an order for a 'pair of dogs', and tell him how they wanted them to look. He would take his hammer and beat them to look just that way.

"Rollers pressed out the hot iron for machines and for special lengths and things that had to be flat. Railroad ties were pressed out in these rollers. Once the man that handled the hot iron to be pressed through these rollers got fastened in them himself. He was a big man. The blood flew out of him as his bones were crushed, and he was rolled into a mass about the thickness and width of my hand. Each roller weighed about 2,000 pounds.

"The man who got killed was named Alex Golightly. He taught the boys my age how to swim, fish and hunt. His death was the worst thing that had happened in the community. The man who worked at the foundry, made Alex a coffin. It had to be made long and thin because he was mashed up so bad. In those days coffins were nothing but boxes anyway, but Alex's coffin was the most terrible thing that I have ever seen. I reckon if they had had pretty coffins then like they do now, folks would have bought them to sleep in.

"Hundreds went to Alex's funeral, white and black, to see that long narrow coffin and the grave which was dug to fit it. On the way to the graveyard, negroes sang songs, for Alex was a good man. They carried him to the Cherokee graveyard on the old Smith Ford Road, and there they buried him. My father helped to build the coffin and he helped haul him to the graveyard. Pa worked at the Iron Foundry until he was very old. He worked there before I was ever born.

"My father was sold four times during slavery. When he was brought to Virginia he was put on the block and auctioned off for $4,000. He said that the last time he was sold he only brought $1,500. He was born in Alabama. When he was bought he was carried from Alabama to Virginia. It was Col. Elmore who took him. He wanted to go to Alabama again, so Col. Elmore let a speculator take him back and sell him. He stayed there for several years and got homesick for South Carolina. He couldn't get his marster to sell him back here, so he just refugeed back to Col. Elmore's plantation. Col. Elmore took him back and wouldn't let anybody have him.

"Pa married twice, about the same time. He married Dorcas Cooper, who belonged to the Coopers at Staunton Military Academy. I was the first child born in Camden. She had sixteen children. I was brought to Spartanburg County when I was little. Both ma and pa were sold together in Alabama. The first time pa came to South Carolina he married a girl called Jenny. She never had any children. When he went to Alabama, Dorcas went with him, but Jenny stayed with Col. Elmore. Of course, pa just jumped the broom for both of them.

"When pa left Alabama to refugee back, he had to leave Dorcas. They did not love their marster anyway. He put Dorcas up on the block with a red handkerchief around her head and gave her a red apple to eat. She was sold to a man whose name I have forgotten. When they herded them she got away and was months making her way back to South Carolina. Those Africans sure were strong. She said that she stayed in the woods at night. Negroes along the way would give her bread and she would kill rabbits and squirrels and cook and eat in the woods. She would get drunk and beat any one that tried to stop her from coming back. When she did get back to Col. Elmore's place, she was lanky, ragged and poor, but Col. Elmore was glad to see her and told her he was not going to let anybody take her off. Jenny had cared so well for her children while she was off, that she liked her. They lived in the same house with pa till my mother died.

"Col. Elmore said that negroes who were from Virginia and had African blood could stand anything. He was kind to ma. He fed her extra and she soon got fat again. She worked hard for Col. Elmore, and she and pa sure did love him. One time a lot of the negroes in the quarter got drunk and ma got to fighting all of them. When she got sobered up she was afraid that Col Elmore was going to send her back to Alabama; so she went and hid in the woods. Pa took food to her. In about a month Col. Elmore asked where she was, and pa just looked sheepish and grinned. Col. Elmore told pa to go and bring her back, for he said he was tired of having his rations carried to the woods; so ma came home. She had stayed off three months. She never felt well anymore, and she died in about three more months. Pa and Jenny kept us till we got big and went off to ourselves.

"Jenny was born and raised in South Carolina, and she was good to everybody and never fought and went on like ma did. Ma liked her and would not let anybody say anything against her. She was good to pa till he died, a real old man. Jenny never had any children. She was not old when she died, but just a settled woman. We felt worse over her death than we did over ma's, because she was so good to us and had cared for us while ma and pa were in Alabama; then she was good to us after Dorcas died and when she hid in the woods.

"It seems that folks are too tender now. They can't stand much. My ma could stand more than I can. My children can't stand what I can right now."

Source: Emanuel Elmore (77). Sycamore St., Gaffney, S.C.
Interviewer: Caldwell Sims, Union, S.C. 11/16/37

Code No.
Project, 1885-(1)
Prepared by Annie Ruth Davis
Place, Marion, S.C.
Date, December 16, 1937

MOM RYER EMMANUEL
Ex-Slave, Age 78

RYER EMMANUEL

"Oh, my Lord, child, I ain' know nothin bout slavery time no more den we was just little kids livin dere on de white people plantation. I was just a little yearlin child den, I say. Been bout six years old in slavery time. Well, I'll say dat I bout 80 some odds, but I can' never seem to get dem odds together. I was a big little girl stayin in old Massa yard in dem days, but I wasn' big enough to do nothin in de house no time. My old Massa been Anthony Ross en he had set my age down in de Bible, but my old Missus, she dead en I know dem chillun wouldn' never know whe' to say dat Bible at dese days. Old Miss, she been name Matt Ross. I wish somebody could call up how long de slaves been freed cause den dey could call up my age fast as I could bat my eyes. Say, when de emancipation was, I been six years old, so my mammy tell me. Don' know what to say dat is, but I reckon it been since freedom."

"I been born en bred right over yonder to dat big patch of oak trees bout dat house what you see after you pass de white people church cross de creek dere. De old man Anthony Ross, he been have a good mind to his colored people all de time. Yes, mam, my white folks was proud of dey niggers. Um, yes'um, when dey used to have company to de big house, Miss Ross would bring dem to de door to show dem us chillun. En my blessed, de yard would be black wid us chillun all string up dere next de door step lookin up in dey eyes. Old Missus would say, 'Ain' I got a pretty crop of little niggers comin on?' De lady, she look so please like. Den Miss Ross say, 'Do my little niggers want some bread to gnaw on?' En us chillun say, 'Yes'um, yes'um, we do.' Den she would go in de pantry en see could she find some cook bread to hand us. She had a heap of fine little niggers, too, cause de yard would be black wid all different sizes. Won' none of dem big enough to do nothin. No, mam, dey had to be over 16 year old fore old Massa would allow dem to work cause he never want to see his niggers noways stunt up while dey was havin de growin pains. Den when dey was first grow up, dey would give some of dem a house job en would send de others in de field to mind de cows en de sheep en bring dem up. Wouldn' make dem do no heavy work right to start wid. But dem what was older, dey had to work in de field. I reckon dey would be workin just bout like dey is now from sunrise in de mornin till sunset in de evenin."

"Yes, honey, I been come here under a blessin cause my white folks never didn' let dey colored people suffer no time. Always when a woman would get in de house, old Massa would let her leave off work en stay dere to de house a month till she get mended in de body way. Den she would have to carry de child to de big house en get back in de field to work. Oh, dey had a old woman in de yard to de house to stay dere en mind all de plantation chillun till night come, while dey parents was workin.

Dey would let de chillun go home wid dey mammy to spend de night en den she would have to march dem right back to de yard de next mornin. We didn' do nothin, but play bout de yard dere en eat what de woman feed us. Yes'um, dey would carry us dere when de women would be gwine to work. Be dere fore sunrise. Would give us three meals a day cause de old woman always give us supper fore us mammy come out de field dat evenin. Dem bigger ones, dey would give dem clabber en boil peas en collards sometimes. Would give de little babies boil pea soup en gruel en suck bottle. Yes, mam, de old woman had to mind all de yearlin chillun en de babies, too. Dat all her business was. I recollects her name, it been Lettie. Would string us little wooden bowls on de floor in a long row en us would get down dere en drink just like us was pigs. Oh, she would give us a iron spoon to taste wid, but us wouldn' never want it. Oh, my Lord, I remember just as good, when we would see dem bowls of hot ration, dis one en dat one would holler, 'dat mine, dat mine.' Us would just squat dere en blow en blow cause we wouldn' have no mind to drink it while it was hot. Den we would want it to last a long time, too. My happy, I can see myself settin dere now coolin dem vitals (victuals)."

"Like I speak to you, my white folks was blessed wid a heap of black chillun, but den dere been a odd one in de crowd what wasn' noways like dem others. All de other chillun was black skin wid dis here kinky hair en she was yellow skin wid right straight hair. My Lord, old Missus been mighty proud of her black chillun, but she sho been touches bout dat yellow one. I remember, all us chillun was playin round bout de step one day whe' Miss Ross was settin en she ax dat yellow child, say, 'Who your papa?' De child never know no better en she tell her right out exactly de one her mammy had tell her was her papa. Lord, Miss Ross, she say, 'Well, get off my step. Get off en stay off dere cause you don' noways belong to me.' De poor child, she cry en she cry so hard till her mammy never know what to do. She take en grease her en black her all over wid smut, but she couldn' never trouble dat straight hair off her noway. Dat how-come dere so much different classes today, I say. Yes, mam, dat whe' dat old stain come from."

"My mammy, she was de housewoman to de big house en she say dat she would always try to mind her business en she never didn' get no whippin much. Yes, mam, dey was mighty good to my mother, but dem other what never do right, dey would carry dem to de cow pen en make dem strip off dey frock bodies clean to de waist. Den dey would tie dem down to a log en paddle dem wid a board. When dey would whip de men, de boards would often times have nails in dem. Hear talk dey would wash dem wid dey blood. Dat first hide dey had, white folks would whip it off dem en den turn round en grease dem wid tallow en make dem work right on. Always would inflict de punishment at sunrise in de mornin fore dey would go to work. Den de women, dey would force dem to drop dey body frock cross de shoulders so dey could get to de naked skin en would have a strap to whip dem wid. Wouldn' never use no board on de women. Oh, dey would have de lot scatter bout full of dem what was to get whip on a mornin."

"You see, de colored people couldn' never go nowhe' off de place widout dey would get a walkin ticket from dey Massa. Yes, mam, white folks would have dese pataroller walkin round all bout de country to catch dem colored people dat never had no walkin paper to show dem. En if dey would catch any of dem widout dat paper, dey back would sho catch scissors de next mornin."

"Well, I don' know as de white folks would be meanin to kill any of dey niggers, but I hear talk dey would whip dem till dey would die some of de time en would bury dem in de night. Couldn' bury dem in de day cause dey wouldn' have time. When dey would be gwine to bury dem, I used to see de lights many a time en hear de people gwine along singin out yonder in dem woods just like dey was buryin buzzards. Us would set down en watch dem gwine along many a night wid dese great big torches of fire. Oh, dey would have fat lightwood torches. Dese here big hand splinters. Had to carry dem along to see how to walk en drive de wagon to haul de body. Yes, child, I been here long enough to see all dat in slavery time. All bout in dese woods, you can find plenty of dem slavery graves dis day en time. I can tell bout whe' dere one now. Yes, mam, dere one right over yonder to de brow of de hill gwine next to Mr. Claussens. Can tell dem by de head boards dere. Den some of de time, dey would just drop dem anywhe' in a hole along side de woods somewhe' cause de people dig up a skull right out dere in de woods one day en it had slavery mark on it, dey say. Right over dere cross de creek in dem big cedars, dere another slavery graveyard. People gwine by dere could often hear talk en couldn' never see nothin, so dey tell me. Hear, um—um—um, en would hear babies cryin all bout dere, too. No'um, can' hear dem much now cause dey bout to be wearin out. I tell you, I is scared every time I go along dere. Some of dem die wicked, I say."

United States. Work Projects Administration

Source: Ryer Emmanuel, colored, age 78, Claussens, S.C. Personal interview by Annie Ruth Davis, Dec., 1937.

Slave Narratives

Project 1885-(1)
Prepared by Annie Ruth Davis
Place, Marion, S.C.
Date, December 26, 1937

MOM RYER EMMANUEL
Ex-Slave, Age 78

RYER EMMANUEL

"Well, how you feelin dis mornin, honey? I had tell Miss Sue dat I would be keepin a eye out dat door dere en when I is see a car stop up to de house, I would try en make it up dere dis mornin. Yes, mam, Miss Sue tell me you was comin today en I promise her I would be up dere, but I ain' been feelin so much to speak bout dis mornin. Den you see, I know I gwine be obliged to run down to de woods en fetch me up some wood en kindlin fore night fall. I been 'spect to make Koota break me up some splinters, but he ain' no count worth nothin. Yes, mam, he my grandson. Cose I tries to knock bout somewhe' en let me get out in de cotton patch, I can put in a good sturdy job any day. You see, my eyes does be pretty good cause dey got on dey second glove, I say. Can see good to my age. But oh, my Lord, right in my chest here, it does thump sometimes just like a drum beatin in dere en I can' never stand to hurry en walk hard no more dese days."

"No, mam, it don' bother me noways to leave dat door open. I keeps it dat way bout all de time, so as I can look out en see what gwine along de road dere. What de matter, honey, you don' loves to smell dem chitlin I got boilin dere on de stove? I hear some people say dey can' stand no chitlin scent nowhe' bout dem, but I loves dem so much dat it does make my mouth run water to think bout how me en Koota gwine enjoy dem dis evenin. No, mam, us don' never eat us heavy meal till dat sun start gwine down behind dem trees cross de creek yonder. You see, I does keep some 'tatoes roastin dere in de coals on de hearth en if us belly sets up a growlin twixt meals, us just rakes a 'tatoe out de ashes en breaks it open en makes out on dat. My God, child, I think bout how I been bless dat I ain' never been noways scornful bout eatin chitlins. Yes, mam, when I helps up dere to de house wid hog killin, Mr. Moses, he does always say for me to carry de chitlin home to make me en Koota a nice pot of stew."

"I tellin you, when us been chillun comin up, people sho never live like dey do dis day en time. Oh, I can remember just as good when I used to go dat Hopewell Presbyterian Church cross de creek dere. Yes, mam, dat been de white people slavery church en dat dey slavery graveyard what settin right dere in front de church, too. Dat sho a old, old slavery time church, I say. Massa Anthony Ross would make us go dere to preachin every Sunday en dey was mighty strict bout us gwine to prayer service, too. Us would go up dem steps in dat little room, what been open out on de front piazza to de church, en set up in de gallery overhead en de white folks let down dere below us. Yes, mam, dat whe' de colored people went to church in dem days en some of dem go dere till dey die cause dat whe' dey been join de church. Some of dem does go dere often times dese days, too, when de white people axes dem to sing to dey church. I remember, when I been baptize dere, I was just a little small child.

Oh, de white preacher baptized all us little niggers dere. Old Massa, he tell all his hands to carry dey chillun up dere en get dem baptized. Oh, my happy, dey been fix us up dat day. Put on us clean homespuns en long drawers, dat been hang down round us ankles like boots, en all us get a new bonnet dat day. I recollects, dey would march us right up to de front of de church en de preacher would come down to whe' we was standin wid a basin of water in one hand en a towel in de other hand. He would take one of us chillun en lay he wet hand on dey head en say, 'I baptize dee in de name of, etc.' Den dat one would have to get back en another one would step up for dey turn. De preacher, he would have a big towel to wipe his hands wid en every child's mammy would be standin right behind hind dem wid a rag to wipe de (drain) dren water out dey eyes."

"Oh, my Lord, when de Yankees come through dere, I hear dem say it was de Republicans. Mr. Ross had done say dat he hear talk dat dey was comin through en he tell his niggers to hurry en hide all de plantation rations. Yes, mam, dey dig cellars under de colored people houses en bury what meat en barrels of flour dey could en dat what dey couldn' get under dere, dey hide it up in de loft. Mr. Ross say, 'Won' none of dem damn Yankees get no chance to stick dey rotten tooth in my rations.' We say, 'Ma, you got all dese rations here en we hungry.' She say, 'No, dem ration belong to boss en you chillun better never bother dem neither.' Den when Mr. Ross had see to it dat dey had fix everything safe, he take to de swamp. Dat what my mammy say cause he know dey wasn' gwine bother de womens. Lord, when dem Yankees ride up to de big house, Miss Ross been scared to open her mouth cause de man was in de swamp. No, child, dey didn' bother nothin much, but some of de rations dey get hold of. Often times, dey would come through en kill chickens en butcher a cow up en cook it right dere. Would eat all dey wanted en den when dey would go to leave, dey been call all de little plantation niggers to come dere en would give dem what was left. Oh, Lord, us was glad to get dem vitals, too. Yes, mam, all dey had left, dey would give it to de poor colored people. Us been so glad, us say dat us wish dey would come back again. Den after dey had left us plantation, dey would go some other place where dere was another crowd of little niggers en would left dem a pile of stuff, too. Old Massa, he been stay in de swamp till he hear dem Yankees been leave dere en den he come home en would keep sendin to de colored people houses to get a little bit of his rations to a time. Uncle Solomon en Sipp en Leve, dey been eat much of boss' rations dey wanted cause dey been know de Yankees was comin back through to free dem. But my mammy, she was a widow woman en old man Anthony Ross never left nothin to her house."

"I tell you, honey, some of de colored people sho been speak praise to dem Yankees. I don' know how-come, but dey never know no better, I say. Dey know en dey never know. One old man been ridin one of dese stick horses en he been so glad, he say, 'Thank God! Thank God!'"

Source: Ryer Emmanuel colored, age 78, Claussens, S.C. Personal interview by Annie Ruth Davis, Marion, S.C. December, 1937.

Code No.
Project, 1885-(1)
Prepared by Annie Ruth Davis
Place, Marion, S.C.
Date, January 7, 1938

MOM RYER EMMANUEL
Ex-Slave, 78 Years

RYER EMMANUEL

"Good evenin, child. How you is? How Miss Sue gettin along over dere to Marion? I hope she satisfied, but dere ain' nowhe' can come up to restin in your own home, I say. No, Lord, people own home don' never stop to cuss dem no time. Dere Koota's mamma all de time does say, 'Ma, ain' no need in you en Booker stayin over dere by yourself. Come en live wid us.' I say, 'No, child. Father may have, sister may have, brother may have, en chillun may have, but blessed be he dat have he own.' I tell all my chillun I rather stay here under my own roof cause when I takes a notion, I can go in en bake me a little hoecake en draw me a pot of coffee en set down to eat it in satisfaction."

"After you was gone de other day, I thought bout right smart to speak to you, but when I gets tired, I just get all fray up somehow. My sister, she come to see me Sunday en I had dem all laughin bout what I say dat I had tell you. My sister, she make out like she don' know nothin bout dem olden times. Her husband, he done gone en die en she out lookin round for another one. Reckon dat what ails her. I tell her, I ain' see none nowhe' dat I would be pleased to take in. But I don' care what she say, us sho been here in slavery time cause my mother didn' have but one free born child en dat one come here a corpse."

"I remember, Ma used to tell we chillun bout how dey couldn' never do nothin in slavery time, but what de white folks say dey could do. I say, 'If I been big enough in dem days, I would sho a let out a fight for you.' You see, I was a little small child den en I never know no better den to speak dat way."

"My mother, she was de house woman to de big house in slavery time, but she never didn' get no money for what she been do. No, mam, white folks never didn' pay de poor colored people no money in dat day en time. See, old boss would give dem everything dey had en provide a plenty somethin to eat for dem all de time. Yes'um, all de niggers used to wear dem old Dutch shoes wid de brass in de toes en de women, dey never didn' have nothin 'cept dem old coarse shoes widout no linin. Couldn' never wear dem out. Yes'um, dey always give us a changin of homespuns, so as to strip on wash day en put on a fresh one."

"Den I recollects we chillun used to ax us mammy whe' us come from en she say, 'I got you out de hollow log.' Well, just like I tell you, slavery chillun had dey daddy somewhe' on de plantation. Cose dey had a daddy, but dey didn' have no daddy stayin in de house wid dem. White folks would make you take dat man whe' if you want him or no. Us chillun never didn' know who us daddy been till us mammy point him out cause all us went in Massa Anthony Ross' name. Yes, mam, all us had a different daddy, so my mammy say."

"Who dat come here wid you? Lord, dat don' look like no wife. How long you is been married, honey? You ain' say so. Look like you is just bloomin, I say."

"Oh, I tell you, I see a heap of things in dem days, but I ain' got my studyin cap on right now en I can' call up nothin right sharp. Us never know nothin bout us was gwine get free in dat day en time. Us was same as brutes en cows back dere cause us been force to go by what white man say all de time. Oh, dey would beat de colored people so worser till dey would run away en stay in de swamp to save dey hide. But Lord a mercy, it never do no good to run cause time dey been find you was gone, dey been set de nigger dog on you. Yes, mam, dey had some of dese high dogs dat dey call hounds en dey could sho find you out, too. Oh, dem hounds would sho get you. Don' care whe' you was hidin, dem dogs would smell you. If you been climb up a tree, de dog would trail you right to de foot of dat tree en just stand up en howl at you. Dey would stand right dere en hold you up de tree till some of de white folks been get dere en tell you to come down out de tree. Den if you never do like dey say, dey would chop de tree down en let you fall right in de dog's mouth. Would let de dog bite you en taste your blood, so dey could find de one dey was lookin for better de next time. Yes, mam, white people would let de dog gnaw you up en den dey would grease you en carry you home to de horse lot whe' dey would have a lash en a paddle to whip you wid. Oh, dey would have a swarm of black people up to de lot at sunrise on a mornin to get whip. Would make dem drop dey body frock en would band dem down to a log en would put de licks to dem. Ma was whip twice en she say dat she stay to her place after dat. I hear talk dey give some of dem 50 lashes to a whippin. Dat how it was in slavery time. Poor colored people couldn' never go bout en talk wid dey neighbors no time widout dey Massa say so. I say, 'Ma, if dey been try to beat me, I would a jump up en bite dem.' She say, 'You would get double portion den.' Just on account of dat, ain' many of dem slavery people knockin bout here now neither, I tell you. Dat first hide dey had, white folks just took it off dem. I would a rather been dead, I say. I remember, we chillun used to set down en ax Ma all bout dis en dat. Say, 'Ma, yunnah couldn' do nothin?' She say, 'No, white people had us in slavery time.'

"My God a mercy, I think now de best time to live in cause I ain' gettin no beatin dese days. If I had been big enough to get whip in slavery time, I know I would been dead cause I would been obliged to fight dem back en dey would kill folks for dat in dem days. If anybody hurt me, dey got to hurt back again, I say. Cose us had us task to do in dem days, but us never didn' have to bother bout huntin no rations en clothes no time den like de people be burdened wid dese days. I tell you, what you get in dese times, you got to paw for it en paw hard, but ain' nobody else business whe' you do it or no."

"Oh, de young people, dey ain' nothin dis day en time. Ain' worth a shuck no time. De old ones can beat dem out a hollow anywhe'. Ain' no chillun raise in dese days, I say. After freedom come here, I know I been hired out to white folks bout all de time en, honey, I sho been put through de crack. Lord, I had a rough time. Didn' never feel no rest. Dat how-come I ain' get all my growth, I say."

Source: Mom Ryer Emmanuel, colored, 78 years, Claussens, S.C.

Slave Narratives

Personal interview by Annie Ruth Davis, Marion, S.C.
[HW: See ES XVII, MS. #14.]

United States. Work Projects Administration

Project 1885-1
FOLKLORE
Spartanburg—Dist. 4
May 18, 1937

Edited by:
Elmer Turnage

STORIES FROM EX-SLAVES

EUBANKS PEN

"White folks. I sho nuff did ride wid de 'Red Shirts' fer Marse Hampton. Dar was two other darkies what rid wid us. Dey is bof daed now. One was Jack Jones, and de t'othern I does not recollect his name. Him and Jack is both daed. Dat leave me de onliest living one what rid in de company.

"I rid in de company wid Marse Jimmie Young and he was de Cap'un. He live out yonder at Sardis Church. Ev'ybody know Marse Jimmie. He ain't quite as aged yet as I bees. Mr. J.T. Sexton, he rid from up around Cross Keys, he got de 'hole in de wall' and I calls on him yit, and us talks over de olden days. Miss Bobo's husband, he rid in Marse Jimmie's company. (Mr. Preston B. Bobo) Our company camped at de ole Brick church out whar de mansion set now. It has allus been called de Lower Fairforest Baptist Church, whar de white folks still goes, 'cept de done move de church down on de new road, further from de mansion and de ole graveyard. I lows dat you knows I is speaking o' de new mansion—Mr.

Emslie Nicholson's house on de forest at de Shoals. I is got memory, but I ain't got no larning; dat I is proud of, kaise I is seed folks wid larning dat never knowed nothing worth speaking about. All de way 'fru', I is done tuck and stuck to my white folks—de Democratic white folks, dat I is.

"Sho was a pretty sight to see 'bout a hun'ded mens up on fine horses wid red shirts on. I still sees dem in my mind clear as day. Our red shirts fastened wid a strong band 'round de waist. Dar wasn't nar'y speck o' white to be seed no whars on 'em. Dey was raal heavy and strong. Fact, dey was made from red flannel, and I means it was sho 'nough flannel, too. I had done kept one o' mine here till times got hard and den I tuck and tore it up fer me a undershirt, here past it been two winters when it got so cold.

"One night us sot up all night and kept a big fire. Next morning it was de biggest frost all over de ground; but us never got one mite cold. De good white ladies of de community made our red shirts fer us. I 'spects Marse Jimmie ken name some fer you.

"I got eve'y registration ticket in my house, and I still votes allus de democratic ticket. I has longed to de Democratic club ever since de red shirt days and I has voted dat way all de time. I was jes' turn't seventeen when I jined de Red Shirts and got into de Democratic Club, and I has been in it ever since. It ain't gwine out neither.

"I sho seed Hampton speak from Dr. Culp's porch. I voted fer him. At dat time, I lived on de Keenan place. Marse Jimmie Young, he de overseer fer Mr. Keenan. Mr. Charles Ray owns and lives on it now. Dat brick church straight up de road from de Keenan place; straight as a bee line. Dat whar us met most o' de time fer de Red Shirt gatherings. Our Red Shirt Club was called de 'Fairforest' club atter de Lower Fairforest white folks Baptist church. De church has allus sot on de banks o' Fairforest Creek. Atter us got organized, I used to tote our flag. I was de onliest darky dat toted it.

"I is done handed you a few names: dey is all Democratic names. Lots of dem 'scapes my knowledge, it has all been so long ago. Dar was Mr. Gilmer Greer. Miss Gilmer Blankenship what lives out dar, she his niece. Mr. John Sims 'nother white man I members. Dar was lots o' companies in dis county, but I does not recall how many.

"Captain Jimmie Young would allus notify when dar was to be a meeting. Us darkies dat 'longed 'ud go and tell de white mens to come to de church. Us met sometime right 'fo de 'lection and all de companies come together at de ole courthouse dat stood right whar de new one is now.

"Robinson's Circus come to Union. De circus folks gib everbody a free ticket to de circus dat 'longed to de Democratic Club. Dey let all de scalawag niggers in fer registration tickets dat de Republicans had done give dem to vote fer Chamberlain. Dem niggers wanted to go to de circus wu'se dan dey wanted to do anything else. Dey never dre'mt dat dey was not a going to git to vote like de carpetbaggers, and de scalawags had done tole dem to do. Fact is, dey never much cared jes' since de got in de circus. Dem dat wanted de registration tickets back when de come out, never seed nobody to git 'em from nohows. Robinson's Circus was so big dat dey never showed it all in Union, but what dey had was out on McClure's field. It wasn't no houses dar den, and, o' course, dar wasn't no mill no whar about Union in dem days. All de tents dat was staked was staked in McClure's ole field over on 'Tosch' Branch. In dem days, dat field was de biggest territory in de clear around Union. Atter dat, all de Red Shirts met on de facade in front o' de courthouse. Mos' all de mens made a speech. Another darky sung a song like dis: 'Marse Hampton was a honest man; Mr. Chamberlain was a rogue'—Den I sung a song like dis: 'Marse Hampton et de watermelon, Mr. Chamberlain knawed de rine.' Us jest having fun den, kaise us had done 'lected Marse Hampton as de new governor of South Ca'linia."

> Source: "Uncle Pen" Eubanks, Hampton Ave. Union, S.C. (age 83)
> Interviewer: Caldwell Sims, Union, S.C. (5/4/37)

Project #1655.
W. W. Dixon,
Winnsboro, S. C.

LEWIS EVANS
EX-SLAVE 96 YEARS

LEWIS EVANS

ewis Evans lives on the lands of the estate of the late C.L. Smith, about ten miles southwest of Winnsboro, S.C. The house is a two-room frame structure, with a chimney in the center. He has the house and garden lot, free of rent, for the rest of his life, by the expressed wish of Mr. Smith before his demise. The only other occupant is his wife, Nancy, who is his third wife and much younger than Lewis. She does all the work about the home. They exist from the produce of the garden, output of fowls, and the small pension Lewis receives. They raise a pig each year. This gives them their meat for the succeeding year.

"Who I b'long to? Where was I born? White folks tell me I born after de stars fell, (1833), but maybe I too little to 'member de day. Just have to go by what I hear them say. Think it was 'bout 1841. All accounts is, I was born a slave of Marster John Martin, near Jenkinsville. Old Mistress, his wife, named Miss Margaret. All I can 'member 'bout them is dis: They had 'bout fifteen slaves, me 'mongst them. His daughter married a doctor, Doctor Harrison. I was sold to Maj. William Bell, who lived 'bout ten or twelve miles from old Marster. I's a good size boy then. Maj. Bell had ten families when I got dere. Put me to hoein' in de field and dat fall I picked cotton. Next year us didn't have cotton planters. I was took for one of de ones to plant de cotton seed by drappin' de seed in de drill. I had a bag 'round my neck, full of seeds, from which I'd take handfuls and sow them 'long in de row. Us had a horse-gin and screwpit, to git de cotton fit for de market in Charleston. Used four mules to gin de cotton and one mule to pack it in a bale. Had rope ties and all kinds of bagging. Seems to me I 'members seein' old flour sacks doubled for to put de cotton bales in, in de screw-press.

"Us raised many cows, hogs, sheep, and goats on de Bell place. Us worked hard. Us all had one place to eat. Had two women cooks and plenty to eat, cooked in big pots and ovens. Dere was iron pegs in and up de kitchen chimneys, chain and hooks to hold pots 'bove de fire. Dat's de way to boil things, meats and things out de garden.

"Whippin's? Yes sir, I got 'most skinned alive once, when I didn't bring up de cows one Sunday. Got in a fight wid one of Miss Betsie Aiken's hands and let de cows git away, was de cause of de whippin'. I was 'shamed to tell him 'bout de fight. Maj. Bell, dis time, whipped me hisself.

"My white folks was psalm singers. I done drove them to de old brick church on Little River every Sabbath, as they call Sunday. Dere was Miss Margaret, his wife, Miss Sallie and Miss Maggie and de two young marsters, Tom and Hugh. De two boys and me in front and my mistress and de two girls behind. Maj. Bell, when he went, rode his saddle horse.

"Who-ee! Don't talk to dis nigger 'bout patrollers. They run me many a time. You had to have a pass wid your name on it, who you b'long to, where gwine to, and de date you expected back. If they find your pass was to Mr. James' and they ketch you at Mr. Rabb's, then you got a floggin', sure and plenty. Maj. Bell was a kind master and would give us Saturday. Us would go fishin' or rabbit huntin' sometime.

"Us had two doctors, Doctor Furman and Doctor Davis. White folks care for you when you sick. I didn't have no money in slavery time, didn't have no use for none. Us had no quarters, houses just here and dere on de place, 'round de spring where us got water.

"My Marster went to de old war and was a major. He had brass buttons, butterflies on his shoulders, and all dat, when he come back.

"De Yankees come. Fust thing they look for was money. They put a pistol right in my forehead and say: 'I got to have your money, where is it?' Dere was a gal, Caroline, who had some money; they took it away from her. They took de geese, de chickens and all dat was worth takin' off de place, stripped it. Took all de meat out de smoke-house, corn out de crib, cattle out de pasture, burnt de gin-house and cotton. When they left, they shot some cows and hogs and left them lying right dere. Dere was a awful smell round dere for weeks after.

"Somethin' d'rected me, when I was free, to go work where I was born, on de Martin place. I married Mary Douglas, a good-lookin' wench. A Yankee took a fancy to her and she went off wid de Yankee. She stayed a long time, then come back, but I'd done got Preacher Rice to marry me to Louvinia then. Dis second wife was a good gal. I raised ten chillun by her, but I's outlived them all but Manuel, Clara and John. When Louvinia passed out, I got Magistrate Smith to jine me and Nancy. She's still livin'. Home sick now, can't do nothin'.

"White people been good to me. I've been livin' in dis home, free of rent, given me for life by Mr. Jim Smith, 'cause I was his faithful servant twenty years.

"Many times I's set up in de gallery of de old brick church on Little River. They had a special catechism for de slaves, dat asked us who made you, what He made you out of, and what He made you for? I ain't forgot de answers to dis day.

"Marster Major give us Chris'mas day and a pass to visit 'bout but we sho' had to be back and repo't befo' nine o'clock dat same day.

"I got my name after freedom. My pappy b'long to Mr. David R. Evans. His name was Steve; wasn't married reg'lar to my mammy. So when I went to take a name in Reconstruction, white folks give me Lewis Evans.

"I b'longs to de Baptist church. Am trustin' in de Lord. He gives me a conscience and I knows when I's doin' right and when de devil is ridin' me and I's doin' wrong. I never worry over why He made one child white and one child black. He make both for His glory. I sings 'Swing Low, Sweet Chariot, Jesus Gwine Carry Me Home.' Ain't got many more days to stay. I knows I'm gwine Home."

Project #1655
W. W. Dixon,
Winnsboro, S.C.

PHILLIP EVANS
EX-SLAVE 85 YEARS OLD.

PHILLIP EVANS

Phillip Evans, his wife, Janie, and their crippled son live together in a two-room frame house with one fireplace. The old woman has been a wet nurse for many white families in Winnsboro. Neither Phillip nor his boy can work. The wife nurses occasionally.

"I was born at de General Bratton Canaan place 'bout six miles, sort of up a little, on de sunrise side of Winnsboro. I hopes you're not contrary like, to think it too much against dis old slave when I tells you de day. Well sir, dat day was de fust day of April but pray sir, don't write me down a fool 'cause I born on dat p'ticular April Fool Day, 1852. When I gits through wid you, I wants you to say if dat birthday have any 'fect on dis old man's sensibility.

"My pappy was name Dick. Him was bought by General Bratton from de sale of de Evans estate. My pappy often tell mammy and us chillun, dat his pappy was ketched in Africa and fetched to America on a big ship in a iron cage, 'long wid a whole heap of other black folks, and dat he was powerful sick at de stomach de time he was on de ship.

"My mammy was name Charlotte. Her say her know nothin' 'bout her daddy or where he come from. One of my brothers is de Reverend Jackson C. Evans, age 72. Richard, another brother, is 65 years old. All of us born on de Canaan Bratton place. General Bratton love dat place; so him named it proud, like de Land of Canaan.

"I help to bring my brother Richard, us calls him Dick, into de world. Dat is, when mammy got in de pains, I run for de old granny on de place to come right away. Us both run all de way back. Good us did, for dat boy come right away. I 'members, to dis hour and minute, dat as soon as dat boy got here, he set de house full of noise, a-cryin' like a cat squallin'. All chillun does dat though, as soon as they come into de world. I got one sister older than me; her name Jenny Watson. Her live in a house on de Canaan place, callin' distance from where I live. Us is Methodists. A proud family, brought low by Mr. Hoover and his crowd. Had to sell our land. 'Spect us would have starved, as us too proud to beg. Thank God, Mr. Roosevelt come 'long. Him never ask whether us democrat or 'publican nor was us black or white; him just clothe our nakedness and ease de pains of hunger, and goin' further, us goin' to be took care of in our old age. Oh, how I love dat man; though they do say him got enemies.

"My brother, de preacher, says dat occasioned by de fact dat de President got a big stick and a big foot, dat sometime he tromp on de gout foots of some of them rich people. Howsomever, he say dat as long as de Lord, de Son, and de Holy Ghost is wid de President, it'll be all right for us colored folks. It makes no difference 'bout who is against de President. He says us niggers down South can do nothin' but be Methodist, pray to de Lord, and shout for de President. I's goin' to try to do some of de prayin' but dis voice too feeble to do much shoutin'.

"What kind of house us live in at slavery time? Nice plank house. All de houses in de quarters made dat way. Our beds was good. Us had a good marster. Our livin' houses and vittles was better and healthier than they is now. Big quarters had many families wid a big drove of chillun. Fed them from big long trays set on planks. They eat wid iron spoons, made at de blacksmith's shop. What they eat? Peas, beans, okra, Irish 'tators, mush, shorts, bread, and milk. Dere was 'bout five or six acres to de garden. Us kept fat and happy.

"Who was de overseers? Mr. Wade Rawls was one and Mr. Osborne was another. There was another one but 'spect I won't name him, 'cause him had some trouble wid my Uncle Dennis. 'Pears like he insult my aunt and beat her. Uncle Dennis took it up, beat de overseer, and run off to de woods. Then when he git hungry, him come home at night for to eat sumpin'. Dis kept up 'til one day my pappy drive a wagon to town and Dennis jined him. Him was a settin' on de back of de wagon in de town and somebody point him out to a officer. They clamp him and put him in jail. After de 'vestigation they take him to de whippin' post of de town, tie his foots, make him put his hands in de stocks, pulled off his shirt, pull down his britches and whip him terrible.

"No sir, Marster General Bratton didn't 'low his slaves' chillun to work. I just played 'round, help feed de stock and pigs, bring in de fruit from de orchard and sich like.

"Yes sir, marster give me small coins. What I do wid de money? I buy a pretty cap, one time. Just don't 'members what I did wid it all.

"Us went fishin' in de Melton Branch, wid hooks. Ketch rock rollers, perch and catfish. They eat mighty good. I like de shortnin' bread and sugar cane 'lasses best and de fust time I ever do wrong was 'bout de watermelons.

"Our shoes was made on de place. They had wooden bottoms. My daddy, being de foreman, was de only slave dat was give de honor to wear boots.

"Dere was just two mulattoes on de place. One was a daughter of my aunt. All de niggers was crazy 'bout her and wid de consent of my aunt, marster give her to some kinfolks in Arkansas. De other was name, Rufus. My marster was not his daddy. No use to put down dere in writing just who his pappy was.

"Stealing was de main crime. De whippin's was put on de backs, and if you scowled, dat would git you a whippin' right dere and then.

"Yes sir, dere is haunts, plenty of them. De devil is de daddy and they is hatched out in de swamps. My brother say they is demons of hell and has de witches of de earth for their hosses.

"De neighbors 'bout was de Neils, de Rawls, de Smiths, and de Mobleys. Marse Ed Mobley was great for huntin'. Marse General Bratton was a great sheep raiser. In spite of dat, they got along; though de dogs pestered de sheep and de shotguns peppered de dogs sometimes.

"My marster was a general in de Secession War. After dat, him a controller of de State. Him run old 'Buttermilk' Wallace out of Congress. Then he was a Congressman.

"My mistress was Miss Bettie. Her was a DuBose. Her child, Miss Isabella, marry some big man up North and their son, Theodore, is de bishop of de high 'Piscopal Church of Mississippi.

"Now I repeats de question: Does you think I's a fool just 'cause I's born on dat fust day of April, 1852?

"You made me feel religious askin' all them questions. Seem like a voice of all de days dat am gone turn over me and press on de heart, and dis room 'fect me like I was in a church. If you ever pass de Canaan place I'd be mighty happy to see you again."

Project 1885-1
FOLKLORE
Spartanburg Dist. 4
June 16, 1937

Edited by:
Elmer Turnage

STORIES FROM EX-SLAVES

PHILLIP EVANS

"I was born in old Abbeville County, S.C. about 1861; was reared in what is now Greenwood County. My father was Winston Arnold and my mother, Sophronia Lomax Arnold. They belonged to the Arnold family during slavery time. I was just a small child during the Confederate War, and don't remember anything about it. I heard my mother tell about some things though. The slaves earned no money and were just given quarters to live in and something to eat. My father was a blacksmith on master's place, and after the war, he was blacksmith for himself. I heard him tell about the patrollers. They had lots of cornshuckings and cotton pickings, but they never worked at night.

"I remember the night-riders, but don't remember that they did any harm much except they got after a man once.

"When any of us got sick we sent for a doctor, but old-time folks I heard about, would use herbs, tree barks, and the like of that to make teas to drink.

"I married in a negro church when I was young. I married Frank Fair who came from Newberry County, S.C. After the ceremony, the neighbors gave me a nice dinner at the church.

"I don't remember anything about Lincoln or Jeff Davis, but I think Booker Washington is a leading colored man and has done good.

"I joined the church when I was nine years old, because my father and mother belonged, and so many young people were joining. I think everybody ought to join a church."

Source: Eugenia Fair (76). Greenwood, S.C.
Interviewed By: G.L. Summer, Newberry, S.C. (6/10/37)

Project 1885-1
Folklore
Spartanburg, Dist. 4
Oct. 14, 1937

Edited by:
Elmer Turnage

STORIES FROM EX-SLAVES

CAROLINE FARROW

"I lives in Newberry in a small three-room house which belongs to my son. He helps me some 'cause I can't work except jest a little 'round de house.

"I don't know much 'bout de war times. All I know is what I told you befo'. I 'member when de war quit and freedom come. Most of de slaves had to find work where dey could. Some had to work as share-croppers, some fer wages, and later on, some rented small plots of land. Many niggers since de war moved to town and worked as day hands, such as carpenters, janitors, dray drivers and de like.

"De old time folks had blacksmith shops on de farm and made most of de tools dey used. Dey had plenty to eat. We never wanted fer nothing and always lived good. I had it better den dan I does now.

"In slavery when de patrollers rode up and down de roads, once a nigger boy stole out to see his gal, all dressed up to kill. De patrollers found him at his gal's house and started to take off his coat so dey could whip him; but he said, 'Please don't let my gal see under my coat, 'cause I got on a bosom and no shirt'. (The custom was to wear stiff, white bosoms held up around the neck when no shirt was on. This gave the appearance of a shirt.)

"My sister-in-law and mother-in-law both come from Virginia but I don't 'member anything dey said 'bout dat country. My sister-in-law went back dere atter freedom come, but her mama died here.

"Us slaves went to de white folks' church at Cross Roads, and our mistress made us go. She often would teach us to read and write at home when we would try to learn. Mistress had a nigger driver fer her carriage, and when he drove he wore a high beaver hat and a long coat. Our white folks had a big kitchen way off from de house. Dey had a big wide fireplace where dey cooked over de fire in skillets. My mistress had me to work in de house, kind of a house-girl, and she made me keep clean and put large ear rings in my ears so I would look good. When Christmas come, Marse and Mistress always give de slaves good things to eat. Dey had lots of cows, and dey give us good butter and milk, molasses, meats and other good things to eat. We always worked on week days except Saturdays, and sometimes on dat day until 12 o'clock. We always had Christmas and Easter holidays.

"We had corn-shuckings and cotton-pickings. De niggers would sing: 'Job, Job, farm in a row; Job, Job, farm in a row'. Sometimes on moonlight nights we had pender pullings and when we got through we had big suppers, always wid good potatoes or pumpkin pies, de best eating ever. We made corn bread wid plenty of milk, eggs and lard, and sometimes wid sweet potatoes, de best corn bread in de world. 'Simmon bread was made wid sifted 'simmon juice cooked wid flour.

"I married first time to Joe Todd, and had a big wedding what my mistress give me in her back yard. She had a big shoat killed fer de wedding dinner. My mistress den was Miss Cornelia Ervin. When I married de second time, I married in town to West Farrow, in de colored people's Baptist church, by Rev. West Rutherford, a nigger preacher, de pastor. My second husband died, too, a few years ago.

"I can't 'member much 'bout old songs, but a Baptist song was: 'Down to de water, River of Jordon; Down to de water, River of Jordon; Dere my Savior was baptized.'

Another version went thus:

> "Come along, come along, my dear loving brother,
> Come along and let's go home;
> Down into de River where my Savior was baptized.'

"De present generation of niggers ain't like de ones when I come along. Dey don't work like I did.

"I don't know much about 'Abramham' Lincoln, Jefferson Davis or Booker Washington. I just hear about Booker Washington, reckon he is all right.

"I think slavery helped me. I did better den dan I do now. When I joined de church I was grown and married, and had two chilluns. I joined de church because I thought I ought to settle down and do better fer my family, and quit dancing and frolicing."

United States. Work Projects Administration

Source: Caroline Farrow (N. 80), Newberry, S.C.
Interviewer: G.L. Summer, Newberry, S.C. (9/16/37)

Project 1885-1
FOLKLORE
Spartanburg Dist. 4
May 24, 1937

Edited by:
Elmer Turnage
STORIES FROM EX-SLAVES

CAROLINE FARROW

"I was born in Newberry County. Near Chappells depot. My master, in slavery time, was John Boazman. He was a good man to his slaves. I was raised in the big-house, and helped as a servant-girl. My mistress smoked a pipe, and sometimes she would have me to get a red coal from de fire and put it in her pipe. I did dat wid tongs. I lived there a long time. I come to Newberry over 40 years ago and worked wid de white people in town.

"I married twice. My first husband was Joe Todd, and after he died, I married West Farrow. He was a dray-man in town for many years.

"The folks back home had fine farms, good gardens, and took pride in raising all kinds of things in the garden. They allus planted Irish potatoes the second time in one season.

"They cooked in big open fireplaces, in kitchens that set away off from the house. A big spider was always used for cooking over the fireplace.

"After de war, we stayed on awhile. My mistress took me to de white folks' church and made me sit in the gallery; then brought me home."

Source: Caroline Farrow (80), Newberry, S.C.
Interviewer: G.L. Summer, Newberry, S.C. (5/18/37)

Project 1885-1
FOLKLORE
Spartanburg Dist. 4
June 28, 1937

Edited by:
Elmer Turnage
STORIES FROM EX-SLAVES

GUS FEASTER

"I do not knows when er whar I was born. My father was Price Feaster; mother was Lucy Richards Feaster. She belonged to Mr. Berry Richards dat lived 'tween Maybinton and Goshen Hill Township, on de 'Richards Quarter'. My sister name Harriet; brothers was Albert and Billy, and dats all de chilluns dere was in de family. My furs' recollection dat I knows was when we went to de Carlisles. I was so young dat I can't recall nothing much 'bout de Feaster plantation. Our beds was home-made and had ropes pulled tight frum one side to de other fer de slats. No sir, I doesn't know nothing 'bout no grandmaw and grandpaw.

"De furs' work dat I done was drapping peas. Albert was plow-hand when I come into de world. Harriet was up big enough to plant corn and peas, too. Billy looked atter de stock and de feeding of all de animals on de farm. My furs' money was made by gathering blackberries to sell at Goshen Hill to a lady dat made wine frum dem. I bought candy wit de money; people was crazy 'bout candy den. Dat's de reason I ain't got no toofies now.

"Ole lady Abbie looked out fer our rations. De mens eat on one side and de gals on t'other side de trough. We eat breakfast when de birds furs' commence singing off'n de roost. Jay birds 'ud allus call de slaves. Dey lowed: 'it's day, it's day,' and you had to git up. Dere wasn't no waiting 'bout it. De whipperwill say, 'cut de chip out de whiteoak,' you better git up to keep frum gitting a whipping. Doves say, 'who you is, who you is.' Dat's a great sign in a dove. Once people wouldn't kill doves, ole marse sho would whip you if you did. Dove was furs' thing dat bring something back to Noah when de flood done gone frum over de land. When Freedom come, birds change song. One say, 'don't know what you gwine to do now.' 'n other one low, 'take a lien, take a lien.' Niggers live fat den wid bacon sides.

"Mr. Billy Thompson and Mr. Bill Harris' daddy give liens in dem days; dese big mens den. Captain Foster clothed de niggers atter Freedom.

"Ole lady Abbie give us mush and milk fer breakfast. Shorts and seconds was mixed wid de mush; no grease in de morning a-tall. Twelve o'clock brung plenty cow-peas, meat, bread and water. At night us drunk milk and et bread, black bread made frum de shorts. Jes' had meat at twelve o'clock, 'course 'sharpers' 'ud eat meat when marster didn't know. Dey go out and git 'em a hog frum a drove of seventy-five er a hund'ed; dat one never be missed.

"I is awful to hunt; come to Union to sell my rabbits and 'possums. Mr. Cohen dat run a brick yard, he buy some. Ole man Dunbar run'ed a market. He was ole man den. He's de beef market man; he take all de rabbits and sell 'em when I couldn't git a thing fer 'em. Ole lady living den, and when I git home she low is I got any 'loady' (something to eat). I come in wid beef and cow heads. Cow foots was de best meat. Dey throws all sech as dat away now. Dere was allus a fuss in de house iffen I never had no 'loady'. Somehow er another I was allus a family man and was lucky to git in wid mens dat help me on. Never suffered wid help frum dese kind men. Dat's de way I got along as well as I has. Ole Missus and Marse learn't me to never tell a lie, and she teached me dat's de way to git along well. I still follows dat.

"Up in age, I got in wid cap'n Perram (Mr. George Perrin). He was de banker. He say 'bout me, 'what I likes 'bout Gus, he never tell a lie'.

"Befo' dat, I work fer Lawyer Monroe. He had a brother named Jim and one named George, his name Bill. His sister named Miss Sally. Dar I farm fer dem and work on half'uns. De Yankees camped on his place whar Mr. Gordon Godshall now got a house. N'used to go dar mi'night ev'y night and ev'y day. Dey had a pay day de furs' and de fifteenth of de month. Dey's terrible fer 'engans' (onions) and eggs. Dey git five marbles and put dem in a ring; put up fifty cents. Furs' man knocks out de middle-man (marble) got de game. Dey's jes' sporty to dat. Never had nothing but greenbacks den. Fifteen cents and ten cents pieces and twenty-five and as high as fifty cents pieces was paper in dem times.

"Dey larn't us a song: 'If I had ole Abe Lincoln all over dis world, but I know I can't whip him; but I fight him 'till I dies'. Dey low'd, 'we freeded you alls'.

"Another song was: 'Salvation free fer all mankind; Salvation free fer all mankind'. I was glad er all salvation.

'Salvation free fer me'; got up dat song furs' on a moonlight night, and us sing it all night long, going from house to house.

"'Motherless chilluns sees hard times; just ain't got no whar to go; goes from do' to do',' dat's de song dey got up. I doesn't know whar it come from. 'Nother one was: 'When de sun refuse to shine; Lord I wants to be in de number, when de sun refuse to shine. If I had a po' mother she gone on befo', Lord I promise her I would meet her when de saints go marching in.' Dat's what lots people is still trying to do.

"We sot mud baskets fer cat fish; tie grapevines on dem and put dem in de river. We cotch some wid hooks. I went seining many times and I set nets; bought seins and made de nets. Pull up sein after a rain and have seventy-five or eighty fish; sometimes have none. Peter Mills made our cat fish stew and cooked ash-cake bread fer us to eat it wid. Water come to our necks while we seining and we git de fish while we drifting down stream.

"We wear cotton clothes in hot weather, dyed wid red dirt or mulberries, or stained wid green wa'nuts—dat is de hulls. Never had much exchanging of clothes in cold weather. In dat day us haul wood eight or ten feet long. De log houses was daubed wid mud and dey was warm. Fire last all night from dat big wood and de house didn't git cold. We had heavy shoes wid wood soles; heavy cotton socks which was wore de whole year through de cold weather, but we allus go barefeeted in hot weather. Young boys thirteen to fifteen years old had de foots measured. When tracks be seed in de wa'melon patch, dey was called up, and if de measurements of dere tracks fitted de ones in de wa'melon patch, dat was de guilty nigger. I 'clar, you had to talk purty den. When I go in de wa'melon patch, I git de old missus to say fer me to go; den I could eat and nothing was said 'bout it.

"Sunday clothes was died red fer de gals; boys wore de same. We made de gals' hoops out'n grape vines. Dey give us a dime, if dey had one, fer a set of hoops.

"Twan't no dressing up fer marring in slavery times; just say, 'gwine to be a marriage tonight' and you see 'bout 40 or 50 folks dar to see it. If it be in wa'melon time, dey had a big feast atter de wedding. Old man preacher Tony would marry you fer nothing. De keep de wedding cake fer three weeks befo' it was eat."

Source: Gus Feaster (97), 20, Stutz Ave., Union, S.C.
Interviewer: Caldwell Sims, Union, S.C.

United States. Work Projects Administration

Project 1885-1
FOLKLORE
Spartanburg Dist. 4
July 7, 1937

Edited by:
Elmer Turnage

STORIES FROM EX-SLAVES

GUS FEASTER

"I ain't never give you dis information. Miss Susie and Miss Tommie Carlisle, Marse Tom's onliest daughters, died befo' de surrender. Miss Susie slipped one day wid de scissors in her hand, and when she did dem scissors tuck and stuck in one her eyes and put it plum' smack out and she never did see out'n it no mo'. Dat made it so sad, and everybody cried wid her but it never done her narry bit of good.

"When dem young ladies died, I left out and run off from my ma and come to Union. Mr. Eller kept a big sto' jest as you come into town. It was jest about whar Mr. Mobley Jeter's is now. Dat's in de middle of town, but in de fur off days I is speaking about, it was de very outskirts of dis town. I is seed dis town grow, dat is what I is. Mr. Eller tuck me to be his driving boy, and dat sto' sot jest exactly whar de Chevet Charage (Chevrolet Garage) sets now.

"When I been dar six years, my ma come to Union and she found me dar. Us was dat glad to lay eyes on one another dat we jest shouted fur joy and my Ma tuck and smacked me wid her lips right in de mouth. She told me dat my pa had done got shot a fixing dem old breastworks down in Charleston and dat called fur a big cry from me and her both. Mr. Eller, he went out'n de back of his sto' 'till us quit. He let me go back home to de Carlisle place wid my ma. Everything done changed and I brung my ma back to Union and kept her, kaise I was a man in full den.

"Lawyer Shand tuck my ma to work fur him and I started being his coachman. He ole and he live in Columbia now. When he done dat, me and ma lived in one of his houses. He lived on what you knows as Douglas Heights and he had de biggest house dar. Dat was way befo' Captain Douglas moved from Goshen Hill. Den Captain Douglas tuck de day and built dat house you sees now aheading what dey calls Douglas Heights atter Lawyer Shand's house was to' (torn) down. De house sot right on top de hill in de middle of de street you sees. His driveway was flanked wid water oaks and it retched down to Main street. De grounds was on each side dat drive and dey retched to whar de white folks is got a school (high school) now. On de other side of dat drive his grounds hit Miss Fant's (Mrs. John Fant's property).

"You could clam up Cap Douglas' stairs and git in a run-around (cupola) and see de whole town through dem glass winders. (This cupola is still on the house.) Never had none of dem things in Union afo' dat. Some years atter dat, when Col. Duncan had his house run over (remodeled) he had one of dem run-arounds put on his'n. To dis day wid all de fine fixings folks has in Union, dar ain't narry one got none of dem things and dey sho' is purty.

"Let me drap back, kaise I is gone too fer along; you wants olden times. On our plantation Marse Tom had a nigger driver. He 'hoop and holler and wake us up at break of day. But befo' freedom come 'long, Marse got a bell; den dat nigger driver rung dat bell at break of day. He was a sorry nigger dat never had no quality in him a'tall, no sir-ee.

"Us had to feed de mules in de dark of mornings and de black of night when craps needed working bad. Seed many as a dozen hoe-womens in de field at one time. Dey come when dey finished breakfast and de plows had got a start.

"Dey used mulberry skins from fresh mulberry saplins to tie around dere waists fer belts. If your singletree chain broke, you fixed it wid mulberry skins; same wid your galluses. Mulberry is mighty strong and easy to tie anything dat break.

"Marse Tom never whipped 'bout nothing much but stealing. He never let his overseer do no whipping if he knowed it. He burnt you up 'bout stealing, dat he would.

"Dey never wanted us to git no larning. Edmund Carlisle, smartest nigger I is ever seed. He cut out blocks from pine bark on de pine tree and smooth it. Git white oak or hickory stick. Git a ink ball from de oak trees, and on Sadday and Sunday slip off whar de white folks wouldn't know 'bout it. He use stick fer pen and drap oak ball in water and dat be his ink atter it done stood all night. He larnt to write his name and how to make figures. Marse Jule and Bill, two of Marse Tom's boys, found out dat Edmund could write and dey wanted to whip him, but Marse Tom wouldn't let 'em.

"One morning Edmund was making a big fire 'round all de pots, kaise we was butchering forty hogs. Edmund had his head under de pot a blowing up de fire dat had done tuck and died to embers. Jule and Bill seed him and dey broke and run and pushed Edmund plum' under dem pots. De embers burnt his face and de hair off'n his head. Marse Tom wo' (wore) Bill and Jule out fer it. Missus 'lowed den dat Edmund de smartest nigger on dat plantation.

"We had Sadday afternoons to do our work and to wash. We had all de hollidays off and a big time Christmas and July Fourth.

"Going to funerals we used all Marse's wagons. Quick as de funeral start, de preacher give out a funeral hymn. All in de procession tuck up de tune and as de wagons move along wid de mules at a slow walk, everybody sing dat hymn. When it done, another was lined out, and dat kept up 'till we reach de graveyard. Den de preacher pray and we sing some mo'. In dem days funerals was slow fer both de white and de black folks. Now dey is so fast, you is home again befo' you gits dar good.

"On de way home from de funeral, de mules would perk up a little in dey walk and a faster hymn was sung on de way home. When we got home, we was in a good mood from singing de faster hymns and de funeral soon be forgot.

"As a child everybody in dem days played marbles.

"Ma sung some of de oldest hymns dat I is ever heard: (He sang) 'O Zion, O Zion, O Zion, wanta git home at last'. (Another) 'Is you over, Is you over, Is you over' and the bass come back, 'Yes thank God, Yes thank God, Yes thank God, I is over. How did you cross? At de ferry, at de ferry, at de ferry, Yes, thank God I is over.' If I sing dem now folks laughs at me, but ma sho' teached dem to her chilluns.

"When boys and gals gits up some size dey feels dey-selves. At dat age, we went bird thrashing in de moon light. Den we sing dis vulgar song, 'I'll give you half-dollar if you come out tonight; I'll give you half-dollar if you come out tonight'. Den de gals charmed us wid honeysuckle and rose petals hid in dere bosoms. Now de gals goes to de ten cent sto' and buys cheap perfume. In dem days dey dried cheneyberries (chinaberries) and painted dem and wo' dem on a string around dere necks to charm us.

"When us very little, ma say at night when she want us to go to bed and we be playing marbles, 'Better come on in de house or Raw Hide and Bloody Bones 'll git you. From den on I is seed spooks.

"Our work song was, 'John Henry was a man; he worked all over dis town'. Dey still uses dat song. In slavery some holler when dey be in de field like owls; some like crows; and some like pea-fowls. Missus had de purtiest pea-fowls in de whole country. Don't see none now, but dar ain't nothing dat flies purtier.

"Me and Wade Carlisle was 'possum hunting one night in de fall when de dogs bedded a 'possum in a grave. We dug down and got de 'possum. He was dat big and fat and his hair was so shiny and purty dat we 'lowed dat he de finest 'possum we had cotch dat fall.

"Jest den, Wade struck de box dat de dead man was a-lying in. Jest as he did dat, a light jumped out'n dat grave right in front of us and all over Wade's shovel. Our two dogs tuck and run and holler and stick dey tails betwix dey legs like somebody a-whipping dem. Dem dogs never stopped running and howling 'till dey reached home, me and Wade right behind dem. Wade had dat 'possum in his hand. Dat light now and den jump right in front of us.

"I hollered, 'Wade, fer de Lawd in Heaven sake, drap dat 'possum.' He drapped it and we run 'till we got home. Wade still had dat shovel—or was it a axe—. I jest recollects which, anyway, he still had it in his hand; and when I looked at it, it was still shining. I pinted my finger at it, kaise I was dat scared dat no words wouldn't come from my mouth. Wade throwed it in de wood pile and we run in de house wid it still shining at us.

"I stayed dar all night, and I ain't never been hunting in no graveyard at night since dat; and if de good Lawd give me sense I is got now, I ain't never gwine to do it no mo'.

"It ain't no good a-'sturbing dead folks. All befo' dat I is heard it gits you in bad, and now since den I knows it."

Source: Gus Feaster (col. 97), 20 Stutz Ave., Union, S.C.
Interviewer: Caldwell Sims, Union, S.C. (7/1/37)

Project 1885-1
From Misc. Field Notes
District No. 4
May 17, 1937

Edited by:
Martha Ritter

FOLKLORE: NEGRO SLAVE.

Slave Time Customs on the Plantation
of Thomas Anderson Carlisle.

GUS FEASTER

"Cap', my old Master's daughter, Mrs. George Perrin (Ida Rice) and Miss Peake (Mrs. Keitt Peake) 'lows I is done pas' 84. Miss Ida was 84 when she died and I was allus mo' older dan she was, and a long ways at dat. I allus figers dat Ah is 97. Miss Agnes (Mrs. Keitt Peake) and Miss Ida was lil' gals when I driv' dem to and from school ever' day fer ole Marse. You see I had to be a big boy to drive de Marse's chilluns to school, 'specially when dey was lil' gals! I is a great deal older than Mr. Bill Harris. I met him dis mornin' wid sweet 'tater in his pocket. He 'lowed, 'Gus, you is jes' 'bout de oldes' nigger in dis county, ain't you?' I raised my hat to 'im and 'lowed, Yessir, guess I is, Cap.

"Had to stay out and guard de silver and de gold jewels in de pines when my white folks hid it dar to keep de Yankees from a-gittin' it. Dey driv' de waggins in de pines and us unload de jewels and things and den dey would drive de waggins out de wood. When de waggin done got plum away us would take dry pine needles and kivver up all de waggin tracks and hoof prints after us had done raked de dirt smooth over dem. We stayed wid de silver and stuff and drink coffee and eat black crus'; dat de sweetnin' bread dat us had durin' de war. Couldn't git no sugar den. Sometime we used sassafras tea as we never had no coffee to grind. De white folks was jes' as bad off as we was. From de big house dey brung our mess of vittals after dark had done fell.

"Poke salad was et in dem days to clean a feller out. Hit cum up tender every spring and when it cut deep down in sand it looked white. It's an herb. Cut it; wash it and par boil; pour off water and ball up in balls in your hand; put in frying pan of hot grease (grease from ham or strip meat) and fry. Season with black pepper and salt and eat with new spring onions. Tender white stems are better than the salad and of course earlier. Ash cake was good wid poke salad and clabber or butter milk and best of all was sweet milk! Dat not only fill up your belly, but make you fat and strong.

"Sometime de darkies would eat too much and git de colic. Fer dis dey would take and chaw pine needles and it would be all over wid den. On all de plantations dar was old womens, too old to do any work and dey would take and study what to do fer de ailments of grown folks and lil' chilluns. Fer de lil' chilluns and babies dey would take and chaw up pine needles and den spit it in de lil' chilluns mouths and make dem swallow. Den when dey was a teachin' de babies to eat dey done de food de very same way. Dem old wimmens made pine rosin pills from de pine rosin what drapped from de pine trees and give de pills to de folks to take fer de back ache. Dey allus kept de pine trees gashed fer dis purpose. Den day also gashed de sweet gum fer to git gum to chaw. 'Twasn't no sech thing as chawin' gum till thirty years ago. Sweet gum, it's good fer de indigestion and fer de toofies, when it don't git yer mouth all stuck so as you can't say nothing. I 'spects dat de chief reason how come it done gone plum out o' date. I most fergot to inform you dat resin pills is still de best thing dat I knows to start your "water" off when it done stopped on ye.

"It was a special day on each plantation when de Master and de o'seer give out de week's rations, like dis: Four pounds o' bacon; one peck o' meal; quart o' flour; quart o' molasses;—dey was dat black; and dey was de rations fer a whole endurin' week. Had a big choppin' block where all de meat was chopped on. In dem days every bit o' de meat was raised on de plantation from de Master's hogs. Into de grooves o' dis choppin' block would git lodged small pieces o' meat. Choppin' ax was heavy and broad. Heavy rations come out on Friday. On Sad'day come de shoulder meat fer Sunday mornin' brekfas' and de flour come on Sad'day also. Our Master give us hominy fer Sunday mornin' brekfas', kaise us had red meat wid gravy den. My Master was Marse' Tom Carlisle of Goshen Hill. He de one give us dem Sunday specials. De niggers on de other surroundin' plantations never got no sech 'sideration as I ever heard of.

"Me and John minded de Missus' cows. When de red meat choppin' was done all de plantation chilluns would be dar to git what fall in de grooves o' de blocks. One day John 'lowed to me if you puts your ol' black hand on dat block 'fore I does today, I is a gwine to chop it off. I never said nary a word, but I jes' roll my eyes at him. I got dar and broke and run fer de block. I got big piece and when John come up I was eating it. I say, Nigger, you is too late and lazy fer anything. 'Bout that time he reach over fer a scrap I never seed. I push him back and reach fer hit. John took up de choppin' ax and come right down on my finger, 'fore I could git it out de way. Dat's why you see dis scar here now. Dat nigger lay my finger plum wide open, fact is dat he jes' left it a hangin'. Marse's doctor and he fix it back. Den he whip John hisself; never 'low de overseer to do it dat time. Marse Tom pretty good to us; never whip much; never 'low de overseer, Mr. Wash Evans, to whip too much neither. He would have liked to whip mo' dan he did, if de Marse would 'lowed it, but he wasn't so bad. Mr. Evans wasn't no po' white trash, but he was kinder middlin' like. De Evans is done riz high up now.

"Newt and Anderson was my young marsters. Dey was 'long 'bout my own age. Dey went to school at Goshen Hill. De school was near de store, some folks called it de tradin' post in dem days. De had barrels o' liquor settin' out from de store in a long row. Sold de likker to de rich mens dat carried on at de race track near by. Folks in Goshen was all rich in dem days. Rogers Church, where de Carlisles, Jeters, Sims, Selbys, Glens, and lots of other folks went too and de slaves, was de richest country church in dis part o' de whole state, so I is often been told. Ebenezer, over in Maybinton, was de onliest church in de whole country dat tried to strive wid Rogers in de way o' finery and style. De Hendersons, Maybins, Hardys, Douglasses, Cofields, Chicks and Oxners was de big folks over dar. Both de churches was Methodist.

"Every summer de carried on Camp Meetin' at Rogers. All de big Methodist preachers would come from way off den. Dey was entertained in de Carlisle big house. Missus put on de dog (as de niggers says now) den. Every thing was cleaned up jes' 'fore de meetin' like us did fer de early-spring cleanin'. Camp Meetin' come jes' after de craps was done laid by. Den all craps was done laid by befo' July de Fourth. It was unheard of fer anybody to let de Fourth come widout de craps out'n de way. Times is done changed now, Lawd. Den de fields was heavy wid corn head high and cotton up aroun' de darky's waist! Grass was all cleaned out o' de furrow's on de las' go 'round. De fields and even de terraces was put in 'apple pie' order fer de gatherin' o' de craps in de fall.

"As you all knows de Fourth has allus been nigger day. Marse and Missus had good rations fer us early on de Fourth. Den us went to barbecues after de mornin' chores was done. In dem days de barbecues was usually held on de plantation o' Marse Jim Hill in Fish Dam. Dat was not fer from Goshen. Marse Jim had a purty spring dat is still all walled up wid fine rocks. De water come out'n dese rocks dat cold dat you can't hold your hand in it fer more dan a minute at de longes'. Dar is a big flat rock beyond de spring dat I 'specs kivvers more dan an acre and a half o' ground. A creek run along over dis rock, where de mules and de hosses could rest in de shade of de trees and drink all de water dat de wanted. Wild ferns growed waist high along dar den. All kinds of purty flowers and daisies was gathered by de gals. Dem was de best days dat any darky has ever seed. Never had nothing to aggravate your mind den. Plenty to eat; plenty to wear; plenty wood to burn; good house to live in; and no worry 'bout where it was a-coming from!

"Old Marse he give us de rations fer de barbecues. Every master wanted his darkies to be thought well of at de barbecues by de darkies from all de other plantations. De had pigs barbecued; goats; and de Missus let de wimmen folks bake pies, cakes and custards fer de barbecue, jes' 'zactly like hit was fer de white folks barbecue deself!

"Young ones carried on like young colts a-frolicin' in de pasture till dey had done got so full o' vittles dat dey could not eat another bite. Den dey roamed on off and set down somewheres to sleep in de shade o' de trees. When de sun started to going down den de old folks begin to git ready to return back to dey home plantations, fer dar was de master's stock and chickens to feed and put up fer de night, to say nothing o' de cows to milk. The master's work had to go on around de big house, kaise all de darkies had been 'lowed to have such a pleasant day. Next day being Sad'day was on dis occasion not only ration day, but de day to git ready fer de white folks' Camp Meetin' which I has already called to recollection several times.

"I has to drap back to my own plantation now; kaise I guesses dat de same [HR: 'same' was crossed out in the original] thing took place on all de neighborin' places in preparation fer de white folks 'big Meetin'. But I better confine my relations to dat what I really knows. At de barbecue I seed niggers from several neighborin' plantations and I can tell you 'bout dat. But I draps now to de doings o' my own white folks.

"As I has said once, de fields was in lay-by shape and de Missus done already got de house cleaned. De chilluns was put in one room to sleep and dat make more room fer de preachers and guests dat gwine to visit in de big house fer de nex' six weeks. Den de plans fer cooking had to be brung 'bout. Dey never had no ice in dem days as you well knows; but us had a dry well under our big house. It was deep and everything keep real cool down dar. Steps led down into it, and it allus be real dark down dar. De rats run aroun' down dar and de younguns skeert to go down fer anything. So us carry a lightwood knot fer light when us put anything in it or take anything out. Dar ain't no need fer me to tell you 'bout de well house where us kept all de milk and butter, fer it was de talk o' de country 'bout what nice fresh milk and butter de missus allus had. A hollow oak log was used fer de milk trough. Three times a day Cilla had her lil' boy run fresh cool well water all through de trough. Dat keep de milk from gwine to whey and de butter fresh and cool. In de dry well was kept de canned things and dough to set till it had done riz. When company come like dey allus did fer de camp meetings, shoalts and goats and maybe a sheep or lamb or two was kilt fer barbecue out by Cilla's cabin. Dese carcasses was kept down in de dry well over night and put over de pit early de next morning after it had done took salt. Den dar was a big box kivvered wid screen wire dat victuals was kept in in de dry well. Dese boxes was made rat proof.

"Whilst de meats fer de company table was kept barbecued out in de yard, de cakes, pies, breads, and t'other fixings was done in de kitchen out in de big house yard. Baskets had ter be packed to go to camp meetin'. Tables was built up at Rogers under de big oak trees dat has all been cut down now. De tables jes' groaned and creeked and sighed wid victuals at dinner hour every day durin' de camp meetin'.

"Missus fetch her finest linens and silver and glasses to out-shine dem brung by de t'other white folks o' quality. In dem days de white folks o' quality in Union most all come from Goshen Hill and Fish Dam. After de white folks done et all dey could hold den de slaves what had done come to church and to help wid de tables and de carriages would have de dinner on a smaller table over clost to de spring. Us had table cloths on our table also and us et from de kitchen china and de kitchen silver.

"Young gals couldn't eat much in public, kaise it ain't stylish fer young courting gals to let on like dey has any appetite to speak of. I sees dat am a custom dat still goes amongst de wimmen folks, not to eat, so heavy. Cullud gals tried to do jes' like de young white missus would do.

"After everything was done eat it would be enough to pack up and fetch back home to feed all de hungry niggers what roams roun' here in Union now. Dem was de times when everybody had 'nuff to eat and more dan dey wanted and plenty clothes to wear!

"During de preaching us darkies sot in de back o' de church. Our white folks had some benches dar dat didn't nobody set on 'cept de slaves. Us wore de best clo'es dat us had. De Marse give us a coat and a hat and his sons give all de old hats and coats 'round. Us wore shirts and pants made from de looms. Us kept dem clean't and ironed jes' like de Marster and de young marsters done their'n. Den us wore a string tie, dat de white folks done let us have, to church. Dat 'bout de onliest time dat a darky was seed wid a tie. Some de oldest men even wore a cravat, dat dey had done got from de old marster. Us combed our hair on Sunday fer church. But us never bothered much wid it no other time. During slavery some o' de old men had short plaits o' hair.

"De gals come out in de starch dresses fer de camp meeting. Dey took dey hair down out'n de strings fer de meeting. In dem days all de darky wimmens wore dey hair in string 'cep' when dey 'tended church or a wedding. At de camp meetings de wimmens pulled off de head rags, 'cept de mammies. On dis occasion de mammies wore linen head rags fresh laundered. Dey wore de best aprons wid long streamers ironed and starched out a hanging down dey backs. All de other darky wimmens wore de black dresses and dey got hats from some dey white lady folks; jes' as us mens got hats from our'n. Dem wimmens dat couldn't git no hats, mostly wore black bonnets. De nigger gals and winches did all de dressing up dat dey could fer de meeting and also fer de barbecue.

"At night when de meeting dun busted till nex' day was when de darkies really did have dey freedom o' spirit. As de waggin be creeping along in de late hours o' moonlight and de darkies would raise a tune. Den de air soon be filled wid the sweetest tune as us rid on home and sung all de old hymns dat us loved. It was allus some big black nigger wid a deep bass voice like a frog dat ud start up de tune. Den de others mens jine in, followed up by de fine lil voices o' de gals and de cracked voices o' de old wimmens and de grannies. When us reach near de big house us soften down to a deep hum dat de missus like! Sometime she his't up de window and tell us sing 'Swing Low Sweet Cha'ot' for her and de visiting guests. Dat all us want to hear. Us open up and de niggers near de big house dat hadn't been to church would wake up and come out to de cabin door and jine in de refrain. From dat we'd swing on into all de old spirituals dat us love so well and dat us knowed how to sing. Missus often 'low dat her darkies could sing wid heaven's 'spiration (inspiration).

Now and den some old mammie would fall out'n de waggin a shoutin' Glory and Hallelujah and Amen! After dat us went off to lay down fer de night.

"Young Newt and Anderson was de boys what was near de age of me and John. Co'se dey went to school every day it was in session. Dey had dey own hosses and dey rid 'em to school. When dey come home dey would throw de reins to me and John and us took dem hosses and rub dem down and feed 'em.

"Lots of times Newt and Anderson would tell me and John to come and git under de steps while ole Marse was eating his supper. When he git up from de table us lil' niggers would allus hear de sliding o' his chair, kaize he was sech a big fat man. Den he go into de missus room to set by de fire. Dar he would warm his feets and have his Julip. Quick as lightning me and John scamper from under de steps and break fer de big cape jasamine bushes long de front walk. Dar we hide, till Anderson and Newt come out a fetching ham biscuit in dey hands fer us. It would be so full of gravy, dat sometime de gravy would take and run plumb down to de end o' my elbow and drap off, 'fo I could git it licked offn my wrists. Dem was de best rations dat a nigger ever had. When dey had honey on de white folks table, de boys never did fail to fetch a honey biscuit wid dem. Dat was so good dat I jest take one measley lil' bite of honey and melted butter on my way to de 'quarter. I would jest taste a leetle. When I git to Mammy den me and Mammy set off to ourself's and taste it till it done all gone. Us had good times den; like I never is had befo' or since.

"Soon atter dat dey sent me and John to de field to larn drapping. I had to drap peas in every other hill and John had to drap de corn in de rest. De overseer, ole man Wash Evans, come down dar to see how us was a doing. Den us got dat skeert dat us got de corn and peas mixed up. He started to hit us wid de whip dat he had hung 'round his waist. Bout dat time Marse Tom rid up. He made de overseer git out'n dem corn rows and let us 'lone. After dat us got 'long fine wid our drapping. When it come up everybody could see dem rows dat us had done got mixed up on when de overseer was dar. Marse Tom was dat good to his hands dat dey all love him all de time. But one day when ole man Evans come through de field and see dem rows he did call me and John off and whip us. Dat de most dat I ever got whipped. Marse got shed o' de overseer soon after dat.

"It was just like dis. Ole man Wash Evans was a wicked man. He take 'vantage of all de slaves when he git half chance. He was great source of worriment to my Mammy, ole lady Lucy Price and 'nother 'oman, ole lady Lucy Charles. Course he 'vantage over all de darkies and fer dat reason he could sway everything his way, most all de time. But my mammy and ole lady Lucy was 'ligious wimmens. Dat didn't make no diffuns wid wicked old man Evans. One day Missus sent my mammy and de other ole lady Lucy to fetch her some blackberries by dinner.

"Me and John was wid dem a pickin' and fillin' o' de big buckets from de lil' buckets when ole man Evans come riding up. He argued wid both mammy and ole lady Lucy and dey kept telling him dat de missus want her berries and dat dey was 'ligious wimmens anyhow and didn't practice no life o' sin and vile wickedness. Finally he got down off'n his hoss and pull out his whip and low if dey didn't submit to him he gwine to beat dem half to death. That me and John took to de woods. But we peep. My mammy and old lady Lucy start to crying and axing him not to whip dem.

"Finally dey act like dey gwine to indulge in de wickedness wid dat ole man. But when he tuck off his whip and some other garments, my Mammy and ole lady Lucy grab him by his goatee and further down and hist him over in de middle of dem blackberry bushes. Wid dat dey call me and John. Us grab all de buckets and us all put out fer de 'big house' fas' as our legs could carry us. Ole man Evans jest er hollering and er cussing down in dem briars. Quick as us git to de big house us run in de kitchen. Cilla call Missus. She come and ax what ailing us and why we is so ashy looking. Well, my Mammy and ole lady Lucy tell de whole story of dey humiliations down on de creek.

"Missus 'lowed dat it didn't make no diffuns if Marse was in Union, she gwinter act prompt. So she sent fer Mr. Evans and he took real long to git dar, but when he do come, Missus, she 'low—'Mr. Evans, us does not need yo' services on dis plantation no mo', Sir!' He 'low Marse aint here. Missus 'low—'I does not want to argue de point wid ye, Mr. Evans, fer yo' services has come to an end on dis plantation!' Wid dat ole man Evans go off wid his head a-hanging in shame. Us niggers went out and tole de news wid gladness shining out from our eyes, kaise us was dat glad dat we did not know what to do.

"All de fields was enclosed wid a split rail fence in dem days. De hands took dey rations to de field early every morning and de wimmens slack work round eleven by de sun fer to build de fire and cook dinner. Missus 'low her niggers to git buttermilk and clabber, when de cows in full, to carry to de field fer drinking at noon, dat is twelve o'clock. All de things was fetched in waggins and de fire was built and a pot was put to bile wid greens when dey was in season. Over coals meat was baked and meal in pones was wrapped in poplar leaves to bake in de ashes. 'Taters was done de same way, both sweet 'taters and irish. Dat made a good field hand dinner. Plenty was allud had and den 'lasses was also fetched along. Working niggers does on less dese days.

"Does you know dat de poplar leaves was wet afo' de meal pone was put in it? Well, it was, and when it got done de ashes was blowed off wid your breath and den de parched leaves folded back from de cooked pone. De poplar leaves give de ash cake a nice fresh sweet taste. All forks and spoons was made out'n sticks den; even dem in de big house kitchen. Bread bowls and dough trays was all made by de skilled slaves in de Marse's shop, by hands dat was skilled to sech as dat.

"Young chilluns and babies was kept at home by de fire and nursed and cared fer by de ole wimmens dat couldn't do no field work. De chief one on our plantation during my 'membrance was ole aunt Abbie. She had head o' de chilluns all over de plantation when dey mamies was a working in de field. Marse Tom used to ride through de 'quarters' every day to see about ole lady Abbie and de chilluns when dey parents was at work in de fields during de working season. Ole lady Abbie had to see to it dat dey was kept warm by de fire and dat dey clothes was kept up wid while dey mammies was in de field. Dem chilluns on our plantation was well looked after. De seamstresses also kept our work clothes patched and darned, till new ones was wove fer us.

"Sides dat dem chilluns was fed. Each child had a maple

fork and spoon to eat wid. Lil' troughs was made fer dem to eat de milk and bread from. 'Shorts', low stools, was made fer dem to set up to de troughs to, whilst dey was eating. De other ole ladies helped wid de preparations of dey messes o' vittals. One ole woman went her rounds wid a wet rag a wiping dem chilluns dresses when dey would spill dey milk and bread. Marse Tom and sometime Missus come to see de lil' babies whilst dey was a eating. De other ole ladies 'tended to de small babies. Sometimes it was many as fifteen on de plantation at one time dat was too little to walk.

"Dey mammies was not worked on our plantation till de babies was big 'nough to take a bottle. And in dem days no bottle was given no baby under a year old. De wimmins in family way was better cared for den dese young niggers now-a-days. Marse Tom never bred no slaves but he did care fer his niggers when dey married and got dey own chilluns. I has done related to you how dey fixed de medicines and things. Dem babies was washed every day if dey mammies was in de field, dat never made no diffuns, kaise it was de old ladies' jobs to see to it dat dey was. Younguns on de plantation was bathed two or three times a week. Mullein leaves and salt was biled in great big pot to put in de babies' wash water and also in de chilluns' water. Dis would keep 'em from gitting sick. Den dey was allus greased after de washing to keep de skin from busting open. Mosely dey was greased wid tallow from de mutton. Mr. Anderson took medicine and after dat he doctor all de slaves fer his paw free.

"While de Yankees had everything closed up down in Charleston it was hard to git anything in dis country into de sto's. Us allus traded at de post (Goshen Hill Trading

Post). If I recollects correctly it was during dis period dat Marse Tom let my Mammy go up to de post to fetch back her a bonnet.

"Up dar dey took cotton and corn and anything like dat in trade dat dey could sell to de folks dat was working on de railroad bed dat was gwine through dat country (Seaboard Airline). So Mammy took a lot of cotton wid her to de post. She knowd dat it was gwine to take lots to git dat bonnet. It weren't but three and a half miles de short way to de post from our place.

"I's gwine long wid her and so I had to wear some pants to go to de post as dat was big doings fer a lil' darky boy to git to go to de trading center. So aunt Abbie fotched me a pair of new pants dat was dat stiff, dat dey made me feel like I was all closed up in a jacket, atter being used to only a shirt-tail!

"Well, it wasn't fur and us arriv' dar early in de day. Mammy said 'howdy' to all de darkies what dar and I look at dem from behind her skirts. I felt real curious-like all inside. But she never give me no mind whatever. She never act like she knowd dat I was pulling her dress at all. I seed so many things dat I never had seed befo', not in all my born days. Red sticks o' candy was a laying right dar fo' my eyes, jes' like de folks from de big house brung us at Christmas. It was not near Christmas den, kaise it was jest cotton picking time and I wondered how-come dey was having candy in de store fer, now-how.

"Mammy look down at me and she say to de white man wid a beard, 'Marse, please sir, give me five cent worth peppermint candy.' Den when he hand her de bag she break off lil' piece and hand it to me, and wall her eyes at me and say in a low voice, 'Don' you dare git none dat red on yo' clean shirt, if you wants to git home widout gitting wo' plumb smack out.'

"Den she talk about de bonnets. Finally she git one fer ten dollars worth o' cotton. Money wasn't nothing in dem times. By dis time us had done started on our return home and I was starting to feel more like I allus felt.

"Nigger, what dat you is done gone and got on dat clean shirt? Didn't you hear me tell you not to git dat new shirt all red? Look dar a streaming down off'n your chin at dar red. How is I gwine to ever teach you anything, when you act jest like a nigger from some pore white trashes poor land?'

"When we gits to dat branch now I's got to stop and wash dat dirty black mouth and den I can't git dat red candy off'n dat shirt. What ole lady Abbie gwine to say to ye when she see you done gone and act like you ain't never seed no quality befo'?

"Atter I has done tole you all de way from home how you must act at de post den you goes and does like you is. Aint never gwine to carry you nowhars 'gin long as I lives.

"Bend dat lazy, good-fer-nothing back so as I won't git you wet all de way down your belly, you hear me? Now you is looking like you belongs to Marse Tom 'gin. Gimme dat candy right now; I gwine to see to it dat you gits back home looking like somet'ing after all my worriments wid ye.'

"Mammy seed dust a flying and de hoss come a-bringing Marse Tom down de road. Mammy drap everything in the dust and grab her apron to drap a curtsy. She 'low—'Git dat hat off dat head and bow your head fo' he git hear."

"Howdy, Lucy, what is you and dat youngun been, anyhow?' 'Us been to git me a bonnet, Marse Tom, and it took all de ten dollars worth of cotton to fetch it back wid.' 'Yes, Lucy, money does not go far these days, since the Yankees got everything'. 'No Sir, No Sir, Marse,' and he rid on, leaving us behind in de dust."

Source: Interview with Gus Feaster (C-97), ex-slave, living at 20 Stutz Ave., Union, S.C.; interviewer - Caldwell Sims,
Union, South Carolina.

Project #-1655
Phoebe Faucette
Hampton County

Approx. 388 words

ANN FERGUSON EX-SLAVE 74 YEARS

ANN FERGUSON

"Aunt Annie" sat in the sun of a fall afternoon on the steps of her house across from the Baptist Church at Estill, S.C. Her short, stout form and her kind, deeply wrinkled face beneath her white cap, were, as always, a pleasingly familiar sight.

"I'se sure you'se come, Missus. I'se been jes' asittin' here awaitin' for somebody to come. I'm gittin' on in years now. Been right here for fourteen years. I was sick last night. Suffers wid high blood, yes'm.

"Could I tell you 'bout de times before de war? Well ma'am, I was jes' a baby den; so I cain't to say know 'bout it for meself, but I knows what me mother told me 'bout it.

"My mother was at Old Allendale when de Yankees come through. She was in de kitchen at de time. I was quite small. 'Round two years old—now how old dat make me, Miss? 74? Well, I knows I is gittin' 'long. I remember dem talkin' 'bout it all. Dey searched de house, and take out what dey want, den set de house afire. Ma, she run out den an' whoop an' holler. De lady of de house wuz dere, but de Massa had went off. De place wuz dat of Dr. Bucknor. My mother been belong to de Bucknors. After dat, dey moved to de old home place of de Bucknors down here at Robertville. Dey had two places. Dey jes' had to start farming all over again. We lived dere a good bit after freedom, ma say. My mother stay wid 'em for about three years after freedom.

"Fore freedom my mother used to go to de white folks church—white and black used to worship together den. She jined at de old Cypress Creek Baptist Church at Robertville. A white preacher baptized her dere. De old church is dere at Robertville now. After freedom de colored folks had dey own churches.

"Dey tell me dat in slav'ry time, some of de overseers treat 'em mighty mean. Some of 'em work 'em in de day, 'en in de night, weaving. Now some of 'em treat 'em good; but some of 'em treat 'em mean. Dey have to run away into de bay.

"Do I know of anybody what sees ghosts? Yes'm, dere's a lady over dere what say she always see a ghost come and whip a woman dat asittin' on de steps. Sometime she say she goin' to report it to de police, but I ain't never seen none, 'ceptin' in my dreams.

"I sure is glad you come, Missus. I been jes' awaitin' for somebody."

Source: Ann Ferguson, ex-slave 74 years, Estill, S.C.

Project, 1885-(1)
Prepared by Annie Ruth Davis
Place, Marion, S.C.
Date, September 21, 1937

Aaron-Ford,
Ex-Slave

AARON FORD

"I was born bout two miles bove Lake View on Zonia Rogers place. Boys used to tell me I was born on Buck Branch. Think I was born de 12th. day of February cause I was bout 16 years old when freedom come. Another person born de same day en de same year en I might look on dey tombstone en get de date."

"Miles Ford was my father en my mother, Jennie Ford, but dey didn' live on de same place. Father belonged to Alias Ford at Lake View en mother come from Timmonsville what used to be called Sparrow Swamp. Railroad run through dere change name from Sparrow Swamp to Timmonsville."

"Just like I tell you, Zonia Rogers was my boss en he wasn' so bad. He whip me a few times when I did things dat I oughtened to do. Sometimes I was pesty en he whip me wid a switch, but he never whip so hard. I tell de truth, Zonia Rogers was a good man. Give his slaves good pole houses to live in up in de quarter. Never had but five slaves to start wid en dat de reason he just had two slave house in de quarter. Sometimes dey slept on de floor en den another time, some had homemade bedstead wid de framework made out of black gum."

"We had meat en corn bread to eat all de time en dey gave us fried meat en rye bread en flour bread to eat every now en den. Made rye bread in time of de war, but didn' get much flour bread to eat. Massa would weigh meat out on his hand. If anybody wanted meat, he hand it to dem on his hand en say, 'Here it is.' Den some of de slaves had gardens dat dey work at 12 o'clock en at night. Never was much to catch possums, but was great hand to catch rabbits. Boss had dog name Trip dat he wouldn' have taken $200.00 for. If I had him now, I wouldn' take $200.00 for him neither cause dat dog would stay at a tree all night. See him stay dere from early in de day till dark."

"Slaves wore one piece garment in de summer en used thick woolen garment in de winter. When I got large, had wrapper en little breeches to wear. Sometimes de clothes was all wool en sometimes dey was just half wool. Yes, sir, I know all bout how de cloth was made in dat day en time. Three treadle made dis here jeanes cloth dat was for de nigger clothes en white people wore four treadle cloth. Had Sunday clothes in slavery time, too, en made de shoes right dere home. Tanned de leather en made shoes called nigger brogans dat dey used in de turpentine woods. Dese here low quarters. I married in 1873. Just had common clothes when I was married."

"I remember my grandfather all right. He de one told me how to catch otters. Told me how to set traps. Heard my grandfather tell bout whippin slaves for stealin. Grandfather told me not to take things dat were not mine. If a pile of corn was left at night, I was told not to bother it. In breakin corn, sometimes people would make a pile of corn in de grass en leave it en den come back en get it in de night. Grandfather told me not to never bother nothin bout people's things."

"De first work dat I remember bout doin in slavery time, I hold mules for my boss. Drove wagon for Mr. Rogers. If people wanted any haulin done, he told me to help dem en collect for it. He never wouldn' ax any questions bout what I collected for de haulin. Just let me have dat money. I remember I bought cloth dat cost 12½ cents a yard wid de first money I get. Den I bought a girl 10 cents worth of candy en sent it to her. Hear she stamped it in de ground wid her foot. Girl never even mentioned it to me en I ain' never bothered wid her again. Dis girl en me bout de same age."

"Don' remember much bout my first Missus only dat she had a bump on her neck. Second Missus was good to me en just like I tell you, Zonia Rogers was a good man. He hired white men to plow, but he never put nobody ahead of me no time. I take dogs en slip out in de woods en hunt rabbits. White man tell on me en my boss ain' never said nothin bout dis to me yet. Never had no overseer en no driver whe' I stay."

"Oh, dere was bout two or three hundred acres in de Rogers place. Slaves worked from daylight till dark in de winter time. Always be up fore day cause my boss generally called de slaves fore day. Hear him say, 'Rob, come, come. Aaron, come, come.' We didn' work hard though. Didn' work in hot sun in June, July en August cause in slavery time dey allow us to take out at 10 or 11 o'clock en go swimmin. Den we had to be back in de field bout three o'clock. Had plenty poor white neighbors bout dere en boss hire me to man like dat one time. Poor man give bout 1½ hours for noon whe' I get two hours back home en I never go back de next day. Boss say, 'Why don' you go back to work?' I tell him dat fellow wouldn' give me long enough time for noon. My boss wouldn' force me to go back when I tell him dat."

"I see one or two slaves whipped in slavery time, but I didn' see anybody whipped bad. If a slave on one place was accused of takin a thing on another place, dey have a trial bout it. Justice might tell dem how many licks to give him en point man to do it. I hear dat some been whipped way off till dey died, but old man Everett Nichols wouldn' never whip his slaves. He had son dat whipped some rough darkies dat he got off another place cause old man Nichols wouldn' want strange darkies to marry girls on his place. I hear way up de country dat dey whipped dem till dey died right dere."

"Dey had jails in slavery time at Marion for de slaves. If dey caught slaves dat had run away, dey would put dem in jail till dey Massa sent after dem. Sometimes dey would hold dem en sell dem for debt. Dey tell me some put on stand en sold dere at Marion, but I never saw any sold. Just hear bout dat, but I remembers I saw dis. Saw six men tied together wid a chain one Saturday evenin dat was comin from Virginia en gwine to Texas."

"Some people helped de slaves to read en write en some of dem didn'. Boy learnt one of my uncles to read, but didn' want him to write. People learn to spell in dem times better den dey do now. Some of de slaves could read de Bible en den others of dem could write dese pass dat dey had to get from dey Massa fore dey could go from one plantation to another. I recollects my mother's father could write a pass."

"Dere wasn' no church on de plantation whe' I stay. Had preachin in Mr. Ford's yard sometimes en den another time de slaves went to white people's church at Bear Swamp. Boss tell slaves to go to meetin cause he say he pay de preacher. Dean Ears, white man, gave out speech to de slaves one day dere to Nichols. Slaves sat in gallery when dey go dere. He tell dem to obey dey Massa en Missus. Den he say, 'God got a clean kitchen to put you in. You think you gwine be free, but you ain' gwine be free long as dere an ash in Ashpole Swamp.' White folks complain bout de slaves gettin two sermons en dey get one. After dat, dey tell old slaves not to come to church till after de white folks had left. Dat never happen till after de war was over."

"I sho remember when freedom come here. Remember when my boss told me I was free. My father come dere en say he wanted his boys. Boss called, 'Aaron, come here, your daddy wants you. I want you to go.' He told me not to go till de news came though. Please me, I felt like a new man."

"I hate to speak what I think bout slavery. Think it a pity de slaves freed cause I know I'm worried more now den in slavery time. Dere got to be a change made. People got to turn. I belong to de Methodist Church en I think everybody ought to belong to de church. God built de church for de people en dey ought to go dere en be up en doin in de church. Dat dey duty."

Source: Aaron Ford, Ex-Slave, Age 80-90, (No other

information given by interviewer.)

Personal interview by H. Grady Davis, June, 1937.

Project 1885 -1-
District #4
Spartanburg, S.C.
May 28, 1937

FOLKLORE: EX-SLAVES

CHARLOTTE FOSTER

Six miles east of Spartanburg on R.F.D. No. 2, the writer found Aunt Charlotte Foster, a colored woman who said she was 98 years old. Her mother was Mary Johnson and her father's name was John Johnson. She is living with her oldest daughter, whose husband is John Montgomery.

She stated she knew all about slavery times, that she and her mother belonged to William Beavers who had a plantation right on the main road from Spartanburg to Union, that the farm was near Big Brown Creek, but she didn't know what larger stream the creek flowed into. Her father lived on another place somewhere near Limestone. She and her mother were hands on the farm and did all kinds of hard work. She used to plow, hoe, dig and do anything the men did on the plantation. "I worked in the hot sun." Every now and then she would get a sick headache and tell her master she had it; then he would tell her to go sit down awhile and rest until it got better.

She had a good master; he was a Christian if there ever was one. He had a wife that was fussy and mean.

"I didn't call her Mistus, I called her Minnie." But, she quickly added, "Master was good to her, just as kind and gentle like." When asked what was the matter with the wife, she just shook her head and did not reply. Asked if she had rather live now or during slavery times, she replied that if her master was living she would be willing to go back and live with him. "Every Sunday he would call us chilluns by name, would sit down and read the Bible to us; then he would pray. If that man ain't in the Kingdom, then nobody's there."

She said her master never whipped any of the slaves, but she had heard cries and groans coming from other plantations at five o'clock in the morning where the slaves were being beaten and whipped. Asked why the slaves were being beaten, she replied rather vehemently, "Just because they wanted to beat 'em; they could do it, and they did." She said she had seen the blood running down the backs of some slaves after they had been beaten.

One day a girl about 16 years of age came to her house and said she'd just as leave be dead as to take the beatings her master gave her, so one day she did go into the woods and eat some poison oak. "She died, too."

On one plantation she saw an old woman who used to get so many beatings that they put a frame work around her body and ran it up into a kind of steeple and placed a bell in the steeple. "Dat woman had to go around with that bell ringing all the time."

"I got plenty to eat in dem days, got just what the white folks ate. One day Master killed a deer, brung it in the house, and gave me some of the meat. There was plenty of deer den, plenty of wild turkeys, and wild hogs.

Master told me whenever I seed a deer to holler and he would kill it."

When slaves were freed her mother moved right away to her father's place, but she said the two sons of her master would not give her mother anything to eat then. "Master was willing, but dem boys would not give us anything to live on, not even a little meal."

"After the Civil War was over and the Yankee soldiers came to our place, dey just took what they wanted to eat, went into de stable and leave their poor, broken-down horses and would ride off with a good horse. They didn't hurt anybody, but just stole all they wanted."

One day she said her master pointed out Abe Lincoln to her. A long line of cavalry rode down the road and presently there came Abe Lincoln riding a horse, right behind them. She didn't have much to say about Jeff Davis, except she heard the grown people talking about him. "Booker Washington? Well, he was all right trying to help the colored people and educate them. But he strutted around and didn't do much. People ought to learn to read the Bible, but if you educate people too high it make a fool out of them. They won't work when they gets an education, just learns how to get out of work, learns how to steal enough to keep alive. They are not taught how to work, how do you expect them to work when they ain't taught to work? Well, I guess I would steal too before I starved to death, but I ain't had to steal yet. No man can say he ever gave me a dollar but what I didn't earn myself. I was taught to work and I taught my chilluns to work, but this present crowd of niggers! They won't do."

She stated her mother had twelve children and the log house they lived in was weatherboarded; it was much warmer in such a house during cold weather than the houses are now. "Every crack was chinked up with mud and we had lots of wood." Her mother made all their beds, and had four double beds sitting in the room. She made the ticking first and placed the straw in the mattresses. "They beat the beds you can get now. These men make half beds, den sell 'em to you, but dey ain't no good. Dey don't know how to make 'em."

Aunt Charlotte said she remembered when the stars fell. "That was something awful to see. Dey just fell in every direction. Master said to wake the chilluns up and let 'em see it. Everybody thought the world was coming to an end. We went out on de front porch to look at the sight; we'd get scared and go back into de house, den come out again to see the sight. It was something awful, but I sure saw it." (Records show that the great falling of stars happened in the year 1833, so Aunt Charlotte must be older than she claims, if she saw this eventful sight. Yet she was positive she had seen the stars falling all over the heavens. She made a sweep of her arm from high to low to illustrate how they fell.)

Source: Aunt Charlotte Foster, RFD #2, Spartanburg, S.C.
Interviewer: F.S. DuPre, Spartanburg, S.C.

Project #1655
Stiles M. Scruggs
Columbia, S.C.

JOHN FRANKLIN
EX-SLAVE 84 YEARS OLD.

JOHN FRANKLIN

"I is the son of John Franklin and Susan Bobo Franklin. I was born August 10th, 1853 in Spartanburg County. My daddy was a slave on the plantation of Marster Henry Franklin, sometimes called Hill and my mammy was a slave on the plantation of Marster Benjamin Bobo. They was brother-in-law's and lived on a plantation joining each other.

"My white marsters and their mistresses was good to us and to all their slaves. We have plenty to eat and wear, on the Bobo plantation, from the time I can remember up to the time I was 'bout eleven years old. In 1861, my marsters go away with their neighbors, to fight the damn Yankees and the plantation was left in charge of the mistresses and worked by the slaves. The slaves all raised 'bundance of rations, but pretty soon there was a scarcity 'cause they was no coffee at the store and stragglin' Yankees or what they call 'Rebel soldiers' come 'long every few days and take all they can carry.

"That shortage begun in 1862, and it kept on gettin' worse all the time, and when Lincoln set all niggers free, there was such a shortage of food and clothes at our white folks houses, that we decided to move to a Dutch Fork plantation. My daddy go 'long with other niggers to fight for 'Uncle Abe' and we never see him no more. Soon after that me and mammy told our mistress goodbye, and move down to her daddy's place, 'bout ten miles from Chapin. I was ten years old that year and we raise corn, beans, 'taters and chickens for ourselves and to sell, when we could go to Columbia and sell it and buy coffee and other things that we could not raise at home. So we do pretty well for a year or two and we keep up our tradin' trips to Columbia, which 'counts for me and Ben Lyles, my cousin 'bout my age, comin' to Columbia on February 16, 1868. We sold out and stayed all night at the home of Ben's uncle. He had us do some tasks 'bout his home on Lincoln Street the next day and it was way in the day befo' we start home. We walk north on what was known then as the Winnsboro road 'til we come to Broad River road, and we take it. There was one or two farm houses north of Elmwood Street on the Winnsboro road at that time and only one house on Broad River road, the farm house of Mr. Coogler, which is still standin'. There was a big woodsland at the forks of the Winnsboro road and Broad River road.

"After we walk 'long the Broad River road, what seem to us for a quarter of a mile, we see four or five old men standin' on the left side of the road wavin' a white flag. We walks out in the woods on the right side opposite and watches. Soon we see what seem lak a thousand men on hosses comin' briskly 'long. The men keep wavin' the white flag. After many had passed, one big bearded man rein up his hoss and speak with the men wavin' the white flag. They tell the soldier there am no 'Rebel soldier' in Columbia and the blue-clad army am welcome; beggin' them to treat the old folks, women and children, well. The Yankee soldier set straight and solemn on his hoss, and when the old men finish and hand him a paper, he salute and tell them, 'Your message will be laid befo' General Sherman'.

"All this time the ground am shakin' from the roar of big guns 'cross the river. Ben and me run thru the woods to our footlog and see thousands still comin' into Columbia, all 'long. We get 'fraid and stayed in the woods 'til we get out of sight of the soldiers. But we ain't got far over the top of the hill 'til we come face to face with more men on hosses. One of the men, who seem to be the leader, stop his hoss and ask us boys some questions. We answer as best we can, when he grin at us and pull out some money and give us a nickel a piece.

"We travel on toward Chapin and meet our mammies and many other people, some them white. They all seem scared and my mammy and Ben's mammy and us, turns up the river and camps on the hill, for the night, in the woods. We never sleep much, for it was 'most as light as day, and the smell of smoke was terrible. We could see people runnin' in certain parts of Columbia, sometimes. Next mornin' we look over the city from the bluff and only a few houses was standin' and hundreds of tumble-down chimneys and the whole town was still smokin'.

"I dreams yet 'bout that awful time, but I thank God that he has permitted me to live 'long enough to see the city rebuilt and it stretching far over the area where we hid in the trees."

Project #-1655
Cassels R. Tiedeman
Charleston, S.C.

FOLKLORE

EMMA FRASER—EX-SLAVE

EMMA FRASER

Emma Fraser, a pathetic old character, probably on account of many hardships, and the lack of family to care for her properly, shows the wear and tear of years. She was born, in slavery, on a plantation near Beaufort, of a mother whom she scarcely remembers, and cannot recall the name of the plantation, nor the name of her mother's owner. She talks very little but is most emphatic about the time of her birth. "I born in rebel time, on de plantation down by Beaufort. My ma say I a leetle gal when dey shoot de big gun on Fort Sumter. All dem people done dead an' gone now. I aint know dey name any mo'. Wid de troublulation and bombation I hab to tend wid an' de brain all wore down, you aint blame me for not know.

"I wants to go to Hebben now an' when de roll is call up dere an' I be dere, de Lord, he find a hiding place for me. I goes to chu'ch when I kin an' sing too, but ef I sing an' it doan mobe (move) me any, den dat a sin on de Holy Ghost; I be tell a lie on de Lord. No I aint sing when it doan mobe me. You mus'n ax me to do dat.

"One day I see a big automobile on de street wid a old gemmun (gentleman) ob slavery time settin' in em. I goes up to em an' ax how old he t'ink I is, an' he say dat I come way, way back dere in de slavery day, an' he know what he say."

Source: Interview with the writer

Emma Fraser, 98 Coming St, Charleston, S.C.
Approx. 80 years old.

S-260-264-N
Hattie Mobley
Project 935
Richland County

ADELE FROST

EX-SLAVE 93 YEARS OF AGE

ADELE FROST

"I was bo'n in Adams Run, South Carolina, January 21st. 1844. My father name was Robert King, an' my mother was Minder King. My father was bo'n in Adams Run but my mother came from Spring Grove, South Carolina. I had eight brothers an' sisters, Maria, Lovie, Josephine, Eliza, Victoria, Charlie an' Robert King. The other two died w'en dey was babies. Only three of us is alive now. Maria, who lives in Adams Run is 95 years old. I was brought heh at the age of twelve to be maid for Mr. Mitchell, from who' I didn't git any money but a place to stay an' a plenty of food an' clothes. My bed was the ole time four post' with pavilion hangin' over the top.

"I's use to wear thin clothes in hot weather an' warm comfortable ones in the winter. On Sunday I wear a ole time bonnet, a'm hole apron, shoes an' stockin'. My Master was kind to his slaves an' his overseer was all Negroes. He had a large fa'm at Parkers' Ferry. He worked his slaves 'til twelve in the day an' the res' of the day they could do their own work.

"I never gone to school in my life an' massa nor missus ever help me to read.

"On the plantation was a meetin' house in which wen' used to have meetin's every Chuseday night, Wednesday night, an' Thursday night. I use to attend the white church. Doctor Jerico was de pastor. Collud people had no preacher but dey had leader. Every slave go to church on Sunday 'cause dey didn't have any work to do for Massa. My grandma use to teach the catekism an' how to sing.

"Co'n shuckin' was always done in de night. Dere was also a dance. Es de distance was five miles we would walk dere, work an' dance all night an' come back early nex' mornin'.

"Fun'rals was at night an' w'en ready to go to the graveyard every body would light a lightud knot as torch while every body sing. This is one of the songs wen' use to sing,

> 'Goin' to carry dis body
> To the grave-yard,
> Grave-yard don' you know me?
> To lay dis body down.'

"These are some the games wen' use to play,

> Have a han'ful of co'n den say,
> "Trow kissey Wilson let him go."

while the res' is to guess how many co'n is lef in his han's.

We ain't had no doctor, our Missus an' one of de slave' would 'tend to the sick.

The Yankees take t'ree nights to march through I was afraid of dem an' clim' into a tree. One call me down an' say, "I am your frien'". He give me a piece of money an' I wasn't 'fraid no mo.

After de war I still work' as a maid for Mr. Mitchell.

My husband was Dan'l Frost. We didn't have no weddin', jus' married at de jedge office. We had three chillun.

I joined the church 'cause I wanted to be a christian an' I think every body should be. I move here wid my gran' daughter, bout ten year ago.

> Reference: Interview with (Mrs) Adele Frost who is supported by her
> Master's people.

Project #-1655
Martha S. Pinckney
Charleston, S.C.

FOLKLORE

AMOS GADSDEN

"My name is Amos Gadsden, not Gadson, like some call it—the same old name Gadsden"—he added, with a friendly smile.

"I was born at St. Philip's Street; that is where old Miss lived then. (We belonged to old Mr. Titus Bissell) I don't rightly know what year, but I was nineteen years old before the War, when the family Bible was lost; old Mistress had my birth written in the Bible. I keep my age by Mas. Henry, he died three years ago; he was 83, and I was five years older than he was, so I am 88. Oh, yes, I can remember slavery! My grandmother was a 'daily gift' to old Mistress when they were both children. Grandmother was nurse to the children; she lived over a hundred years and nursed all the children and grandchildren. She died at the Bissell's home on Rutledge Avenue years and years after slavery. Mother Ellen was laundress; she died first part of the War. My father tended the yard and was coachman.

"I never got a slap from my mistress; I was treated like a white person; if my mistress talked to me to correct me, I want to cry. Sometime I slept at the foot of my mistress bed." Whatever the occasion, Amos was very proud of it, and mentioned it a second time in his story, and added—"it ain't every little boy that could say that.

"We spent the summers in Charleston—winters on the plantation; Cypress Plantation which belonged to Mr. Bissell's father, Mr. Baker, was near Green Pond. The smoke house was there full of meat; the fields and the gardens were there and everybody had plenty to eat—but still there was bad people just like they are now. You can make yourself respectable, but some never do it. The bad ones had to be punished; they got a few lashes on 'um. Now they go to Court, and they go to jail—If there was a place to whip bad coons, they would be scared to behave like they do now—the jails wouldn't be so full. There was no bad treatment of our people. Some neighbors that never owned any slaves, hired negro help and ill-treated them—old mistress felt so bad about this.

"I grew up with the white children in the family, but I was trained to step aside at all times for white people. My grandmother's name was Affy Calvert; she was a 'daily gift' to old Mistress; she was given to her when they were both children and trained up in her service. Old Mistress died long before her because she lived over a hundred years, and nursed all the children and grandchildren. She brought me up more than my mother; she and I never gave up the family."

Amos makes a strange statement: "Old Mausa, Mr. T.L. Bissell, (voice lowered) was a Yankee, but he lived long before the War," with an indulgent smile, and in a lower voice, with his hand up to his mouth he continued as though communicating a dangerous confidence, "Oh, yes, Ma'am—but he was a Yankee!" What Amos meant will remain a family secret.

"I was trained by old Tony for yard boy before the War. I looked out that no harm came to the older children, but one day they got away from me," Amos chuckled, "they went to play on the logs in the lumber yard, around what is now Halsey's Mill. The water was full of timber, open to the river, (Ashley) and the tide was running out. One of the boys got on a log, and two others on another log, and the little scamps paddled the logs out, but when they found themselves in the tide they were scared, and screamed at the top of their voices. I wasn't far off and heard them. I was scared too. I jumped into the water and swam to get a bateau; when they saw me they hushed. The tide had carried them some distance before I caught up with them—was down near Chisolm's Rice Mill. Mr. Chisolm saw it; he gave me a five dollar bill, Confederate money, for saving the children."

Amos throws a new light on old history;—"Before the War come here it was down in Beaufort, on the Port Royal Road; Confederates on one side, Yankees on the other, and things happen here that belong to War. One evening, early dusk, because it was winter, I was with two white boys on the corner of Hasell street and East Bay. We stopped to watch a balloon slowly floating in the sky. I never saw anything like it before—it looked so pretty—and while we were looking a streak of fire came straight down from the balloon to Russell's Planing Mill at the foot of Hasell street,[1] right by us. In a short time the mill was on fire; nothing could put it out. One place after another caught, and big flakes of fire were bursting up and flying through the air, and falling on other buildings. (illustrating with his arms, hands, and whole body) The first church that burned was the Circular Church on Meeting Street; then Broad street and the Roman Catholic Church, and St. Andrews Hall. Yes, Ma'am, 'course I remember St. Andrews Hall, right next to the Roman Catholic Cathedral on Broad Street! That was 1861, before I went to Virginia with Dr. H. E. Bissel. That balloon went on down to Beaufort, I s'pose. Yes Ma'am, I saw it drop that fire on Russell's Mill.

"I went to Virginia with Dr. H.E. Bissell in the Army; he was a surgeon. A camp of Negroes went ahead to prepare the roads; pioneers, they called them. I remember Capt. Colcock, (he mentioned several other officers,) Honey Hill—terrible fighting—fight and fight! had to 'platoon' it. I was behind the fighting with Dr. Bissell. I held arms and legs while he cut them off, till after a while I didn't mind it. Hard times came to the Army; only corn to eat. When the bombardment came to Charleston the family moved to Greenville; I was in Virginia with the Doctor. The railroad bridge across the Ashley River was burned to prevent the Yankees from coming into Charleston; the ferry boat 'Fannie' crossed the river to make connections with the Savannah Railroad. The 54th Massachusetts Regiment was coming down to Charleston; they destroyed railroads as they came. Sherman set fire everywhere he went—didn't do much fighting, just wanted to destroy as he went.

"After Freedom, we went back to the Plantation; lived catch as catch can. The smoke house had been emptied by the Yankees, and no money. Lieutenant Duffy, at the Citadel, fell in love with me and offered me a place to work with him for money. I took it and worked for him til he left—but I didn't give up the family. I work for Mas. Titus now; haven't stopped calling Mr. Orvel Bissell 'Mas' today; I raised him but I still call him Mas. Orvel.

My young Missus was the one who taught me; she kept a school for us; we took it for a play school; when I was a little boy I knew the alphabet.

"We buried our valuables in sacks in holes, then put plants over the hiding places. The silver was buried by Cypress Pond; and we saved all buried valuables.

"To show how Mas. Titus (Bissell) will look out for me—a man I rented from wanted to put some 'coon' in my room. I had paid him the rent, but one day I came and find my things being put out. I went right to Mas. Titus and told him. He was mad, and, excusing the words, he said, 'do you mean that damned so-and-so is putting your things out, well, we'll go there'—so we went, and the man was so scared he wanted to put the things back but Mas. Titus said: 'He sha'nt bother with any such damned person as you are. I'll find a proper place for him,' and he found me a good room on Short Street where I stayed for 8 years until the house was sold—that make I move on Elliott street where I am now.

"My wife is long dead, and I have no children—this is my niece; my brother's daughter. He went from this State three years ago and we have never heard a word from him since. I take care of her. Does she do right by me? She got to! I make her!"

Source: Amos Gadsden, 88, 20 Elliott Street, Charleston, S.C.

[1] King, William L. in "The Newspaper Press of Charleston, S.C." Lucas and Richardson (Book Press) 1882—200p—pp-120-121. Charleston Library Society.

Confirms the statement that the fire of 1861 started in

the Russell's Planing Mill, though no mention is made of its origin.

Project 1886 -1-
District #4
Spartanburg, S.C.
From Field Notes
Folk-Lore
May 26, 1937

FOLKLORE: EX-SLAVES:

JANIE GALLMAN

Journeying on Cudd Street this morning and stopping at the "Old Ladies' Home" (an institution for negroes), the writer found two ex-slaves sitting on the porch passing the time of day with those who passed the house. They both spoke very respectfully and asked me to come in.

One was seated and she asked me to have a seat by her. Her name was Janie Gallman and she said she was 84 years of age. Upon my telling her my name she stated she knew my father and grandfather and had worked for them in days gone by. "If your father or Mr. Floyd was living I wouldn't want for a thing".

She was born in slavery on the plantation of Bill Keenan in Union County. The place was situated between Pacolet River and Fairforest Creek and near where Governor Gist had a plantation. Her mother and father were both owned by Bill Keenan and he was a good master. She never saw any of the slaves get a whipping and never saw any slave in chains. When she, her father, and mother were set free, she said, "My master gave my father a barrel of meal, a cow and a calf and a wagon of corn when he sot him free. He gave every one of his slaves the same. He had a big plantation, but I don't know how many acres of land there was, but it was a big place."

She was married three times and her mother had 12 children, but she has never had any.

Her young life was spent in playing with the children of the white overseer. They used to jump rope most of the time. Whenever the overseer left home to spend the night anywhere, his wife would send for her to spend the night with the family. The overseer was "poor white trash". She had plenty to eat in slavery days. Her father and mother had their own garden, and she did her share of eating the vegetables out of the garden. She remembered seeing plenty of wild turkeys as a child, but as for hogs and cattle, she did not remember them running wild. She had heard of conjuring, but she did not know how it was done—never saw anybody who had been conjured—yet she had seen ghosts two or three times. One night she saw a light waving up against a piece of furniture, then come towards her, then flicker about the room, but she wasn't able to see anybody holding the light. She had heard of headless men walking around, yet had never seen any.

A neighbor told her a woman ghost came to her house one night, just sat on the front steps and said nothing, repeated her visits several nights in succession, but said no word as she sat on the front step. One night the neighbor's husband asked the ghost what did she want, why she sat on the steps and said nothing. The ghost then spoke and told him to follow her. He followed her and she led him to the basement of the house and told him to dig in the corner. He did and pretty soon he unearthed a jar of money. The woman ghost told him to take just a certain amount and to give the rest to a certain person. The ghost told the man if he didn't give the money to the person she named, she would come back and tear him apart. He very obediently took the small amount of the money and gave the balance where the ghost directed, and he never saw the woman sitting on his steps any more.

Another time she heard footsteps approaching a certain house in the yard, but she could never see anybody walking, though she could distinctly hear the gravel crunching as the ghost walked along. "God is the only one who can do any conjuring. I don't believe anybody else can."

Source: Aunt Janie Gallman, 391 Cudd St, Spartanburg, S.C.
Interviewer: F.S. DuPre, Spartanburg, S.C.

United States. Work Projects Administration

Project 1885 -1-
Spartanburg, S.C.
May 31, 1937
District #4

Edited by:
Martha Ritter

FOLKLORE: EX-SLAVES

LUCY GALLMAN

"I was born in Edgefield County, S.C. (now called Saluda County) in 1857. My father and mother was Bill and Mary Kinard who was slaves of John Kinard. The year I was born, I allus heard say, there was a big fire near Columbia, S. C. It started in the woods near the river, spread over all parts there and the people, womens with new-born infants, had to leave in a hurry, going back from the fire and crossing the river, to Edgefield County. I 'member there was a big fire in Prosperity back in about 1875.

"I was a girl in slavery, worked in the fields from the time I could work at all, and was whipped if I didn't work. I worked hard. I was born on John Bedenbaugh's place; I was put up on the block and sold when a girl, but I cried and held tight to my mistress's dress, who felt sorry for me and took me back with her. She was Mrs. Sarah Bedenbaugh, as fine a woman as ever lived.

"Marse Bedenbaugh had a 5-horse farm, and about 20 slaves. We didn't have time to teach them to read and write; never went to church—never went to any school. After the war some started a nigger school and a brush-arbor church for niggers.

"When the Yankees went through their soldiers stole everthing, all horses and supplies. The soldiers stopped at places, and like the soldiers who come home foot-sore, they was lousy and dirty. Our soldiers come with canteen shoes and and old blankets swung on their backs and shoulders. The people would send wagons out to meet them and bring them in, some of them could hardly walk. The Yankee soldiers would take our rations at our gates and eat them up. They would blow bugles at we children and beat drums. Our old Missus would take victuals to them.

"The paterollers down there where we lived was Geo. Harris, Lamb Crew, Jim Jones, and Theo. Merchant. They bothered us lots. On the first day of the month, some was put up on the whipping block and whipped with an oak paddle with holes in it to make blisters; then de blisters were cut open with cowhide whips.

"When freedom come, all slaves went to some place to get work. My father give me six cuts a day to work in the house to spin the yarn. My mistress used to have me pick up de sheckles for her when she was making a homespun dress. In the winter time we had homespuns, too, but sometimes had flannel underwear. I helped at the corn mill, too, always went there and tote a half bushel corn many days. The mill belonged to Capt. McNary. I worked hard, plowed, cut wheat, split cord wood, and other work just like a man.

"When any niggers died they had funerals like they do

now, 'cept the pallbearers den would sing. They carried the bodies in wagons, and the preacher would say words while they was going to the grave.

"When the soldiers was here, I 'member how they would sing:

> "I'm all de way from Georgia,
> I'm all the way to fight,
> I left my good old mother,
> To come here to fight."

> "Joe Bowers, Joe Bowers,
> He had another wife,
> He's all de way from Missouri,
> To come here to fight."

"I didn't like slavery. I'd rather live like now.

"I thought Abraham Lincoln was a big man, a fine man. I thought Jeff Davis was all right. I don't know nothing about Booker Washington."

Source: Lucy Gallman (80), Newberry, S.C.
Interviewer: G. Leland Summer, 1707 Lindsey St, Newberry, S.C.

United States. Work Projects Administration

Slave Narratives

Project 1885-1
FOLKLORE
Spartanburg Dist. 4
May 24, 1937

Edited by:
Elmer Turnage

STORIES FROM EX-SLAVES

SIMON GALLMAN

"I was born about 1857, and belonged to Marse George Gallman who lived in the Dutch Fork, on de old road to Pomaria, S.C. There was not a better man to his slaves. When the Ku Klux went through, they never hurt anybody at our place. The Padder-rollers never did harm any of Marse George's slaves—he would not allow it.

"After the war when I married, I moved to Newberry, but first, I moved to the Jalapa section and lived there ten years.

"I allus 'member the old wheat mill dat old Captain Ellerson had in Dutch Fork, on Cannons Creek. All the neighbors would take their wheat there to grind."

Source: Simon Gallman (80), Newberry, S.C.
Interviewer: G. L. Summer, Newberry, S.C. (5/18/37).

Project 1885-1
Folklore
Spartanburg, Dist. 4
Oct. 25, 1937

Edited by:
Elmer Turnage

EX-SLAVES STORIES

SIMON GALLMAN

"I live in de house wid my grandniece and her husband. It is a two-room house which dey rent; and dey take care of me. I am old, weak and in bed much of de time. I can't work any, now. My grandniece had to give up her job so she could stay home and take care of me. Dat makes it hard fer us.

"I don't remember much about de war nor de Ku Klux 'cept what I done tole you befo'. Dey never bothered us. My master would not let 'em bother us. He was George Gallman and he had a big farm and lots of slaves. Just atter freedom come he made a coffin shop in back of his house in a little one-room shack. He made coffins fer people about de country. It got to be han'ted, and sometimes niggers could see ghosts around dere at night, so dey say, I never saw none, myself.

"Master George and his mistress was good to de niggers. Dey always give dem plenty to eat. I had it good, and never bothered about nothing den. De slaves never learn't to read and write; but dey went to de whitefolks' church. Dey had to go, and set in de back or in de gallery.

"When freedom come, de slaves hired out mostly as share-croppers. A little later, some got small farms to rent. Since dat time dey have worked at most anything dey could get to do. De ones dat moved to town worked at odd jobs, some at carpenter work, janitor work or street work; but most of dem worked in fields around town.

"I married Hattie Eckles. When she died I went to Jalapa and lived ten years dere; den atter I got too old to work, I come to town and lived wid my kin.

"I was about twelve years old when dey made me go to de field to work. Befo' dat and after dat, too, I worked around de barn and took care of de stock.

"As fer eats, we had plenty. We had good collards, turnips and other good vegetables. De master has his own hogs, too, and we had plenty meat to eat.

"Christmas was a big day fer us. We never worked dat day. We had good dinner, and could do what we wanted to do. We never had to work in de fields on Saturday. We would do washing or go hunting or something else.

"All I know about slavery being all right, is dat I had a good time, better dan now. Abraham Lincoln was a good man. I don't know nothing agin' him. Never heard anything about Jefferson Davis. I think Booker Washington is a good man. He do good fer de niggers in giving dem education.

"I joined de church when I was young because others

was joining. I think everybody ought to belong to de church."

   Source: Simon Gallman (80), Newberry, S.C.
   Interviewer: G.L. Summer, Newberry, S.C. (9/3/37)

United States. Work Projects Administration

Project 1885
District #4
Spartanburg, S.C.
June 1, 1937

Edited by:
Martha Ritter

FOLKLORE: EX-SLAVES

LAURENCE GARY

"I was born in 1861, at Gary's Lane, in Newberry County, S.C. My father and mother and me were slaves of Dr. John Gary who lived in a big fine house there. They had lots of slaves, and a large plantation. After freedom come he told them they could go where they wanted to, but they stayed on with Doc Gary. He was a good master; he never allowed any paderollers around his place; he always give the slave a pass when he went off. When de Ku Klux went up and down the road on horses, all covered with white sheets, old Doc wouldn't allow them on his place.

"We was allowed to hunt, and we hunted rabbits, 'possums, a few foxes in the neighborhood, partridges, squirrels, and doves.

"We went to school after freedom come; we had a school for niggers and had a church for niggers, too.

"Doc Gary had a big piano in his house, and most

everybody else had a fiddle or Jews harp. He had a wide fireplace in his kitchen where he cooked over it, in skillets.

"I think Abe Lincoln was a fine man and Jeff Davis was all right. Booker Washington is a smart fellow."

Source: Laurence Gary (76), Newberry, S.C. (Helena)
Interviewer: G. Leland Summer, 1707 Lindsey St, Newberry, S.C.

Code No.
Project 1885-(1)
Prepared by Annie Ruth Davis
Place, Marion, S.C.
Date, December 2, 1937

No. _____
Reduced from_____words
Rewritten by

————————-

LOUISA GAUSE
Ex-Slave, Age 70-75

LOUISA GAUSE

"I been born down yonder to old man Wash (Washington) Woodberry's plantation. Pa Cudjo, he been keep my age in de Bible en he tell me dat I come here de first year of freedom. Monday Woodberry was my grandfather en Celina Woodberry, my grandmother. I tell you, I is seen a day, since I come here. My mammy, she been drown right down dere in de Pee Dee river, fore I get big enough to make motion en talk what I know. Dat how-come it be dat Pa Cudjo raise me. You see, Pa Cudjo, he been work down to de swamp a heap of de time en been run boat en rafter up en down dat river all bout dere. Ma, she get word, one day, she better come cross de river to de Sand Hills to see bout grandmammy cause she been took down wid de fever en was bad off. Pa Cudjo tell her de river been mighty high, but dat he would risk to take us. Say, Ma, she get in de boat wid Pa Cudjo en take me in her lap en dey start cross de river. De wind, it begin gettin higher en higher en de boat, it go dis way en den it go de other way. Cose I never recollect nothin bout dat day cause I won' nothin, so to speak, but a sucklin child den. But I hear Pa Cudjo speak bout de water wash rougher en rougher en knock side dat boat just like it been comin out de ocean. Say, fore he think bout he in trouble, de wind just snatch he hat right out in de water en when he reach out after it, he hear Ma holler en de next thing he know, us all been throwed right out in de water. Yes, mam, de boat turned over en dumped us all out in dat big old crazy river. Pa Cudjo say, if he ain' never had no mind to pray fore den, he know, when he see dat boat gwine down dat stream, dere won' nothin' left to do, but to pray. Pa Cudjo tell dat he make for de bank fast as he could get dere cause he know de devil been in de river dat day en he never know whe' he might go. I reckon you hear talk bout, Pa Cudjo, he been a cussin man. Never had no mind what he was gwine let loose no time. But poor Ma, she been a buxom woman, so dey tell me, en when she hit de bottom of dat river, she never didn' come to de top no more. Like I tell you, I never been long come here den en I ain' been fast gwine under de water cause dere won' no heaviness nowhe' bout me. Pa Cudjo say, he pray en he cuss en when he look up, he see a boat makin up de river wid two men in it en me lyin dere 'tween dem. You see, dey had come along en pick me up bout a mile from dere floatin down de river. Now, I tellin you what come out of Pa Cudjo mouth. Pa Cudjo say, when he see me, he been so happy, he pray en he cuss. Say, he thank de Lord for savin me en he thank de devil for lettin me loose. Yes, mam, I tell you, I been raise up a motherless child right dere wid Pa Cudjo en I been take de storm many a day. I say, if you is determine to go through wid a thing, God knows, you can make it. Cose Pa Cudjo, he been mighty good to me, but he used to have dem cussin spells, my Lord. Been love to keep up fun all de time."

"Oh, de colored people never had no liberty, not one speck, in slavery time. Old man Wash Woodberry, he was rough wid his niggers, but dem what lived on Miss Susan Stevenson's plantation, dey been fare good all de time. I know what I talk bout cause I been marry Cato Gause en he tell me dey been live swell to Miss Susan's plantation. Dat whe' he been born en raise up. Hear Pa Cudjo talk bout dat Miss Harriet Woodberry whip my mother one day en she run away en went down in Woodberry en stayed a long time. Say, some of de Woodberry niggers stayed down dere till after freedom come here. Yes, mam, white folks would whip dey colored people right dere, if dey didn' do what dey tell dem to do. Oh, dey was awful in dat day en time. Colored people had to live under a whip massa en couldn' do nothin, but what he say do. Yes, mam, dey had dese head men, what dey call overseers, on all de plantations dat been set out to whip de niggers. I tell you, it was rough en tough in dem days. Dey would beat you bout to death. My grandfather en my grandmother, dey die wid scars on dem dat de white folks put dere."

"Oh, my Lord, dey would give de colored people dey allowance to last dem a week to a time, but dey never didn' give dem nothin widout dey work to get it en dat been dey portion. I remember, I hear Cato tell bout Mr. Bobbie say, "Mom Dicey, dey tell me dey catch Bacchus stealin Pa's watermelons out de field de other night." (Bacchus was Mom Dicey's son). Grandmother Dicey say, "Oh, he never take nothin but dem little rotten end ones."

Den Mr. Bobbie say, "Well, dey tell me, dey catch Bacchus stealin de horse's corn out de feed trough de other night." En grandmother Dicey say, "Well, if he did, he never take nothin, but what been belong to him." Dat it, some white folks was better to dey colored people den others would be. Would give dem so much of meal en meat en molasses to last dem a week en dey would feed all de nigger chillun to de big house 'tween meals. Have cook woman to give dem all de milk en clabber dey wanted dere to de white people yard."

"De overseer, he would give you a task to do en you had to do it, too, if you never been want your neck broke. Yes, mam, de overseer would stock you down en whip you wid a buggy whip. Some of de time, when de colored people wouldn' do what dey been put to do, dey would hide in de woods en stay dere till de overseer come after dem. Oh, dey would find dem wid de nigger dog. When de overseer would find out dey had run away, he would send de nigger dog to hunt dem. My God, child, dem dogs would sho find you. Some of de time, dey would run you up a tree en another time, dey would catch you whe' dere won' no tree to go up en grab you en gnaw you up. Yes, mam, de overseer would hear you hollerin or else he would hear de dog barkin at you up de tree. Dem nigger dogs, I know you is see dem kind of dogs. Dey is high, funny lookin dogs. Don' look like no other kind of dog. When dey would find de one dey was huntin, dey would just stand right dere en look up in de tree en howl."

"De colored people never had no church dey own in slavery time cause dey went to de white people church. Yes, mam, I been dere to de Old Neck Church many a day. In dat day en time, when de preacher would stand up to preach, he would talk to de white folks en de colored people right dere together. But when de colored people would get converted in dem days, dey never been allowed to praise de Lord wid dey mouth. Had to pray in dey sleeve in dem days. De old man Pa Cudjo, he got right one day to de big house en he had to pray wid he head in de pot."

"No, mam, de colored people never didn' have no liberty no time in dem days. Cose dey had dey little crop of corn en 'tatoe en thing like dat bout dey house, what dey would work at night, but dat won' nothin to speak bout. Oh, dey would put fire in a fry pan en fetch it up on a stump to see to work by."

"No, child, white people never teach colored people nothin, but to be good to dey Massa en Mittie. What learnin dey would get in dem days, dey been get it at night. Taught demselves."

"Now, Pa Cudjo, if he been here, my Lord, I couldn' never say what he might could tell you. Like I say, he been a cussin man en he die wid a bright mind. Cose I never come here what dey call a slavery child, but I been hear slavery people speak dey mind plenty times."

Source: Louisa Gause, colored, age 70-75; Brittons Neck, S.C.
Personal interview by Annie Ruth Davis.

United States. Work Projects Administration

Project #1665
W.W. Dixon
Winnsboro, S.C.

GRACIE GIBSON

EX-SLAVE 86 YEARS OLD.

GRACIE GIBSON

"I was born at Palatka, Florida. I was a slave of Captain John Kinsler. Wish all white men was just like him, and all white women like Miss Maggie Dickerson, de lady that looks after me now.

"Captain John wouldn't sell his niggers and part de members of de family. He fetched us all, Daddy George, Mammy Martha, Gran'dad Jesse, Gran'mammy Nancy, and my two brothers, Flanders and Henry, from Florida to Richland County, South Carolina, along wid de rest.

"My mistress was named Mary. Marster John had a daughter named Adelaide, but they call her Ada. I was called up on one of her birthdays, and Marster Bob sorta looked out of de corner of his eyes, first at me and then at Miss Ada, then he make a little speech. He took my hand, put it in Miss Ada's hand, and Say: 'Dis your birthday present, darlin'.' I make a curtsy and Miss Ada's eyes twinkle like a star and she take me in her room and took on powerful over me.

"We lived in a two-room log house daubed wid mud and it had a wood and mud chimney to de gable end of one room. De floor was hewed logs laid side by side close together. Us had all we needed to eat.

"De soap was made in a hopper for de slaves. How dat you ask? A barrel was histed on a stand 'bove de ground a piece; wheat straw was then put into de barrel, hickory ashes was then emptied in, then water, and then it set 'bout ten days or more. Then old fats and old grease, meat skins, and rancid grease, was put in. After a while de lye was drained out, put in a pot, and boiled wid grease. Dis was lye-soap, good to wash wid.

"Slaves had own garden. Some of de old women, and women bearin' chillun not yet born, did cardin' wid hand-cards; then some would get at de spinnin' wheel and spin thread, three cuts make a hank. Other women weave cloth and every woman had to learn to make clothes for the family, and they had to knit coarse socks and stockin's. Mighty nigh all de chillun had a little teency bag of asafetida, on a string 'round they necks, to keep off diseases.

"Us slaves had 'stitions and grieve if a black cat run befo' us, or see de new moon thru de tree tops, and when we start somewhere and turn back, us sho' made a cross-mark and spit in it befo' we commence walkin' again.

"I 'member Wheeler's men come to our house first, befo' de Yankees. They took things just like de Yankees did dat come later. Marster John was a Captain, off fightin' for Confeds but dat didn't stop Wheeler's men from takin' things they wanted, no sir! They took what they wanted. Wasn't long after then dat the Yankees come and took all they could and burnt what they couldn't carry off wid them.

"After de war I marry Abe Smith and had two chillun by him, Clifton and Hattie. De boy died and Hattie marry a man named Lee. She now lives at White Oak.

"My husband die, I marry Sam Gibson, and had a nice trousseau dat time. Blue over-skirt over tunic, petticoats wid tattin' at de borders, red stockin's and gaiter shoes. I had a bustle and a wire hoop and wore a veil over my hair."

United States. Work Projects Administration

Project 1885-1
FOLKLORE
Spartanburg Dist. 4
May 31, 1937

Edited by:
Elmer Turnage

STORIES FROM EX-SLAVES

CHARLIE GILES

"I was Capt. Jack's body-guard in during de whole entire war. I means Capt. Jack Giles, his own self. And I is pushing close to a hundred. Dey used to make likker in de holler down on Dr. Bates' place deep in de forest. De soldiers would drink by de barrels. Mr. Will Bates, Dr. Bates' son, helped me out of skimage one time.

"Don't never go in no war, 'less you is gwine to give orders like my marse Jack. Dat is, onless you is gwine to act as body-guard. Time of de war, old man Sammy Harmon had a state still. He never sold no likker to no private. De bluecoats, dey blockade Charleston and Savannah. Miss Janie couldn't get no spices fer her cakes, neither could she get no linen and other fine cloth fer her 'dornment. Couldn't nothing get by dat blockade. So Mr. Sammy, he make de likker by de barrels. Dem dat had wagins come and fotch it off, as many barrels as de mules could draw, fer de soldiers. I drunk much as I wanted. De drum taps say, 'tram lam-lam, following on de air. De sperrits lift me into a dance, like dis, (he danced some) 'cept I was light on my foots den—atter I had done drunk, anyhow.

"De sharp-shooters got atter me one day. Mr. Dewey, one of de rangers, sent fer de cannon balls. Dese run de bluecoats.

"I went to Petersburg wid Capt. Douglas, dat Miss Janie's second husband. Our train went dat fast, dat it took my breaf away. But de cars goes much faster, gwine to Patter-a-rac now.

"All de picket-men had dogs. Lots of de soldiers had niggers wid dem. At night in de camp when de Yankees would come spying around, de dogs would bark. De niggers would holler. One Confederate officer had a speckledy dog that could smell dem Yankees far off. When de Yankees got dare, everything was ready. When us want information fer direction and time, all us had to do was to look up through de pines fer it.

"One song I remembers is, 'would like to catch-a feller looking like me'. Another was, 'I feel as happy as a big sun-flower.' (Charlie can sing them both, and dance accompaniment.)

"At Petersburg, April 1863, de Yankees act like dey was gwine to blow everything up. I crawl along de ground wid my Marster, and try to keep him kivered as best as I could. Us reached Chica-hominy River and go over to Petersburg. Den dey blow up Richmond. De river turn to blood while I was looking at it. De cannons deafened me and I has been hard of hearing ever since. Some de blue tails clumb de trees when us got atter dem.

"Next time I'se gwine to tell you about deserters and

refugees. Ain't nobody got no business in automobiles 'cept lawyers, doctors, and fools."

Source: Charlie Giles, Rt. 3, Box 274, Union, S.C.
Caldwell Sims, Union, S.C. 2/8/37.

United States. Work Projects Administration

Project #-1655
Phoebe Faucette
Hampton County

Folklore

WILLIS GILLISON
Luray, S.C.

WILLIS GILLISON

There is no doubt that "Uncle Gillison" is old. He is knock-kneed and walks slowly. His long thin hands clutch his chair strongly for support as he continually shifts his position. When he brings his hands to the back of his head, as he frequently does, in conversation, they tremble as with palsy. He enjoys talking of the old times as do many of his contemporaries.

"Yes, Maam," he starts off. "I been heah when de war was on. I seen when de drove of people come up. Dey was dress in blue clothes. Call dem Yankees. Had de Scouts, too. But dey was de Southerners. I knowed all dem! I wasn't nuthin' but a little boy but I kin remember it.

"Mr. Jesse Smith wife been my young Missus. Dey lived at Furman. My mother mind Mr. Trowell's father. His name was Mr. Ben Trowell. I call him, Bub Ben. Bub was for brother. Dat de way we call folks den—didn't call 'em by dere names straight out. Mr. Trowell's mother we call, Muss, for Miss. Sort of a nickname. We call Mr. Harry Fitts grandmother, Muss, too.

"My daddy was name Aleck Trowell. After freedom he was call by his own name, Aleck Gillison. After freedom some was call by dere own name—some were, and some weren't. My father was sold from a Gillison, first off.

"How old I is? Well, Missus, I been put on de road to 75 years, but I'm more than dat. I'm between seventy and eighty years old.

"I knows Mr. Tom Lawton. Dey was rich people. My old Massa and him been boys together. Dey was a place call de Trowell Mill Pond right at de Lawton place. Mr. Lawton was sure rich, 'cause we all had a plenty—plenty to eat, and sech likes—Mr. Lawton was rich! When Mr. Trowell got up a little higher than what he was, he trade his Lena place for a place at Stafford. De Stafford place was some better.

"Yes Maam, de records was burn. Dey had a courthouse at Gillisonville in dem times. Dat fact 'bout it Miss. Now I don't want you to say a nigger 'spute your word, or nuthin' like that, (this, in response to the visitor having remarked that the records were burned at Beaufort) but I don't think that Beaufort was built up till after the war. Gillisonville was right muchly built up. I don't think de records was burn at Beaufort. I think it was at de courthouse at Gillisonville dey was burn up. Now de district was call Beaufort District, but de courthouse was at Gillisonville. Gillisonville was where dey had de trial of de Mr. Martin dat kill Mr. Peeples. De Morrisons lived at Gillisonville. Plenty of 'em!

"I kin tell you where two of de old Robert homes used to be. One was back dis way toward Scotia from Robertville. Dat was de Mr. John H. Robert' place. Had a whole string of cedar trees going up to his place. Now den, 'bout two miles out from Robertville going from de white folk' church out toward Black Swamp was another Robert place. Dat where old Major Robert lived. He had a whole tun (turn) of slaves. Dere was no Robert live right in de village of Robertville. De Lawtons was de only people live right in Robertville—and one family of Jaudons. I don't know of no other Robert home.

"Dat's all I kin tell you 'bout de old times, Missus. I don't want to tell you what ain't true."

Source: Willis Gillison, 75 years old, (Ex-slave) Luray, S.C.—R.F.D.

United States. Work Projects Administration

Project 1885-1
FOLKLORE
Spartanburg Dist. 4
June 10, 1937

Edited by:
Elmer Turnage

STORIES FROM EX-SLAVES

BRAWLEY GILMORE

"We lived in a log house during the Ku Klux days. Dey would watch you just like a chicken rooster watching fer a worm. At night, we was skeered to have a light. Dey would come around wid de 'dough faces' on and peer in de winders and open de do'. Iffen you didn't look out, dey would skeer you half to death. John Good, a darkey blacksmith, used to shoe de horses fer de Ku Klux. He would mark de horse shoes with a bent nail or something like that; then atter a raid, he could go out in the road and see if a certain horse had been rode; so he began to tell on de Ku Klux. As soon as de Ku Klux found out dey was being give away, dey suspicioned John. Dey went to him and made him tell how he knew who dey was. Dey kept him in hiding, and when he told his tricks, dey killed him.

"When I was a boy on de 'Gilmore place', de Ku Klux would come along at night a riding de niggers like dey was goats. Yes sir, dey had 'em down on all-fours a crawling, and dey would be on dere backs. Dey would carry de niggers to Turk Creek bridge and make dem set up on de bannisters of de bridge; den dey would shoot 'em offen de bannisters into de water. I 'clare dem was de awfulest days I ever is seed. A darky name Sam Scaife drifted a hundred yards in de water down stream. His folks took and got him outen dat bloody water and buried him on de bank of de creek. De Ku Klux would not let dem take him to no graveyard. Fact is, dey would not let many of de niggers take de dead bodies of de folks no whars. Dey just throwed dem in a big hole right dar and pulled some dirt over dem. Fer weeks atter dat, you could not go near dat place, kaise it stink so fer and bad. Sam's folks, dey throwed a lot of 'Indian-head' rocks all over his grave, kaise it was so shallah, and dem rocks kept de wild animals from a bothering Sam. You can still see dem rocks, I could carry you dere right now.

"Another darky, Eli McCollum, floated about three and a half miles down de creek. His folks went dere and took him out and buried him on de banks of de stream right by de side of a Indian mound. You can see dat Indian mound to dis very day. It is big as my house is, over dere on de Chester side.

"De Ku Klux and de niggers fit at New Hope Church. A big rock marks de spot today. De church, it done burnt down. De big rock sets about seven miles east of Lockhart on de road to Chester. De darkies killed some of de Ku Klux and dey took dere dead and put dem in Pilgrims Church. Den dey sot fire to dat church and it burnt everything up to de very bones of de white folks. And ever since den, dat spot has been known as 'Burnt Pilgrim'. De darkies left most of de folks right dar fer de buzzards and other wild things to eat up. Kaise dem niggers had to git away from dar; and dey didn't have no time fer to fetch no word or nothing to no folks at home. Dey had a hiding place not fer from 'Burnt Pilgrim'. A darky name Austin Sanders, he was carring some victuals to his son. De Ku Klux cotch him and dey axed him whar he was a gwine. He lowed dat he was a setting some bait fer coons. De Ku Klux took and shot him and left him lying right in de middle of de road wid a biscuit in his dead mouth.

"Doctor McCollum was one of dem Ku Klux, and de Yankees sot out fer to ketch him. Doc., he rid a white pony called 'Fannie'. All de darkies, dey love Doc, so dey would help him fer to git away from de Yankees, even though he was a Ku Klux. It's one road what forks, atter you crosses Wood's Ferry. Don't nobody go over dat old road now. One fork go to Leeds and one to Chester. Well, right in dis fork, Mr. Buck Worthy had done built him a grave in de 'Woods Ferry Graveyard'. Mr. Worthy had done built his grave hisself. It was built out of marble and it was kivered up wid a marble slab. Mr. Worthy, he would take and go dar and open it up and git in it on pretty days. So old Doc., he knowed about dat grave. He was going to see a sick lady one night when dey got atter him. He was on old Fannie. Dey was about to ketch de old Doc. when he reached in sight of dat graveyard. It was dark. So Doc., he drive de horse on pass de fork, and den he stop and hitch her in front of some dense pines. Den he took and went to dat grave and slip dat top slab back and got in dar and pulled it over him, just leaving a little crack. Doc. lowed he wrapped up hisself in his horse blanket, and when de Yankees left, he went to sleep in dat grave and never even woke up till de sun, it was a shinning in his face.

"Soon atter dat, my sister took down sick wid de

misery. Doc., he come to see her at night. He would hide in de woods in daytime. We would fetch him his victuals. My sister was sick three weeks 'fore she died. Doc, he would take some blankets and go and sleep in dat grave, kaise he know'd dey would look in our house fer him. Dey kept on a coming to our house. Course we never know'd nothing 'bout no doctor at all. Dar was a nigger wid wooden bottom shoes, dat stuck to dem Yankees and other po' white trash 'round dar. He lowed wid his big mough dat he gwine to find de doctor. He told it dat he had seed Fannie in de graveyard at night. Us heard it and told de doctor. Us did not want him to go near dat graveyard any more. But Doc, he just laugh and he lowed dat no nigger was a gwine to look in no grave, kaise he had tried to git me to go over dar wid him at night and I was skeer'd.

"One night, just as Doc was a covering up, he heard dem wooden shoes a coming; so he sot up in de grave and took his white shirt and put it over his head. He seed three shadows a coming. Just as dey got near de doc, de moon come out from 'hind a cloud and Doc, he wave dat white shirt and he say dem niggers just fell over grave-stones a gitting outen dat graveyard. Doc lowed dat he heard dem wooden shoes a gwine up de road fer three miles. Well, dey never did bother the doctor any more.

"Doc, he liked to fiddle. Old Fannie, she would git up on her hind legs when de doc would play his fiddle."

Source: Brawley Gilmore (col), 34 Hamlet St., Union, S.C.
Interviewer: Caldwell Sims, Union, S.C. (12/3/36)

Project 1885-1
Ex-slave—(Pick Gladdeny, Pomaria, Rt. 3, S.C.
Interviewer: Caldwell Sims, Union, S.C.

EARLY RECOLLECTIONS.
Typist: Louise Dawkins, Rt. 4, Union, S.C.

PICK GLADDENY

"Ah sees all through 'im now. Naw, sir, Ah doesn't know whar Ah wuz bawn, maybe in Fairfield, maybe in the Dutch Fork, Ah doesn't know, Ah won't dar. It wuz on May 15, 1856. Ah 'spec Ah could've been born on Mr. Joe Hellar's place, you knows dat down on Hellar Creek.

"Ah'se old enough to go to de speechin' dat Dan White made on "Maybinton Day" (emancipation speech at Maybinton, S.C.). You axes me more than I can answer, Site of folks dar all day, settin' aroun. Us clam trees, so us could see and hear. I sho did listen but I don't 'member nothin' what de man say. I knows dis dat I still hears dat band music ringing in my ears. At dat time I was so young dat all I cared about on dat day, was the brass band what let out so much music. Niggers being free never meant nothing to us chaps, cause we never had no mind fer all such as that nohow. Dat de first band dat I ever seed, and to tell you de truf I never seed no more till the World War fotch de soldiers all through here. Bands charms me so much dat dey just plumb tickles the tips of my toes on both feets.

"Squire William Hardy was de man dat I worked for when I had done turned five. Dey teach me to bring in chips, kindling wood, fire wood and water. I learnt to make Marse's fire ever morning. Dat won't no trouble, cause all I had to do was rake back de ashes from the coals and throw on some chips and lightwood and de fire come right up. Won't long 'fore I was big enough to draw water and bring in big wood. You knows what big fire places they got down dar cause Squire Hardy—Mr. Dick's Pa, and Pa and Heyward and Frank's grandpa.

"Squire Hardy was a good man so was Mr. Dick. Mr. Dick was dat smart till he just naturally never forgot nothing that was told to him. If he was a-living, he could tell you way back before de Squire's time. I was right dar at Squire Hardy's dat day Freedom come and de band come to Maybinton.

"Going farther back than this, droves of niggers used to come down the road by Squire Hardy's front gate. Yes, sir, a overseer used to come through here driving niggers; just like us drives cows and hogs up around this big road these days and times. One day Squire Hardy went out and stopped a drove coming down de road in the dust. He pick him out a good natured looking darky and give the overseer one eye contrary niggers, what nobody didn't like for the good-natured ones. Ain't got no more to say. I does not remember but I has heared about the time when my ma moved from Hellar's Plantation in the Dutch Fork to the Tom Lyles quarter in Fairfield. My ma's name Sally Murphy. Her master was Dave Murphy. He stayed at Tom Lyles. Mistus Betsy (Dave Murphy) cared for her. Mr. Dave Murphy overseed for Capt. Tom Lyles who lived about two miles from Lyles' Ford on Broad River.

"I don't know what things has gone to. So much diffence in everthing now than it was back in dem days. Don't know nothing about no Booker T. Washington. I sees much but hears little 'bout dat what I doesn't see, Yes, siree boy, all such little 'muck' go in one ear and come out tother'n wid me. Dat's de talk fer dese young niggers dats eddicated, and I ain't dat bad off.

"Winnsboro fust town I ever seed, but it don't favor itself now.

"Maybinton the place I love best in all the world. Most my life is right here. I'll be buried in Hardy graveyard, whar my white folks dat was so good to me lie sleeping, and dat's whar my ma and pa and others that I loves lies too.

"Post office at Maybinton is whar Miss Bessie Oxner stay. Bill Oxner, her pa kept de post office from de time it started till they stopped it, fur as I knows. It look better then than it does now. Mr. Bill Oxner pretty good man.

"He was a settled man. His wife was a good-looking lady who before her marriage was a Bethune.

"Dar was a big store at the end of Mr. W. B. Whitney's plantation. Dis along to'd first of Freedom. Mr. Slattery lived twixt the Maybins and the Whitney's house. The store upon the end was kept by Mr. Pettus Chick and Mr. Bill Oxner. It was a good store. Didn't have to go to Newber'y to git no candy and 'Bacco. And Dr. Jim Ruff was de doctor what tended to folks in dem parts when dey got sick.

"De old Buck when I first knowed it was run fer a dwelling house by Mr. Jeff Stewart. I been knowed

Maybinton all my life. But when I come along stages had done gone out but that's where dey stopped when they come from Spring Hill. I'se heared dat de Buck had large stables and a lots of folks stop there and rested overnight on their way to the Springs. (Glenn's, Chick's, and West Springs.)

"Used to rather dance than to eat. Started out at sundown and git back to the Whitney's at daybreak, den from dar run all de way to Squire Hardy's to git dar by sunup. Pats our feets and knocks tin pans was the music dat us niggers danced to all night long. Put on my clean clothes dat was made right on the plantation and wear them to the dance. Gals wore their homespun stockings. Wore the dresses so long dat they kivered their shoes. My britches were copperus colored and I had on a home wove shirt with a pleated bosom. It was dyed red and had wristbands. I wore that shirt for five years.

"Didn't have no nigger churches down dar den. We went to Chapman's stand. It had a brush top and log seats. The darkies from the Hardy Plantation walked five miles to hear a nigger from Union preach. He driv a one horse waggin and course he stayed around from place to place and the folks take care of him and his mule. Big Jim Henderson owned Chapman's stand which was in the Glymp quarter. The Glymp quarter still got the best land in our settlement yet. All my 'quaintances done left me, fac' is, most of them done crossed over de river. Folks meets me and speaks familiar. I axes, "Who is that?" I used to deal with Mr. Bee Thompson in Union.

"I'se got some business to tend to in Union soon and I spec I be up there in short to see is it anything familiar dar."

Project #1655
W.W. Dixon
Winnsboro, S.C.

HENRY GLADNEY
EX-SLAVE 82 YEARS OLD.

HENRY GLADNEY

Henry Gladney lives with his wife, his son, Murdock, his daughter-in-law, Rose, and seven grandchildren. They live near White Oak, S.C., in a two-room frame house with a one-room box board annex. He works a one-horse farm for Mr. Cathcart and piddles a little at the planing mills at Adgers. His son does the ploughing. The daughter-in-law and grandchildren hoe and pick cotton and assist in the farm work. Henry is of medium height, dark brown complexion, and is healthy but not vigorous.

"I lives out on de John H. Cathcart place, close to White Oak. In slavery time my mammy b'long to old Marse Johnnie Mobley, and us lived in de quarter 'bout three miles to de west of Woodward station, tho' dere was no station dere when I was a boy. De station was down de railroad from dere and then it was called Yonguesville. My mammy name Lucy, my pappy name William, my sisters was Louise, Elsie, and Adeline. My brudders name Tim and Curtis.

"I wasn't a very big boy in slavery time, tho' I 'member

choppin' cotton, and pickin' cotton and peas 'long 'side mammy in de field. Pappy was called 'Bill de Giant', 'cause him was so big and strong. They have mighty bad plantation roads in them days. I see my pappy git under de wagon once when it was bogged up to de hub and lift and heft dat wagon and set it outside de ruts it was bogged down in. Him stayed at de blacksmith shop, work on de wagons, shoe de mules and hosses, make hinges, sharpen de plow points and fix de iron rings in de wagon wheels.

"My pappy didn't 'low other slave men to look at my mammy. I see him grab Uncle Phil once, throw him down on de floor, and when him quit stompin' Uncle Phil, they have to send for Dr. Newton, 'cause pappy done broke Uncle Phil's right leg. My old marster no lak dat way one of his slaves was crippled up. Him 'low to whip pappy for it. Pappy tell mammy to go tell Marse John if he whip him, he would run off and go to de North. She beg for pappy so, dat nothin' was done 'bout it. 'Spect Marse John fear to lose a good blacksmith wid two good legs, just 'bout a small nigger man wid one good leg and one bad leg.

"It come to de time old marster have so many slaves he don't know what to do wid them all. He give some of them off to his chillun. He give them mostly to his daughters, Miss Marion, Miss Nancy, and Miss Lucretia. I was give to his grandson, Marse John Mobley McCrorey, just to wait on him and play wid him. Little Marse John treat me good sometime and kick me 'round sometime. I see now dat I was just a little dog or monkey, in his heart and mind, dat 'mused him to pet or kick as it pleased him. Him give me de only money I ever have befo' freedom, a big copper two-cent piece wid a hole in it. I run a string thru dat hole and tied it 'round my neck and felt rich all de time. Little niggers always wanted to see dat money and I was proud to show it to them every time.

"Little Marse John's mother was another daughter of old Marster John. Her name was Dorcas. They live in Florida. I was took 'way down dere, cried pow'ful to leave my mammy, but I soon got happy down dere playin' in de sand wid Marse John and his little brudder, Charlie. Don't 'member nothin' 'bout de war or de Yankees. Freedom come, I come back to de Mobley quarters to mammy. I work for old Marster John up 'til after Hampton was 'lected. I marry Florie Williams, a pretty black gal on de Mobley quarters. Us is had seventeen chillun. So far as I know they is all livin'. Some in Florida, some in Sparrows Point, Virginia, some in Charlotte, N.C., and some in Columbia, S.C. Murdock and his wife, Katie, and deir six chillun live in de same house wid me.

"My old marster have two daughters dat marry McCroreys. Miss Lucretia marry James McCrorey and Miss Dorcas marry John McCrorey. Miss Lucretia have a son name John. Miss Dorcas have a son name John. In talkin' wid old mistress, 'fusion would come 'bout which John of de grandsons was bein' meant and talked 'bout. Old Marster John settle dat.

"Old Marster John and old mistress (her name Katie) had de same birthday, March de 27th, tho' old Marster John was two years older than old Mistress Kate. They celebrate dat day every year. All de chillun-in-laws and grandchillun come to de mansion, have a big dinner and a big time. After dinner one day, all de men folks 'semble at de woodpile. De sun was shinin' and old marster have me bring out a chair for him but de balance of them set on de logs or lay 'round on de chips. Then they begun to swap tales. Marse Ed P. Mobley hold up his hand and say: 'See dis stiff finger? It'll never be straight agin. I got out of ammunition at de secon' battle of Bull Run, was runnin' after a Yankee to ketch him, threw my gun 'way to run faster, ketch him as he was 'bout to git over a fence and choked his stiff neck so hard in de scuffle dat I broke dat finger. General Lee hearin' 'bout it, changed me from de infancy (infantry) to de calvary (cavalry) dat I might not run de danger any more.' Old marster laugh and say: 'Jim, can you beat dat?' Marse Jim Mobley say: 'Well, you all know what I done at Gettysburg? If all had done lak me dat day, us would have won de war. Whenever I see a bullet comin' my way, I took good aim at de bullet wid a double charge of powder in my musket. My aim was so good dat it drove de enemy ball back to kill a Yankee and glanced aside at de right time to kill another Yankee. I shot a thousand times de fust day of de battle and two thousand times de secon' day and kilt six thousand Yankees at Gettysburg!' Old marster slap his sides and fell out de chair a laughin'! When him git back in de chair, him say: 'Zebulon, what you got to say?' Marse Zeb, p'intin' to his empty pants leg, say: 'Me and some officers 'tended a chicken fight on de banks of de Chickenhominy River de day befo' de battle of Shilo. De cocks fight wid gaves on deir heels. Dere was five hundred fights and two hundred and fifty roosters was kilt. Us have big pots of chicken and big pots of hominy on de banks of de Chickenhominy Creek dat night and then de battle of Cold Harbor come de nex' day. I had eat so much chicken and hominy my belly couldn't hold it all. Some had run down my right leg. Us double quicked and run so fast thru swamps nex' day, after Yankees, my right leg couldn't keep up wid my left leg. After de battle I went back to look for dat leg but never could find it. Governor Zeb Vance tell me afterwards, dat leg of mine run on to Washington, went up de White House steps, and slushed some of dat chicken and hominy on de carpet right befo' President Lincoln's chair.'

"Everybody laugh so loud dat old mistress come out and want to know what for they was laughin' 'bout. All dat had to be gone over agin. Then her laugh and laugh and laugh. She turnt 'round to my young Marster John and say: 'John, can you beat dat?' He say: 'Henry, go git grandma a chair.' I done dat. Then my young marster start. Him say: 'One day down in Florida, I saddle my pony, took Henry dere up behind me and went a fishin' on de St. John River. I had some trouble a gittin' thru de everglades when I want to fish but us got dere. Big trees on de banks and 'round, wid long moss hangin' from de limbs. I baited my hook wid a small, wigglin', live, minnow and throwed out into de water. Nothin' happen. In de warm sunshine I must have gone to sleep, when I was startle out my doze by Henry a shoutin': 'Marse Johnnie, Marse Johnnie, your cork done gone down out of sight!' I made a pull but felt at once it would take both hands to land dat fish. I took both hands, put my foot 'ginst de roots of a great live oak and h'isted dat fish in de sky. It was so big it shut out de light of de sun. When it come down, dat fish strip off de limbs of de trees it hit while comin' to de ground. I sent Henry back to de house on de pony, for de four-hoss wagon and all de men on de place, to git de fish home. When us got it home and cut it open, dere was 119 fishes varyin' from de size of de minnow up to de big fish. Marse Ed P. say: 'Was de little minnow dead or 'live when you found him in de belly of de 119th fish? 'He was still wigglin', say my young marster. Old marster say: 'It was a whale of a fish, wasn't it, grandson?' Young marster say: 'It was, grandpa. De river bank show dat de water went down two inches after I pulled him out.' 'Maybe it was a whale', said Marse Ed P. 'In fact, it was', said Marse Johnnie,' 'cause on one of de ribs under de belly was some tatooin'.' 'What was de tatooin'?' ask old mistress, just as innocent as a baby. 'De word Nenivah', say Marse little John. 'Why it might have been de whale dat swallowed Jonah', say Miss Katie. 'It was', say my young marster, 'for just under Nenivah was de name Jonah.' After a good laugh old marster say: 'Your name is changed from John Mobley McCrorey to John Munchawsome McCrorey.' Kin folks call him Barron after dat. Him lak dat but when they got to callin' him, lyin' John McCrorey him git red in de face and want to fight.

"Poor Marse Johnnie! Wonder if him still livin'. Him marry a rich woman in Florida but her soon 'vorce him. What her 'vorce him for? 'Pattybility and temper, they say. What I means by pattybility? I 'spect dat mean de time they was gittin' up in de mornin' and her lam him 'cross de head wid de hairbrush and him take dat same hairbrush, push her down 'cross de bed and give her a good spankin'. Now you're laughin' agin but it was no laughin' wid her dat mornin', de way I hear them tell it."

Project 1885-1
FOLKLORE
Spartanburg Dist 4
July 15, 1937

Edited by:
Elmer Turnage

STORIES FROM EX-SLAVES

EMOLINE GLASGOW

"I was born in Newberry County, South Carolina. Near Indian Creek above Jalapa. My mammy and pa was Charlie and Frances Gilliam. We belonged to Marse Pettus and Harriet Gilliam who had a big plantation. I married George Glasgow in the yard of Reid place, by a nigger preacher. My husband died about 15 years ago.

"I was a young child when de war stopped, and don't remember so much about slavery times. Marse Pettus and Miss Harriet was good to us. I never got a whipping, except Misses whipped me once wid just one lick. Dey give us a small patch of 'bout half acre fer us to raise cotton or anything we wanted to on it. De master had a big garden and give his slaves plenty vegetables. We had plenty to eat all de time. My pa, Charlie, was de foreman of a crowd of slaves, and dere was a white overseer, too.

"Master Gilliam had a boy dey called 'Bud'. He still lives in Arkansas. Dey all moved to state of Arkansas sometime atter de war. My master was a good man, a church man, and he was steward in Tranquil Methodist

Church. Around de place at home he was always singing and in good humor. I 'member one song he sung dat was like dis:

> "Lord, Lord, Heaven—Sweet Heaven,
> Lord, Lord, Heaven—Sweet Heaven,
> How long will it be?
> (repeated three times)

"De first time I come to town was when I was a little child, and when we got to College Hill, about ten miles from home, I started to run back home because I heard de train whistle blow.

"Miss Harriet always give us chilluns 'mackaroot tea' fer worms. It's made from roots of a plant dat grow in de woods. We had to drink it before breakfast, and it shore had a bitter taste.

"Slavery wasn't good much, I reckon, but I had a good time ... didn't nothing bother me. When freedom come, all of us stayed with de master until he and his folks moved away.

"Old Dr. Clark was de best doctor in de state. He lived at Jalapa. He used to give barbecues at his home in de yard under big trees. He had niggers dere, too. Dey eat by demselves. Old Mrs. Sligh lived above dere. I waited on her when she was sick. When she died, she made her son promise not to hold against me what I owed her—just let it go—and told him not to ever let me go hungry.

"Once when Master Gilliam took one of his slaves to church at old Tranquil, he told him dat he mustn't shout dat day—said he would give him a pair of new boots if he didn't shout. About de middle of services, de old nigger couldn't stand it no longer. He jumped up and hollered: 'Boots or no boots, I gwine to shout today'.

"I jined de church atter I got married, 'cause I wanted to do right and serve de Lord."

Source: Emoline Glasgow (78), Newberry, S.C.
Interviewer: G.L. Summer, Newberry, S.C. (7/8/37)

Project 1885-1
FOLKLORE
Spartanburg Dist. 4
Sept. 16, 1937

Edited by:
Elmer Turnage

STORIES FROM EX-SLAVES

SILAS GLENN

"I live on Mr. Sim Bickley's farm, about five miles northwest of Newberry Courthouse. I have a fairly good house to live in. I work on the farm, myself, and make a pretty good living from it. I live with my second wife. I had two children but they both died.

"I was born on Dr. Geo. W. Glenn's plantation, about six miles north of Newberry. My parents, Berry and Frances Glenn, were slaves of Dr. Glenn. I was seven years old when freedom come.

"Dr. Glenn gave us good quarters to live in and plenty to eat. He was a good man and was not hard on slaves; but the mistress was mean to some of the slaves that come from the Glenn side. She was good to the slaves that come into her from her daddy.

"I didn't work much around the place when I was small, just did little things to help. The master had a big garden and raised lots of green vegetables like turnips, collards, cabbages and some okra, but little beans except cornfield beans. We had plenty clothes.

"The master whipped us sometimes when we needed it. They would not learn us to read and write. Some of the slaves went to the white folks' church.

"I was married the first time on the Glasgow place by a colored preacher named Boyd. Her daddy didn't want us to marry; he didn't like me. I slipped to the field where she was working and stole her; went to the preacher and got married. I married the second time in town on College Hill.

"A band of Confederate soldiers in 1865 went past the master's house on their way from war, and Mistress had dinner for them. They eat out under big shade trees in the yard where Master always kept a long table for dinners they had sometimes. When freedom come, the master called all his slaves up to the house one night and spoke to them. He said they was free, but any who wanted to stay on with him and help make the crop that year could stay and he would pay wages. All stayed that year.

"The Ku Klux and Red Shirts didn't like Negroes. They would catch them and whip them.

"It was a long time after the war before the negroes had a school. They went to white folks churchs for a long time. Some of them had 'brush harbors' for their churches, and schools, too.

"I don't know nothing about Abraham Lincoln and Jefferson Davis. I can't give much about Booker Washington, except I heard of him and believe he is a good man and doing a good turn for the negroes.

"I think slavery was wrong; don't think one man ought to own another man.

"I joined the church when I was about 25 or 30 years old."

Source: Silas Glenn (79), Newberry, S.C. RFD
Interviewer: G.L. Summer, Newberry, S.C. 8/9/37.

United States. Work Projects Administration

Project, 1885-(1)
Prepared by Annie Ruth Davis
Place, Marion, S.C.
Date, August 11, 1937

JOHN GLOVER
Ex-Slave, 77 Years
Timmonsville, S.C.

JOHN GLOVER

"Born on Rafter Creek bout 20 miles from Timmonsville on Elija Carson place. My white folks live in big two story house dere cause my Massa was a bankholder in Charleston en dat de reason he go back en forth to Charleston every week or two. My Massa a good man, a good man, en I hope he restin in Heaven dis day."

"De Carsons had bout 2,000 acres of land en 100 head of slaves on dey plantation. Have long row of house up in de quarter whe' all de slaves live. We have a very good livin in dat day en time. Had more to eat den we do dese days cause rations won' scarce like dey is now. Eat potatoes en peas en corn bread en homemade grits mostly, but I likes everything to eat, Captain. Den dey give us a garden to make us greens en things like dat en we is catch possum heap of de time. Uncle Ben (father's father) was a great possum hunter, but he died fore I get big enough to go huntin wid him. He went possum huntin every night till something went up de tree one night en possum talk to him. He used to go huntin on a Sunday night en dat how-come de possum talk to him."

"You didn' see de peoples wear much different clothes like dey wear dese days, but what dey have was very decent. Just have bout one piece, Captain, make out of some kind of homemade cloth wid no extra for Sunday. Wear same kind of pants on Sunday dat wear every day en same kind of shoes call brogans wid brass toes. I ain' see no fittin cloth since dey used to raise sheep en have dey own wool en have loom en spin. Look like God smile on us in dat day en time."

"I work round de white folks house fore freedom come, but I go back to de quarter en sleep when night come. Dem dat live in de quarter have lumber bed wid mattress made out of sacks en hay. Den when dey ring dem bells en blow dem horns in de mornin, dat mean you better get up en go bout your task for dat day."

"Oh, dey work us hard en late in dem times. Work from de sunrise in de mornin to de sundown in de evenin. Dey have a driver dat tote whip en see dat you do what you know to do. Didn' have no jail in dat day, but if you ain' do your task en dey catch you, dey punish you by de whip. Some of de time, dey put em in de screw box what dey press bales of cotton wid. Put em in dere en run press right down whe' can' crush en dey oouldn' move till dey take em out in de mornin en whip em en put em to work. See plenty whipped on de place. Dey make one fellow go over a barrel, en de other peoples hold he head down en de driver whip him. Give em 50 en 75 licks fore dey stop sometimes. Use chains to hold em when dey break ropes so dey couldn' get away."

"I see em sell slaves heap of times. See em gwine along in droves en sayin dey was gwine to market. Sell em if dey ain' stay on de place en work. Bid em off just like horse en mules. What am I bid for dis one? Come en open you mouth en examine you teeth en dey wouldn' miss you a year."

"Oh, Gracious God, didn' get married till after de shake was en I reckon I bout 30 years old den. Captain, we thought it was de Jedgment (Judgment). It come like it was thunderin in de earth, rollin in de earth en de earth was gwine en comin. We pray en all de cows en chickens was yelling. Last dat night bout 30 minutes dat you could look at anything en it look like top spinning. We was all good bout two years after dat."

"My white folks didn' teach none of dey slaves to read en write en didn' let em go bout from one plantation to de other no time. All us know is when we go to dey meetin en dey pray wid us. Peoples used to sing en pray in de quarter on Saturday night en when dey dig grave en have a funeral. Dey didn' do bout buryings den like dey do now. Burying dem times en de funeral would all be over at de burying. Slaves didn' have no way to go to de funeral but to walk. Den a white man would stop you en if you have a ticket wid you dat have pass word on it, you could go on."

"I can tell you all bout when dem Yankees come through dere. Some was on black horses, some on red horses, en some on white horses. De one dat on black horse wear black, de one on white horse wear white, en de one on de red horse wear red. De horses had sense enough to double up when dat man hollo from de top of dem. Dey was wearing soldier clothes en dey come up to you house en set place on fire, kill cow or anything dey want to. Dey burn up Carson house en stay dere till next day. Dey talk to my mamma cause our house de next one to de white folks house. De white folks done been gone. Dey ask her whe' dey hide dey money en she know dey hide it to Stafford Hill, six miles from de house, but she didn' tell dem. Don' know yet what became of de money, but dem Yankees loaded an old chest on de wagon en took all de slaves dat wanted to run away wid dem en left dere."

"Slaves didn' know what to do de first year after freedom en den de Yankees tell de white folks to give de slaves one-third of dey crops. What de slaves gwine buy land wid den, Captain? Won' a God thing to eat in dat time. Had to plow corn wid ox cause de Yankees took all de horses en mules dey wanted. My mother worked on three years dere for de white folks en dey give her one bushel of corn en dey take two. One bushel of corn en dey take two. Measured by de same basket."

"Well, I can' tell you bout people, but I can tell you bout my poor soul. I think I know I'm bless to be here en raise three generation clear up dis world. All my chillun dead en gone en God left me to live among dese wild varments here. I have to cry sometimes when I think how dey die en leave me in dis troublesome world. During slavery time, didn' know what hard times was. I know you see in de Bible dat God sorry he made man done so. I'm sorry dat de last war done. Every time you fight war makes times harder. See three war en every one I see makes time worse. Money gets balled up in one or two hand. Looks bad to me. Didn' know what it was one time to be hungry."

Source: John Glover, Ex-Slave, 77 Years, Timmonsville, S.C.
(Personal interview by Mrs. Lucile Young and H. Grady Davis.)

United States. Work Projects Administration

Slave Narratives

Project, 1885-1
Prepared by Annie Ruth Davis
Place, Marion, S.C.
Date, June 28, 1937

HECTOR GODBOLD
Ex-Slave, 87 Years

HECTOR GODBOLD

"What you gwine do wid me? I sho been here in slavery time. Talk to dem soldiers when dey was retreatin dey way back home. My old Missus was Miss Mary Godbold en den she marry a Haselden. Dey buy my mamma from de old man Frank Miles right over yonder. Harry en Cindy Godbold was my parents. We live in a one room house in de slave quarter dere on de white folks plantation. My God, sleep right dere on de floor. Had gran'parents dat come here over de water from Africa. Dey tell me dat whe' dey come from dey don' never let no man en he wife sleep together cause dey is scared of em catchin disease from one another. Dat sho a good thing, you know dat. I think dat sho a good thing."

"Dey ain' never give none of de colored peoples no money in dat day en time. Coase dey give us plenty something to eat. Fed us out a big bowl of pot licker wid plenty corn bread en fried meat en dat bout all we ever eat. Dey is let us have a garden of we own dat we had to work by de night time. You see de colored folks know dey had to get up soon as dey hear dat cow horn blow en dat been fore daylight come here. Oh, dey work from dark to dark in dat day en time. Didn' but one day out all de year stand dat was a week day en dat was de big Christmas day. Sweet molasses bread was de thing dat day. Coase dey give us a big supper when dey had dem cornshucking day. Oh, dey had a frolic den dat last way up to de midnight."

"I never live dere to de Haselden plantation wid my parents long fore dey hire me out to Massa John Mace en I stay dere till me en Maggie (his wife) come here to live. Nurse six head of chillun for de white folks dere. I hear em say my Missus was a Watson fore she marry Massa John Mace. Lord, Lord, love dem chillun to death. If Moses Mace been livin, you wouldn' be talkin to no Hector Godbold bout here dese days. He de one what give me en Maggie dat four room house you see settin dere. My Missus give me a good beatin one time when I did drop one of dem baby. Just put me head under her foot en beat me dat way."

"Another thing I had to do was to carry de baby cross de swamp every four hour en let my mamma come dere en suckle dat child. One day I go dere en another fellow come dere what dey call John. He en my mamma get in a argument like en he let out en cut my mamma a big lick right cross de leg en de blood just pour out dat thing like a done a what. My mamma took me en come on to de house en when Miss Jane see dat leg, she say, "Cindy, what de matter?" My mamma say, "John call me a liar en I never take it." Miss Jane tell em to send after Sam Watson right den. Sam Watson was a rough old overseer en he been so bowlegged dat if he stand straddle a barrel, he be settin down on it just as good as you settin dere. Sam Watson come dere en make dat fellow lay down on a plank in de fence jam en he take dat cat o' nine tail he have tie round his waist en strike John 75 times. De blood run down off him just like you see a stream run in dat woods. Dat sho been so cause all we chillun stand bout dere en look on it. I suppose I was bout big enough to plough den. When dey let John loose from dere, he go in de woods en never come back no more till freedom come here. I tellin you when he come back, he come back wid de Yankees."

"Oh, de colored peoples never know nothin more den dogs in dem times. Never couldn' go from one plantation to de other widout dat dey had a ticket wid em. I see Sam Watson catch many of dem dat had run way en buff en gag em. Never have no jails nowhe' in dat day en time. Dey sho sell de colored peoples way plenty times cause I see dat done right here to Marion. Stand em up on a block en sell em to a speculator dere. I hear em bid off a 'oman en her baby dere en den dey bid off my auntie en uncle way down to de country. Dey wouldn' take no whippin off dey Massa en dat how-come dey get rid of em. My gran'pappy been worth $1,000 en it de Lord's truth I tellin you, he drown fore he let em whip him. Den my gran'mammy use to run way en catch rides long de roads cause de peoples let em do dat den. Coase if dey catch her, dey didn' never do her no harm cause she was one of dem breed 'omans."

"Never know nothin bout gwine to school in dem times. Just pick up what learnin we get here, dere, en everywhe'. Learnt something to de white folks meetin house dere to Antioch settin on de back side of dat church on dem benches what de slaves had to set on. I is know dis much dat I voted three times to de courthouse in Marion way back in dem days."

"Sho, we chillun play game en frolic heap of de time. Shinny was de thing dat I like best. Just had stick wid crook in de end of it en see could I knock de ball wid dat. I sho remembers dat. Den I was one of de grandest hollerers you ever hear tell bout. Use to be just de same as a parrot. Here how one go: O—OU—OU—O—OU, DO—MI—NICI—O, BLACK—GA—LE—LO, O—OU—OU—O—OU, WHO—O—OU—OU. Great King, dat ain' nothin."

"Ain' never believe in none of dem charms people talk bout en ain' know nothin bout no conjuring neither, but I know dis much en dat a spirit sho slapped Maggie one night bout 12 o'clock. Den another time me en her was comin home from a party one night en I had a jug of something dere wid me en Maggie ax me for it. Say something was followin after her. De next thing I know I hear dat jug say, gurgle, gurgle, gurgle. I look back en she been pourin it out on de ground. She say she do dat to make de spirit quit followin after her. Dat spirit sho been dere cause I see dat licker disappear dere on de ground wid me own eyes."

"Sho, dey had doctors in dat day en time. Had plant doctors dat go from one plantation to another en doctor de peoples. Dr. Monroe was one of dem doctor bout here en dere ain' never been no better cures nowhe' den dem plant cures was. I get Maggie so she can move bout dat way. She won' able to walk a step en I boil some coon root en put a little whiskey in it en make her drink dat. It sho raise her up too. Dem coon root look just like dese chufas what you does find down side de river. Dat sho a cure for any rheumatism what is. I know dat all right."

"Mighty right, I remembers when freedom was declare. I think dat must a been de plan of God cause it just like dis, if it hadn' been de right thing, it wouldn' been. I know it a good thing. De North was freed 20 years head of de South en you know it a good thing. I a history man en I recollects dat de history say de North was freed 20 years fore de South was."

"I sho hear dem guns at Fort Sumter dere en I remembers when dem soldiers come through dis way dat de elements was blue as indigo bout here. Had parade bout five miles long wid horses dancin bout en fiddles just a playin. Some of dem Yankees come dere to de white folks house one of dem time, when my Massa was way from home workin dere on de Manchester Railroad, en ax my Missus whe' dey horses was. Dem horses done been hide in de bay en dey never get nothin else dere neither, but a little bit of corn dat dey take out de barn."

"I 87 year old now en I here to tell you dat I never done nobody no mean trick in all me life. I does fight cause I cut a man up worth 19 stitches one of dem times back dere. Two of em been on me one time en I whipped both of em. I tellin you I been good as ever was born from a 'oman. It just like dis, I say fight all right, but don' never turn no mean trick back. Turn it to God, dat what do. Dem what go to church in de right way, dey don' have no vengeful spirit bout em. I sho goes to church cause de church de one thing dat does outstand everything—everything."

Source: Hector Godbold, ex-slave, age 87, Pee Dee, Marion Co., S.C.
(Personal interview, June 1937).

United States. Work Projects Administration

Project #1855
Stiles M. Scruggs
Columbia, S.C.

DANIEL GODDARD
EX-SLAVE 74 YEARS OLD.

DANIEL GODDARD

"My name is Daniel Goddard. I was born in Columbia, S.C. Feb. 14, 1863, to slave parents. You know I recall no contacts I made in slavery for I was too young during that period. You know too, if I had been born in Massachusetts, for example, I should have been free, because all slaves in the United States had been set free when President Lincoln, shortly before my birth, January, 1863, struck the shackles from bondage.

"The Confederate states had seceded from the Union and they paid no attention to the freedom proclamation during the war. So the slaves in the South, generally speaking, stayed on until the Confederacy collapsed in April, 1865, and even then, some of the slaves were slow to strike out for themselves, until the Federal government made ample preparations to take care of them.

"Now you ask, if I heard about escapes of slaves. Sure I did and I heard my parents discuss the efforts of slaves to shake off the shackles. This was probably true because my father's brother, Thomas, was a member of the slave ship which was taking him and 134 others from Virginia to New Orleans. A few miles south of Charleston, the slaves revolted, put the officers and crew in irons, and ran the ship to Nassau.

"There they went ashore and the British Government refused to surrender them. They settled in the Bahama Islands and some of their descendants are there today. That was about 1830, I think, because my Uncle Thomas was far older than my father. I heard about the other slave revolts, where that African prince, one of a large number of slaves that were kidnaped, took over the Spanish ship L'Amada, killing two of the officers. The remaining officers promised to return the slaves to Africa but slyly turned the ship to port in Connecticut. There the Spanish minister at Washington demanded the slaves, as pirates. Appeal was made to the courts and the United States Court ruled that slavery was not legal in Spain and declared the slaves free.

"The Nat Turner insurrection in Virginia and the Vesey uprising in Charleston was discussed often, in my presence, by my parents and friends. I learned that revolts of slaves in Martinique, Antigua, Santiago, Caracas and Tortugus, was known all over the South. Slaves were about as well aware of what was going on, as their masters were. However the masters made it harder for their slaves for a while.

"I have a clipping, now worn yellow with age, which says the Federal census of 1860, showed there were 487,970 free Negroes and 3,952,760 slaves in the United States at that time. I am not at all surprised at the number of free Negroes. Many South Carolina families freed a number of their slaves. Some slaves had the luck to be able to buy their freedom and many others escaped to free areas. The problem of slavery as a rule, was a question of wits, the slave to escape and the master to keep him from escaping.

"I once talked with Frederick Douglass, perhaps the most eminent Negro to appear so far in America. He told me he was born a slave in Maryland, in 1817, and that he served there as a slave for ten years. He escaped to Massachusetts, where he was aided in education and employment by the Garrisons and other abolitionists, and became a leader of his race. He was United States Minister to Haiti at the time I met him and was eminent as an orator. He died in 1895.

"You ask, what do I think of the Presidents. Well, I have always been such an admirer of Andrew Jackson, a South Carolinian, that I may be prejudiced a little. The reason I admire him so much, is because he stood for the Union, and he didn't mean maybe, when he said it. He served his time and God took him, just as he took Moses.

"Then Lincoln was raised up for a specific purpose, to end slavery, which was a menace to both whites and blacks, as I see it. And President Wilson kept the faith of the fathers, when he decided to put the German Kaiser where he could no longer throw the world into discord. But there has only been one President whose heart was touched by the cry of distress of the poor and needy and his name is Franklin D. Roosevelt. He is one white man who has turned the bias of the Negroes from the bait of partisan politics.

"Yes, sir, I recall the reconstruction period here in Columbia. My parents lived until I was about grown and we kept the middle of the road, in the matter of selling out to the Federal soldiers and carpet-baggers on the one hand, or to designing politicians on the other. But my father was an admirer of General Hampton, because General Hampton owned many Negroes at one time and had treated them well. Between Hampton and Chamberlain for governor, in 1876, most of my Negro friends voted for Hampton.

"What have I been doing since I grew up? Well, I have been busy trying to make a living. I worked for various white folks in this community and sometime for the railroads here, in a minor capacity. My younger years were spent in the quest of an education. For the past thirty years I have been the porter for the State Paper Company, Columbia's morning newspaper. As I became proficient in the work, the Gonzales boys grew fond of me. While the youngest one, Hon. William E. Gonzales, was absent in the diplomatic service in Cuba and in Peru for eight years for President Wilson, I looked after the needs of Mr. Ambrose Gonzales. Shortly before he died, Hon. William E. Gonzales returned. He has since been editor and publisher of the 'State', as well as principal owner.

"You ask, if I have applied for an old age pension. No, I have not. I am old enough to qualify, I guess, but I understand, you cannot get a pension if you have a job. If that is so, I shall never enjoy any pension money. I would not leave serving my friend, Captain William E. Gonzales, for any pension that might be offered me."

N.B. This man is well educated, speaks no dialect. He received his education from Northern teachers in Freedman aid, equal to the modern high school curriculum. He afterward studied in Boston. He reads, writes, and speaks excellent English.

Address: 1022 Divine Street, Columbia, S.C.

United States. Work Projects Administration

Project #-1655
Mrs. Genevieve W. Chandler
Murrells Inlet, S.C.
Georgetown County

FOLKLORE

AUNT ELLEN GODFREY
(Ex-Slave)
(Verbatim Conversation)

ELLEN GODFREY

Aunt Ellen is a misfit in her present environment. Born at Longwood Plantation on Waccamaw in 1837, all she knows is the easy, quiet life of the country. And the busy, bustling 'RACE PATH' near which her Grandson lives with whom she makes her home doesn't make a fitting frame for the old lady. All day she sits in a porch swing and when hungry, visits a neighbor. The neighbors (colored—all) vie with each other in trying to make her last days happy days. She says they do her washing and provide necessary food. When you start her off she flows on like the brook but usually her story varies little. She tells of the old days and of the experiences that made the greatest impression—the exciting times during the 'Confedrick' war—the 'Reb time day.'

Visitor: "Aunt Ellen home?"

Aunt Ellen's neighbor (from the washtub):

"No'um. She right cross there on the 'Race Path'" (So

called because in Conway's early days races were run—horse races—on this street.)

Visitor: "Are you one of the neighbors who take such good care of Aunt Ellen?"

Neighbor: "No'um. I'm off all day. I work for Miss Bernice."

Visitor: "Miss Bernice who?"

Neighbor: "Miss Bernice something nother. I can't keep up with that lady title! See Aunt Ellen white cap yonder?"

Aunt Ellen (Sitting on chair at back door leaning on cane.)

"I want everybody come to my birthday! Seventh o' October coming be a hundred. Baby one dead jew (due) time! Five daughter—one sanctify preacher. Seven one—one Ports-smith Virginia. All dead! All dead! Marry three times; all the husband dead! My last baby child—when the Flagg storm kill everybody on the beach, (1893) the last child I have out my body been a year old!

"Last time I gone see the old Doctor, rap! rap! Doctor: "Come in!" Gone in. Doctor: "Great God! Looker Aunt Ellen! For the good you take care Daddy Harry, God left you live long time!"

Ellen: "Flat 'em all up to Marlboro! (All the slaves) Ten days or two weeks going. PeeDee bridge, stop! Go in gentlemen barn! Turn duh bridge! Been dere a week. Had to go and look the louse on we. Three hundred head o' people been dere. Couldn't pull we clothes off. (On flat.)

Boat name Riprey. Woman confine on boat. Name the baby 'RIPREY!' Mama name Sibby."

(Neighbor: "Aunt Ellen been looking for you all day! Keep saying she got to go home. A white lady coming and she got to be there!")

Aunt Ellen: "Doctor come on boat. By name Doctor Lane. White lady come tend woman. Get to Marlboro where they gwine. Put in wagon. Carry to the street. Major Drake Plantation. One son Pet Drake. Wife leetle bit of a woman.

"I see Abram Lincoln son Johnny! Talk with him! Gimme tobacco. I been to loom. Weave. Sheckle flying—flying sheckle!

> (Singing): "Tech (touch) me all round my waist!
> Don't tech my water-fall!
> Gay gal setting on the rider fence!
> Don't tech my water-fall!"

"Clothes gone to wash this morning. (Can't go today.) Clothes gone.

"I been here so long—I ax Jesus one day carry me next day! Can't make up my bed. Like an old hog sleep on a tussick." (I always heard it 'Toad on a tussock'—and you?)

(Four lean cats prowled about sniffing around the woodpile where a boy was scaling some pale, dead fish.)

Visitor: "Aunt Ellen, how could you cook on the flat?"

Aunt Ellen: "Dirt bank up. Fire make on dirt. Big pot.

Cook. Fry meat. Come PeeDee get off flat. Bake. Bake. Iron oven. Stay PeeDee week. Bake. Pile coals on oven top." (Another slave told of scaffold—four posts buried and logs or planks across top with earth on planks. On this pile of earth, fire was made and on great bed of coals oven could be heated for baking. 'Oven' means the great iron skillet-like vessel with three legs and a snug lid. This oven bakes biscuit, pound cake, and some old timers insist on trusting only this oven for their annual fruit cake. It works beautifully on a hearth. Put your buttermilk biscuit in, lid on and pile live-oak coals on top. Of course only the ones who have done this a long time know when to take the lid off.)

"Dirt camp to stay in—to hide from Yankee." (Her gestures showed earth was mounded up.)

Visitor: "Like a potato bank? A potato hill?"

Ellen: "Dat's it! Pile 'em! Gone in dirt camp to hide we from Yankee. Have a Street Row of house. Yankee coming. Gone in dirt camp.

"I been weave. My loom at door. Six loom on dat side! Six loom on dis side! I see 'em coming. Hat crown high as this." (She measured off almost half of her walking stick—which had a great, tarnished plated silver knob.) "And I tell 'em 'Yankee coming!' I talk with Abram Lincoln own son Johnny and, bless your heart I glad for Freedom till I fool!"

(Singing)

> 'Freedom forever!
> Freedom everymore!
> Want to see the Debbil run

Let the Yankee fling a ball
The Democrack will take the swamp!'

"Massa been hide. Been in swamp." (This is history. All the old men, too old for the army, hid in Marlboro swamps and were fed by faithful slaves until Yankees passed on. My grandmother and mother gave vivid accounts of this—my mother telling of the sufferings of the women—mental—worrying about her feeble old grandfather down there with the mocassins)

Ellen: "Yankee officer come. 'Where Mahams Ward and John J. Woodward? Come to tell 'em take dese people out the dirt camp! Put we in flat. Carry back!' (In first story Aunt Ellen told the Yankee Captain said, 'Tell 'em be Georgetown to salute the flag!')

"Put food and chillun in flat. We been walk." (Walking back to Waccamaw) We gone. (See 'um! See their feet like the children of Israel in Green Pastures!) In man's house. Man say, 'Come out! You steal my turnip!' Brush arbor. Night come. Make camp. Way down the road somewhere! Make a big bush camp. All squeeze under there. Left Marlboro Monday. Come Conway Friday sun down! Hit Bucksville, hit a friend. Say 'People hungry!' Middle night. Snow on ground. Get up. Cook. Cook all night! Rice. Bake tater. Collard. Cook. Give a quilt over you head. I sleep. I sleep in the cotton. I roost up the cotton gone in there." (Burrowed down in the cotton—'rooted' it up) "December. Winter time. Cook all night. Corn-bread, baked tater, collard. Git to Bucksport, people gin to whoop and holler! Three flat gone round wid all the vittles." (And with the very young and very old) Easier coming home. Current helped. Going up against the current, only poles and cant hooks—tedious going. "Git 'Tip Top' (Plantation) all right. Come home den! Git to double trunk (rice-field trunk) at 'Tip Top' Whoop! Come bring flat! Mother Molly dead on flat! Bury she right to Longwood grave-yard. Nuss. (nurse) Sam'l Hemingway bury there. Horse kill 'em in thrashing mill. Child name Egiburt bury there too. Horse gwine round in thrashing. He lick the horse. Horse kick 'em. Whole gang white jury come!

"Sing and pray all the time. Pray your house. Pray all the time. (I wish to God I could get some of you clam!)

"Salem Baptist? I helped build Salem! I a choir in Salem!"

>Aunt Ellen Godfrey
>Age 99 years 10 months
>Conway, S.C.

Project 1655
Genevieve W. Chandler
Georgetown County, S.C.

FOLKLORE

MOM ELLEN GODFREY
(Ex-slave—Age 100)

ELLEN GODFREY

"I'm waitin' on the leese (RELIEF). He was to have my birthday the seven of October.

"Slavery time Maussa buy 'em. We Maussa buy me one good shoe. Send slam to England. Gie me (give me) good clothes and shoe. I been a-weave. When the Yankee come I been on the loom. Been to Marlboro district. A man place they call Doctor Major Drake. Got a son name Cap and Pet. Oh, Jesus! I been here TOO long. In my 99 now. Come seven o' October (1937) I been a hundred.

"Three flat (big flat-boats) carry two hundred head o' people and all they things. We hide from Yankee but Yankee come and get we. Ask where Maussa! Maussa in swamp. I in buckra house. I tell Yankee: 'Them gone! Gone to beach!' Yankee say:

"'Tell 'em to be in Georgetown to bow unto flag'.

"That time I been twenty-three years old. Old Doctor Flagg didn't born then. He a pretty child and so fat. Love the doctor too much. Born two weeks after Freedom. He

Ma gone to town. Melia Holmes? She ain't no more than chillum to me. Laura and Serena two twin sister. When the Freedom I was twenty-three—over the twenty-five. Great God, have-a-mercy! McGill people have to steal for something to eat. Colonel Ward keep a nice place. Gie'em (give them) rice, peas, four cook for chillum, one nurse. Make boy go in salt crick get 'em clam. That same Doctor Flagg Grandpa. Give you cow clabber. Share 'em and put you bittle for eat.

"Gabe Knox? (A very old colored man who has been dead ten years) I nurse Gabe! I nurse 'em. He Pappy my cousin. I been a big young woman when he born.

"Albert Calina? He a Christian-hearted people. Christian-heart boy. I give my age. My birthday get over I want to go right home to Heaven.

"I gone to see Doctor Wardie when I in my 95. He say:

"'Great Dow! Looker Aunt Ellen! In you 95! What make you live to good age you take such good care you husband—Harry Godfrey.'"

Conversation of Aunt Ellen Godfrey—age 99 years, Conway, S.C. June 25th.

ELLEN GODFREY

"Would gone wid you Missus, but I waiting on the 'Relief'. He wuz going to bring me the dress and shoe and ting. My birthday the seven of October coming. We Massa have give we good shoe. Right here Longwood Plantation. Massa was kind—you know. Send slam to England gie me good clothes and shoe. I been a weave when the Yankee come. I been on the loom to Marlboro district. A man place they call Doctor Major Drake. Got a son name Cap and Pet. Oh, Jesus, been here too long! In my ninety-nine now. Come seben of October been a hundred. Three flat" (flat boats used for rice field work) "carry two hundred 'o people and all they things. We hide from Yankee but Yankee come and git we. Ask whey (where) Massa. (Massa in swamp! I in buckra house. I say, 'Dem gone! Gone to beach.' Say, 'Tell 'em to be in Georgetown to bow unto the flag.' Dat time I been twenty-three year old. Doctor Flagg didn't born. He a pretty child and so fat! Love duh Doctor too much! Born two weeks after freedom. He Ma gone Georgetown. Granny git 'em there. Melia Holmes! Ain't no more dan chillun to me!" (Aunt Melia is eighty-eight or nine—bony and cripple) "She have two twin sister Laura and Serena. When the Freedom I wuz twenty-three years old.—over the twenty-five. Great God hab a mercy! Couldn't do dat! Colonel Ward keep a nice place. Doctor McGill people hab to steal for someting to eat. Gie 'em rice—peas. Four cook for chillun. One nurse". (Aunt Ellen said 'Nuss') "Make the boy go get 'em clam. That same Dr. Ward GrandPa. Great big sack 'o clam! Give you cow clabber. Shay'm". (Share them—the clabber) "and put on bittle for eat.

"Hagar Brown! She darter (daughter) got a abscess in her stomach. Save Rutledge! I nuss (nurse) Sabe. I nuss 'em. Her pappy my cousin. I been big young women, I nuss Sabe.

"Albert Calina a christian-hearted people. Christian hearted boy. Relief come. I gie 'em my age. My birthday over, I wanter go right home to Heaven. Great Dow! 'Looker Aunt Ellen!' (That is what Dr. Wardie say when I gone see 'um.) 'In you ninety-five! What make you good, you take care of you husband! 'Harry Godfrey waiting man! Marry twice time. He duh last——

"Andrew Johnson? Dropsy? I have wid every chillun— Oh, I buss (burst) one time. Buss here." (Illustrating by drawing line across stomach.) "Till it get to my groin it stop! Every time I get family I swell. Never have a doctor 'Granny' for me yet. My Mary good old Granny. Catch two set 'o twin for me. Isaac and Rebecca; David and Caneezer.

"Sell all my fowl and ting—five dollars—me and old man two come to town to we chillun.

"Been Marlboro four year. Yankee foot where they put on stirrup red. Most stand lak a Mr. Smoak—Big tall—Abraham Lincoln own son Johnny! 'You jess as free as ribbon on my hat!' That what he say. I been weave. Sheckle!" (Aunt Ellen worked foot and hand and mouth in illustrating how the shuttle worked back and forth—and the music it made).

"Conch? Eat 'm many time! Take 'em bile! Grind 'em up!

"Welcome Beas? She son get kill in Charston, Welcome Beas son courting my gal.

"Tom Duncan? He child to me. He wife Susannah. I know duh fambly. I gone knock to duh door.

"Come in! Come in! Come in! 'Here duh beard!" (And Aunt Ellen measured on her chest to show how long Dr. Flagg's beard was).

> "Old Daddy Rodgers and merry wuz she!
> The old man wuz cripple
> And Mary wuz blind.
> Keep you hat on you head.
> Keep you head warm
> And set down under that sycamore tree!
> My kite! My kite!
> My kite! My kite!
> Two oxen tripe!
> Two open dish 'o cabbage!
> My little dog!
> My spotted hawg!
> My two young pig a starving!
> Cow in the cotton patch. Tell boy call dog drive pig out cotton!
> Heah duh song;
> Send Tom Taggum
> To drive Bone Baggum
> Out the world 'o wiggy waggum!"

(This last song chanted out by Aunt Eleanor Godfrey, age 99, is really a gem. She said 'Bone Baggum' boney old white cow. 'Wiggy waggum' is a picture word making one see the soft, wagging tufts of white cotton.)

    Given by Aunt Eleanor Godfrey
    Age 99 (100 come seben of Oct.)
    June 25th, 1937
    Conway, S.C.

Project 1655
Genevieve W. Chandler
Georgetown County, S.C.

FOLKLORE.

(MOM ELLEN SINGS * * *)
BONE BAGGUM (Bag o' bones?)

ELLEN GODFREY

Send Tom Taggum (a man)
To drive Bone Baggum (a boney critter)
Out the world o' wiggly waggum. (cotton patch)

Rock-a-bye!
Rock-a-bye!
Down come baby cradle and all!
Roll 'em! Roll 'em! Roll 'em!
Roll 'em and boll' em!
And put 'em in the oven!

"I KNOW when I was a woman Ben was boy!" (Ben now 88)

"Go to writin'!":

If you want to know my name
Go to Uncle Amos house.
Big foot nigger and he six foot high.
Try to bussin' at my waterfall! (Kissin' her waterfall—

head-dress.)
Oh, the gay gal
Settin' on the rider (fence 'rider' on 'stake and rider fence')
Gay gal waterfall.
Don't tech (touch) my waist
But bounce my shirt!
Don't touch my waterfall!"

"I sing that sing to 'em and man buss out and cry! 'My God! You talk ME?' I ain't want him! I kick him with that same word.

"They was Zazarus and Lavinia. Dead can't wash for myself. I go wash and lay Lavinia out. And he husband wanter (want to) marry with me. I kick him with that same sing. Hint to wise. If he couldn't understand that he couldn't understand nothing.

"Mr. Godfrey my last husband, he worth all the two I got. I have the chillun. Wenus, Jane, Patient, Kate, Harry, Edmund, Jeemes—"

Source: Mom Ellen Godfrey
Age 100 October 1937
Conway, S.C.

S-260-264-N
Project #1655
Augustus Ladson
Charleston, S.C.

No. Words 1654

MASTER WAS NEVER SO MOROCIOUS
SLAVES CALLED COW-MEAT FISH
SLAVE BORN WITH A 'CALL'

THOMAS GOODWATER

I come frum Mt. Pleasant an' was bo'n January 15, 1855 on Mr. Lias Winning plantation on the Cooper River. I wus den six years ole w'en the war broke out an' could 'member a good many things. My ma an' pa bin name Anjuline an' Thomas Goodwater who had eight boys an' eight gals. I use to help my gran'ma 'round the kitchen who wus the cook for the fambly. I am the older of the two who is alive. Peter, the one alive, live on my place now, but I ain't hear from dem for two years. I don' know for certain dat he's alive or not.

In slavery the people use to go an' catch possums an' rabbits so as to hab meat to eat. De driber use to shoot cows an in de night de slaves go an' skin um an' issue um 'round to all the slaves, 'speciall w'en cows come frum anodder plantation. He go 'round an' tell the slaves dey better go an' git some fish 'fore all go. Any time any one say e hab fish it wus understood e mean cow-meat. Our boss ain't nebber cetch on nor did e ebber miss any cow;

Gie Simmons, de collud driber wus under Sam Black, the white overseer. Sam Black wusn't mean, he jus' had to carry out orders of Lias Winning, our master. Dere wus a vegetable garden dat had things for the year round so we could hab soup an' soup could be in the Big House.

One day w'en I wus 'bout fourteen I did supin an' ma didn' like it. A bunch of gals bin home an' ma wheel my short over my head an' start to be at me right 'fore the gals. Dey begged her not to lick me an' she got mad jus' for dat. I couldn't help myself cuz she tie' de shirt over my head wood a string, my han's an' all wuz tie' in de shirt wood the string. In hot wedder gals an' boys go in dere under shirts an' nothin' else.

Boys in dose days could fight but couldn' throw any one on the groun'. We had to stan' up an eider beat or git beat.

I wus married in 1872 to Catharine, my wife. At our weddin' we had plenty to eat. There wus possums, wine, cake, an' plenty o' fruits. I had on a black suit, black shoes, white tie an' shirt. Catharine had on all white. I stay' wood Catharine people for a year 'til I wus abled to buil' on my lan'. I am a fadder of nineteen chillun; ten boys an' nine gals; only two now livin'.

Lias Winning wusn' a mean man. He couldn' lick pa cus dey grow up togedder or at least he didn' try. But he liked his woman slave. One day ma wus in da field workin' alone an' he went there an' try to rape 'er. Ma pull his ears almos' off so he let 'er off an' gone an' tell pa he better talk to ma. Pa wus workin' in the salt pen an' w'en Mr. Winning tell him he jus' laugh cus e know why ma did it.

Dere wus a fambly doctor on de plantation name James Hibbins. My eye use to run water a lot an' he take out my eye an' couldn' put it back in, dats why I am blin' now. He ax ma an' pa not to say anything 'bout it cus he'd lost his job an' hab his license take 'way. So ma an' pa even didn' say anything even to Mr. Winning as to the truth of my blin'ness.

I wus by the "nigger quarters" one day w'en Blake, the overseer start' to lick a slave. She take the whip frum him an' close de door an' give him a snake beatin'.

Our boss had 'bout shree hund'ed acres o' lan' an' ober a hund'ed slaves. De overseer never wake de slaves. Dey could go in the fiel' any time in the mornin' cus ebery body wus given their tas' work on Monday Mornin'. No body neber work w'en it rain or cole. Nuttin' make Lias Winning so mad as w'en one would steal; it make him morocious. Any one he catch stealin' wus sure to git a good whippin'. He didn' like for any one to fight eider.

Dey tell me dat w'en slaves wus shipped to New Orleans dey had to be dress-up in nice clothes. My pa could read an' write cus he live' in the city here. His missus teach him.

Isaac Wigfall run 'way an' went to Florida an' meet a white man on a horse with a gun. He ax de man for a piece o' tobacco. The man give him de gun to hole while he git the tobacco for him. Isaac take the gun an' point it at the man an' ax 'im, "you know wha' in dis gun?" De man got frighten' an' he tell de man "you better be gone or I'll empty it in you." The man gone an' come back wood a group o' men an' houndogs. He'd jus' make it to de river 'fore the dogs cetch him. He had a piece o' light-wood knot an' ebery time a dog git near he hit um on de neck an' kill' all o' them. The men went back to git more help an' dogs but w'en dey git back Isaac wus gone.

Dere wus a collud church fifteen miles frum Mt. Pleasant w'ere we went to service. De preacher wus name' John Henry Doe. I use to like to sing dis song:

> Run away, run away
> Run away, run away
> Sojus of the cross.
>
> CHORUS
>
> Hole on, hole on
> Hole on, hole on
> Hole on, hole on
> Hole on, sojus of the cross.

Ma too use to sing dat song.

Dere use to be dances almos' ebery week an' the older boys an' gals walk twelve miles dis to be dere. Some time there wus a tamborine beater, some time dey use' ole wash tubs an' beat it wood sticks, an' some time dey jus' clap their han's. W'en any one die dey wus bury in the mornin' or early afternoon.

I always play wood ghost cus I wus bo'n with a "call". I kin see the ghost jus' is plain is ebber. Some time I see some I know an' again others I don' know. Only thing you can' see their feet cus dey walk off de ground. W'en I use to see dem my sister would put sand on de fire den dey would go an' I wouldn' see any for a long time. One mornin' my uncle wus passin' a church an' a ghost appear on the porch. My uncle had a dog wood 'im. He start to run an' the dog start to run too, an' down the road dey went. He didn' hab on anything but his shirt an' he say he run so fas' 'til the wind had his shirt-tail stif as a board. He couldn' out run the dog, nor could the dog out run 'im.

Dis is a spiritual dey use to sing durin' slavery:

> Climb up de walls of Zion
> Ah, Lord,
> Climb up de walls of Zion
> Ah, Lord, Climbin' up de walls of Zion
> Ah, Lord.
> Climbin' up de walls of Zion
> Ah, Lord,
> Great camp meetin' in the promise lan'.

My pa use to sing dis song:

> See w'en' 'e rise
> Rise an' gone,
> See w'en' 'e rise
> Rise an' gone.
>
> Gone to Galilee on a Sunday morning.
> Oh, my Jesus rise an' gone to Galilee
> On a Sunday morning.

Dey use to sing dis in experience meetin's:

> Go round, go round
> Look at the mornin' star,
> Go round, go round

Got a soul to save.

CHORUS

Wuan' for ole satan
I wouldn' have to pray,
Satan broke God's Holy Law
I got a soul to save.

Dey use to sing dis too:

>Room Anough, room anough
>Room anough, room anough
>Room anough in de Heaven I know,
>I can't stay away,
>Room anough in de Heaven I know,
>I can't stay away.

Source: Interview with Thomas Goodwater, 108 Anson Street.

P.S. The variations of words and sentences describe interviews with
individuals, naturally.

Code No.
Project, 1885-(1)
Prepared by Annie Ruth Davis
Place, Marion, S.C.
Date, August 31, 1937

No. Words_____
Reduced from _____words
Rewritten by_____

CHARLIE GRANT
Ex-Slave, 85 Years

CHARLIE GRANT

"I born de 24th day of February, 1852 bout 1½ miles of Mars Bluff. My father, Western Wilson, belonged to Col. William Wilson en my mamma name Chrisie Johnson. She belonged to Dr. William Johnson en we stay dere wid him four or five years after freedom. Dr. Johnson old home still standin yonder. It de Rankin home. I drive carts under dat house lots of times in slavery time." (The house is built high off the ground.)

"Dr. Johnson was a mighty able man, a stiff one, able one. He kill one hundred head of hogs to feed his niggers wid. Oh, I don' know how many acres of land in his plantation, but I reckon dere be bout 1,000 or more acres of land. He have slave house all de way from de side of his house to Tyner. De overseer stay on de lower end of street dat bout ¾ mile long en all de niggers house up from de overseer to Dr. Johnson house. Over hundreds of dem dere."

"Dr. Johnson en his wife was good to dey niggers as dey could want anybody to be. Had plenty to eat en plenty clothes to wear all de time. He give all de slaves out something on Saturday or he give dem more any time dey needed it. Just go en say, 'Boss, I ain' got no rations en I need some.' Dey give us meat en bread en molasses to eat mostly, but didn' have no wheat flour den. Dey plant 10 or 20 acres of sprangle top cane en make de molasses en sugar out dat. Bill Thomas mash it together en cook it for de molasses. Den he take cane en cook it down right low en make sugar, but it wasn' like de sugar you buy at de store now days. Oh, yes, de slaves had dey own garden dat dey work at night en especially moonlight nights cause dey had to work in de field all day till sundown. Mamma had a big garden en plant collards en everything like dat you want to eat."

"All de niggers dat live in de quarters had bunk beds to sleep on what was thing dat have four legs en mattress put on it. Have mixed bed dat dey make out of cotton en shucks. De boy chillun have shuck bed en de girl chillun have cotton bed."

"De peoples bout dere have good clothes to wear in dat day en time. Dey was homemade clothes. My mamma spin en send dem to de loom house en den dey dye dem wid persimmon juice en different things like dat to make all kind of colors. Dey give us cotton suit to wear on Sunday en de nicest leather shoes dat dey make right dere at home. Clean de hair off de leather just as clean as anything en den de shoemaker cut en sew de shoes. Vidge Frank father de shoemaker. Vidge Frank live down dere at Claussen dis side de planing mill."

"I hear dem tell dat my grandparents come from

Africa. Dey fooled dem to come or I calls it foolin dem. De peoples go to Africa en when dey go to dock, dey blow whistle en de peoples come from all over de country to see what it was. Dey fool dem on de vessel en give dem something to eat. Shut dem up en don' let dem get out. Some of dem jump over board en try to get home, but dey couldn' swim en go down. Lots of dem still lost down dere in de sea or I reckon dey still down dere cause dey ain' got back yet. De peoples tell dem dey gwine bring dem to a place whe' dey can live."

"I tellin you dat was a good place to live in slavery time. I didn' have to do nothin but mind de sheep en de cows en de goats in dat day en time. All de slaves dat was field hands, dey had to work mighty hard. De overseer, he pretty rough sometimes. He tell dem what time to get up en sound de horn for dat time. Had to go to work fore daybreak en if dey didn' be dere on time en work like dey ought to, de overseer sho whip dem. Tie de slaves clear de ground by dey thumbs wid nigger cord en make dem tiptoe en draw it tight as could be. Pull clothes off dem fore dey tie dem up. Dey didn' care nothin bout it. Let everybody look on at it. I know when dey whip my mamma. Great God, in de mornin! Dey sho had whippin posts en whippin houses too in dem days, but didn' have no jail. I remember dey whipped dem by de gin house. De men folks was put to de post what had holes bored in it whe' dey pull strings through to fasten dem up in dere. Dey catch nigger wid book, dey ax you what dat you got dere en whe' you get it from. Tell you bring it here en den dey carry you to de whippin post for dat. No men folks whip me. Women folks whip me wid four plaitted raw cowhide whip."

"Niggers went to white peoples church in dat day en time. Dr. Johnson ride by himself en bought carriage for niggers to drive his girls dere to Hopewell Church below Claussen. You know whe' dat is, don' you? Miss Lizzie (Dr. Johnson's daughter) good teacher. She sent me to de gallery en I recollect it well she told me one Sunday dat if I didn' change my chat, dey were gwine to whip me. She say, 'You chillun go up in de gallery en behave yourself. If you don', I gwine beat you Monday.' Dey had catechism what dey teach you en she say, 'Charlie, who made you?' I tell her papa made me. She ax me another time who made me en I tell her de same thing another time. I thought I was right. I sho thought I was right. She took de Bible en told me God made me. I sho thought papa made me en I go home en tell papa Miss Lizzie say she gwine beat me Monday mornin. He ax me what I been doin cuttin up in church. I say, 'I wasn' doin nothin. She ax me who made me en I tell her you made me.' He told me dat God made me. Say he made Miss Lizzie en he made everybody. Ain' nobody tell me dat fore den, but I saved my beaten cause I changed my chat."

"I hear tell bout de slaves would run away en go to Canada. Put nigger dogs after dem, but some of dem would get dere somehow or another. If I was livin on your place, I wouldn' dare to go to another house widout I had a permit from my Massa or de overseer. We slip off en de patroller catch en whip us. One time dey give my daddy a quilting en ax several women to come dere. Dey had a lot of chillun to cover en give a quilting so dey can cover dem up. Mistress tell dem to give so en so dis much en dat much scraps from de loom house. I was settin dere in de corner en dey blow cane. Common reed make music en dance by it. Dat de only way niggers had to make music.

Dance en blow cane dat night at grandmother's house (Wilson place). Dey was just a pattin en dancin en gwine on. I was sittin up in de corner en look up en patrol was standin in de door en call patrol. When dey hear dat, dey know something gwine to do. Dey took Uncle Mac Gibson en whip him en den dey take one by one out en whip dem. When dey got house pretty thin en was bout to get old man Gibson, he take hoe like you work wid en put it in de hot ashes. People had to cut wood en keep fire burnin all de year cause didn' have no matches den. Old man Gibson went to de door en throwed de hot ashes in de patrol face. Dey try to whip us, but de old man Gibson tell dem dey got no right to whip his niggers. We run from whe' we at to our home. Dey tried four year to catch my daddy, but dey couln' never catch him. He was a slick nigger."

"I don' remember what kind of medicines dey use in slavery time, but I know my mamma used to look after de slaves when dey get sick. Saw one child bout year or two old took sick en died en Lester Small want me to dig it up en carry him to de office. I expect dey gwine be dere, but dey never come. I took it out en laid it on de bank in sheet dat dey give me. Den I picked it up en carried it in de house. It smeared me up right bad, but I carried it in de office en he look at it. He put it in de corner en say, 'You can go.' Pay me $2.00. Dr. Johnson want to cut dat child open. Dat what he want wid it. I know dis much dat dey use different kind of roots for dey medicines en I see dem wear dime in dey clothes dat dey tell me was to keep off de rheumatism. Send to Philadelphia to get dat kind of dime."

"I tellin you time hard dese days. I had stroke here en can' work, but I doin de best I can. Miss Robinson help me daughter do de best she can. Do washin en ironin. Miss Robinson say she gwine give me old age pension. I ask Miss Robinson, I say, 'I livin now en can' get nothin. If I die, would you help my chillun bury me?' She say, 'I will do de best I can to help put you away nice.' Miss Robinson good lady."

Source: Charlie Grant, ex-slave, age 85, Florence, S.C.

Personal interview by H. Grady Davis and Mrs. Lucile Young, Florence, S.C., May 11, 1937.

Project #-1655
Phoebe Faucette
Hampton County

Folklore

[HW: Grant, Rebecca Jane]
NINETY TWO YEAR OLD NEGRO TELLS OF EARLY LIFE AS SLAVE

GRANT REBECCA JANE

In Hampton County at Lena, S.C., there lives an old negro woman who has just passed her ninety-second birthday, and tells of those days long ago when man was bound to man and families were torn apart against their will. Slowly she draws the curtain of Time from those would-be-forgotten scenes of long ago that cannot ever be entirely obliterated from the memory.

"Well, just what is it you want to hear about, Missus?"

"Anything, everything, Auntie, that you remember about the old days before the Civil War. Just what you've told your grand-daughter, May, and her friend, Alice, here, many times, is what I want to hear."

"Tell her, mamma," said Alice with a whoop of laughter, "about the time when your Missus sent you to the store with a note!"

"Oh that! Not that Missus?"

"Yes, Auntie that!"

"Well, I was just a little girl about eight years old, staying in Beaufort at de Missus' house, polishing her brass andirons, and scrubbing her floors, when one morning she say to me, 'Janie, take this note down to Mr. Wilcox Wholesale Store on Bay Street, and fetch me back de package de clerk gie (give) you.'

"I took de note. De man read it, and he say, 'Uh-huh'. Den he turn away and he come back wid a little package which I took back to de Missus.

"She open it when I bring it in, and say, 'Go upstairs, Miss!'

"It was a raw cowhide strap bout two feet long, and she started to pourin' it on me all de way up stairs. I didn't know what she was whippin' me bout; but she pour it on, and she pour it on.

"Turrectly she say, 'You can't say "Marse Henry", Miss? You can't say, "Marse Henry"!'

"Yes'm. Yes'm. I kin say. 'Marse Henry'!

"Marse Henry was just a little boy bout three or four years old. Come bout halfway up to me. Wanted me to say Massa to him, a baby!"

"How did you happen to go to Beaufort, Auntie? You told me you were raised right here in Hampton County on the Stark Plantation."

"I was, Miss. But my mother and four of us children (another was born soon afterwards) were sold to Mr. Robert Oswald in Beaufort. I was de oldest, then there was brother Ben, sister Delia, sister Elmira, and brother Joe that was born in Beaufort. My father belong to Marse Tom Willingham; but my mother belong to another white man. Marse Tom was always trying to buy us so we could all be together, but de man wouldn't sell us to him. Marse Tom was a Christian gentleman! I believe he seek religion same as any colored person. And pray! Oh, that was a blessed white man! A blessed white man! And Miss Mamie, his daughter, was a Christian lady. Every Wednesday afternoon she'd fill her basket with coffee, tea, sugar, tobacco and such things, and go round to de houses where dere was old folks or sick folks. She'd give um de things; and she'd read de scriptures to um, and she'd kneel down and pray for um. But we had to leave all de folks we knew when we was took to Beaufort.

"All of us chillun, too little to work, used to have to stay at de 'Street'. Dey'd have some old folks to look after us—some old man, or some old woman. Dey'd clean off a place on de ground near de washpot where dey cooked de peas, clean it off real clean, den pile de peas out dere on de ground for us to eat. We'd pick um up in our hands and begin to eat. Sometimes dey'd cook hoe cakes in a fire of coals. Dey'd mix a little water with de meal and make a stiff dough that could be patted into shape with de hands. De cakes would be put right into the fire, and would be washed off clean after they were racked out from de coals. Sometimes de Massa would have me mindin' de birds off de corn. But 'fore I left Beaufort, I was doin' de Missus' washin' and ironin'. I was fifteen years old when I left Beaufort, at de time freedom was declared. We were all reunited den. First, my mother and de young chillun, den I got back. My uncle, Jose Jenkins come to Beaufort and stole me by night from my Missus. He took me wid him to his home in Savannah. We had been done freed; but he stole me away from de house. When my father heard that I wasn't wid de others, he sent my grandfather, Isaac, to hunt me. When he find me at my uncle's house, he took me back. We walked all back—sixty-four miles. I was foundered. You know if'n a foundered person will jump over a stick of burning lightwood, it will make um feel better."

"Tell us, Auntie, more about the time when you and your mother and brothers and sisters had just gone to Beaufort.

"Well mam. My mother say she didn't know a soul. All de time she'd be prayin' to de Lord. She'd take us chillun to de woods to pick up firewood, and we'd turn around to see her down on her knees behind a stump, aprayin'. We'd see her wipin' her eyes wid de corner of her apron, first one eye, den de other, as we come along back. Den, back in de house, down on her knees, she'd be aprayin'. One night she say she been down on her knees aprayin' and dat when she got up, she looked out de door and dere she saw comin' down out de elements a man, pure white and shining. He got right before her door, and come and stand right to her feet, and say, "Sarah, Sarah, Sarah!"

"Yes, Sir."

"What is you frettin' bout so?"

"Sir. I'm a stranger here, parted from my husband, with five little chillun and not a morsel of bread."

"You say you're parted from your husband? You're not parted from your husband. You're jest over a little slash of water. Suppose you had to undergo what I had to.

I was nailed to the Cross of Mount Calvary. And here I am today. Who do you put your trust in?

"My mother say after dat, everything just flow along, just as easy. Now my mother was an unusually good washer and ironer. De white folks had been sayin', 'Wonder who it is that's makin' de clothes look so good.' Well, bout dis time, dey found out; and dey would come bringin' her plenty of washin' to do. And when dey would come dey would bring her a pan full of food for us chilluns. Soon de other white folks from round about heard of her and she was gettin' all de washin' she needed. She would wash for de Missus durin' de day, and for de other folks at night. And dey all was good to her.

"One day de Missus call her to de house to read her something from a letter she got. De letter say that my father had married another woman. My mother was so upset she say, 'I hope he breaks dat woman's jawbone. She know she aint his lawful wife.' And dey say her wish come true. Dat was just what happened.

"But we all got together again and I thanks de good Lord. I gets down on my knees and prays. I thanks de Lord for His mercy and His goodness to me every day. Every time I eats, I folds my hands and thanks Him for de food. He's de one that sent it, and I thanks Him. Then, on my knees, I thanks him.

"Aunt Jane receives an ample pension since her husband fought on the side with the Federals. He was known as James Lawton before the war, but became, James Lawton Grant after the war."

Source: Mrs. Delacy Wyman, Mgr. Pyramid Pecan Grove,

Lena S.C.
Rebecca Jane Grant, ninety-two year old resident of Lena, S.C.

Project #-1655
Phoebe Faucette
Hampton County

REBECCA JANE GRANT

"Yes, Ma'am," Aunt Beckie said, "I remembers you, you Miss Mamie Willingham' granddaughter. She was sure a good woman. She'd fill her buggy with sugar, tea, coffee and tobacco, and go every Thursday to see the sick and old people. She wouldn't except none—white or colored. No'm she wouldn't except none! That's the kind of folks you sprung from. You's got a good heritage.

"The most of what I remembers before the war was when I was in Beaufort. They used to take care of the widows then. Take it by turns. There was a lady, Miss Mary Ann Baker, whose husband had been an organist in the church. When he died they would all take turns caring for Miss Mary Ann. I remember I'd meet her on de street and I'd say, 'Good mornin' Miss Mary Ann.' 'Morning Janie.' 'How you this mornin' Miss Mary Ann?' She'd say, 'Death come in and make alterations, and hard living make contrivance.' She'd take any old coat, or anything, and make it over to fit her children, and look good, too. She was a great seamstress. You'd see her children when they turn out on de street and they looked the same as some rich white people's children. Nearly all of her children was girls. Had one boy, as well as I kin remember.

"Dey used to make de clothes for de slaves in de house. Had a seamstress to stay there in de house so de mistress could supervise the work. De cloth de clothes was made out of was hand woven. It was dyed in pretty colors—some green, some blue, and pretty colors. And it was strong cloth, too. Times got so hard during de war dat de white folks had to use de cloth woven by hand, themselves. De ladies would wear bustles, and hoops made out of oak. Old times, they'd make underbodies with whalebone in it. There was something they'd put over the hoop they call, 'Follow me, boy'. Used to wear the skirts long, with them long trains that trail behind you. You'd take and tuck it up behind on some little hook or something they had to fasten it up to. And the little babes had long dresses. Come down to your feet when you hold the baby in your lap. And embroidered from the bottom of the skirt all the way up. Oh, they were embroidered up in the finest sort of embroidery.

"One day when I was nursing, my Missus' son—him and I been one age, 'bout the same age—he go up town and buy a false face. Now I didn't see nuthin' like dat before! He put dat thing on and hide behind de door. I had de baby in my arms, and when I start toward de door with de baby, he jump out at me! I threw the baby clean under the bed I was so scared. If it had of killed it, it wouldn't been me. It'd been dem! Cause I ain't never seen sech a thing before.

"You say what schoolin' de slaves got? They didn't get none—unless it was de bricklayers and such like, and de seamstresses. If de masters wanted to learn them, they'd let 'em hold de book. But they wouldn't miss de catechism. And they was taught they must be faithful to the Missus and Marsa's work like you would to your heavenly Father's work.

"Didn't have no colored churches. De drivers and de over-seers, de house-servants, de bricklayers and folks like dat'd go to de white folk's church. But not de field hands. Why dey couldn't have all got in de church. My marsa had three or four hundred slaves, himself. And most of the other white folks had just as many or more. But them as went would sing! Oh they'd sing! I remember two of 'em specially. One was a man and he'd sing bass. Oh, he'd roll it down! The other was a woman, and she'd sing soprano! They had colored preachers to preach to de field hands down in de quarters. Dey'd preach in de street. Meet next day to de marsa's and turn in de report. How many pray, how many ready for baptism and all like dat. Used to have Sabbath School in de white people's house, in de porch, on Sunday evening. De porch was big and dey'd fill dat porch! They never fail to give de chillun Sabbath School. Learn them de Sabbath catechism. We'd sing a song the church bells used to ring in Beaufort. You never hear it any more. But I remembers it."

The old woman sang the song for me as melodiously and beautifully as any young person. The words are:

"I want to be an angel, and with an angel stand,
A crown upon my forehead, a harp within my hand.
Right there before my Saviour, so glorious and so bright,
I'll hear the sweetest music, and praise Him day and night."

"Old Parson Winborn Lawton used to preach for us

after the war until we got our church organized. He had a daughter named Miss Anna Lawton. At the white folk's church at Lawtonville they had a colored man who used to sing for them, by the name of Moses Murray. He'd sit there back of the organ and roll down on them bass. Roll down just like de organ roll! He was Moses Lawton at that time, you know.

"You know how old I am? I'm in my 94th year. Ella has a dream book she looks up my age in and tells me what luck I have, and all that. I generally had good luck."

Source: Rebecca Jane Grant, 93 years old. Lena, S.C.

Project 1885-(1)
FOLKLORE
Spartanburg, S.C.
District No. 4.
May 26, 1937.

Edited by:
R.V. Williams

STORIES OF EX-SLAVES

JOHN GRAVES

"Mos' everybody know my name. You gotta help me. Oh, yeah, dat's what I goes by. It's Brack; dey calls me ole uncle Brack".

"Look out, over dar!" said a negro who was standing nearby. "Uncle Brack, you know you is got mo' names dan dat. Why, everwhar you goes, dey calls you a different name."

"Shet up, you sassy-mouth nigger!" Uncle Brack waved his stick as the younger negro moved out of its reach. Uncle Brack walks with two sticks nearly all the time. He is bent almost double.

"He de greatest nigger rascal a-gwine," Uncle Brack said. "He jest dream all de time, and dreams don't nebber amount to nothin'. Dem dreams what he carries on wid in de daytime, dey is what makes him tell so many lies. De idea, talking like I has a different name everwhar I goes, when I don't go nowhar. Why, I can't hardly hobble to de sto'.

"Dey mus' help me. I took down sick in November. Mr. Rice sent me things. You gov'ment folks ain't sont me much as Mr. Rice and de good white folks what likes me. I'se bawn ten years when Freedom come out. Benn seventy-odd years since Freedom, ain't it, Cap?

"Dr. Jim Gibbs was mighty good to me. You sees dat I'se a-gwine about now. Dr. Gibbs come from Aiken to Union and set up a drug sto' whar Cohen's is now. Dr. Gibbs was a Charleston man, but I is a Kentucky darky. Dr. Gibbs brung me from Kentucky to Charleston when I was five years old. My ma was de one dat dey bought. Dr. Gibbs' wife was a Bohen up in Kentucky. When Dr. Gibbs fetch his wife to Charleston, he bought my ma from his wife's pa, and she fetch me along too.

"It ten o'clock befo' I can creep. Dat de reason dat I has to beg. Wasn't fer my age, I wouldn't ax nobody fer nothing. De Lawd done spared me fer somethin' and I carries on de best dat I can. Doctor say he couldn't do no good. Dat been five years ago de fust time I tuck down. Doctors steadies about money too much. I trustes de Lawd, He spare me to dis day. I can't hardly walk, and I jus' can't bear fer nothing to touch dis foot. I has to use two sticks to walk. (Uncle Brack punched his foot with a stick; then looked up and saw two negro girls approaching.)

"As the girls got opposite Uncle Brack, he threw his stick in front of them and they exclaimed, "Is dat you, Uncle Brack? How did you get up here?" Uncle Brack replied, "I never meant fer you to git by me. Jes kaize I'se ole, ain't no reason fer you not speaking to me." As the girls walked on, Uncle Brack said, "I flirts wid all de colored gals, and I also has a passing word for de white ladies as dey goes by."

"I used to work at the baker shop over dar when Mr. James' chilluns was little saplings. I'se gwine on eighty-six and dem big boys raise dey hats to me. White people has respec' for me kaize I ain't never been in jail. I knows how to carry myself, and I specs to die dat way if I can. Lil chile what jus' could talk good gived me a penny dis mawning.

"I used to could read. I learnt to read in Aiken, when school fust broke out to de colored people. Northern people teached me to read long time ago. Now my eyes is dim."

Source: John Graves, (Col. 86) N. Church St., Union, S.C.
Interviewer: Caldwell Sims, Union, S.C. (2/27/37)

United States. Work Projects Administration

Project 1885-1
FOLKLORE
Spartanburg, Dist. 4:
Sept. 8, 1937

Edited by:
Elmer Turnage

STORIES OF EX-SLAVES

SIM GREELEY

"Miss Alice Cannon give me my age from de foundation of my mother. Dey been bringing my things out to me—is dat what you'se doing, setting down here by me? I was born on de first Christmas Day, I means de 25th of December, 1855; in Newberry County on de Sam Cannon place. You had to turn off de Ashford Ferry Road about seven and a half miles from de town of Newberry. My mother was Frances Cannon of near Cannon Creek Church.

"I'll try to give you a straight definition. Old man Sim Gallman was my old missus' brother; she was Miss Viny Cannon. My boss was overseer for Mr. Geo. Gallman. We was on Mr. George's place. When Mr. Gallman started overseeing, Mr. Sim Gallman come over dar for dem to take his place and care for him.

"My boss, Sam Cannon, promised me a place. Miss Viny Cannon suckled me and her son Henry at de same time, me on one knee and Henry on t'other. Dey calls me 'Timber'. Miss Sallie said to us atter Freedom, 'You ain't got no marsters'. I cried. My Ma let me stay wid Miss Sallie. Mr. Henry Gallman promised to marry Miss Sally Cannon, my young missus; but he went to de war and never come back home no mo'. Mr. Jeff Gallman went, but he come back wid one arm. Mr. Tom Gallman went and married his first cousin, Miss Addie Cannon; he never got to go to de war.

"My father was a full-blooded Indian from Virginia. He was a refugee. But you know dat dey had a way of selling people back den. Somebody caught him and sold him at one of dem sales. De man what bought him was Mr. Jeff Buzzard. He went back to Virginia atter de surrender. I would not go. He took another woman on de place, and my mother would not let me go. De woman's name dat he took was Sara Danby. She had two brothers and a sister—Samuel, Coffee, and Jenny.

"My mother was mixed Indian and African blood. My folks got 'stroyed up in a storm. My grandfather was named Isaac Haltiwanger. My grandmother, his wife, was named Annie. Dey had one child who was my mother; her name Frances. My grandmother's name was Molly Stone.

"My parents, talking 'bout de Africans, how funny dey talked. Uncle Sonny and uncle Edmund Ruff was two of de old 'uns. Old man Charles Slibe was de preacher. He was a Methodist. My father was a Baptist. His white folks, de Billy Caldwells, prepared de barn for him to preach to dere slaves. In dat day, all de Africans was low chunky fellers and raal black. Dey said dat in Africa, little chilluns run 'round de house and de fattest one fall behind; den dey kill him and eat him. Dat's de worst dat I ever heard, O Lawd!

"I hates dat Missus didn't whip me mo' and let me be teached to read and write so dat I wouldn't be so ignant.

"For de neuralgia, take and tie two or three nutmegs around yo' neck. Tie brass buttons around de neck to stop de nose a-bleeding."

Greeley's house has four rooms and it is in great need of repair. It is badly kept and so are the other houses in "Fowler's Row". He lives with his wife, Eula, but she was not home during the visit.

"My house 'longs to a widder woman. She white but I does not know her name. Her collector is Mr. Wissnance (Whisenant). He got a office over here on E. Main St., right up in de town. I rents by de month but I pays by de week—a dollar. De house sho is gwine down. Rest of de houses on de Row is repaired, but mine ain't yet; so she have Mr. Wissnance drap off twenty-five cents, and now I is paying only seventy-five cents a week. Me and Eula has to go amongst de white folks fer bread and other little things. Ain't got no bread from 'Uncle Sam' since last August. See my tater patch, wid knee-high vines.

"De case worker want to git my age and whar I's born. I told her jest what I told you. She say she got to have proof; so I told her to write Mr. Cannon Blease who was de sheriff. I means de High Sheriff, fer nigh thirty years in Newberry. And does you know, she never even heard of Mr. Cannon Blease. Never had no money but Mr. Blease knowed it, so he up and sont my kerrect age anyway. It turn't out jest 'zactly like I told you it was. What worried me de mostest, is dat she never knowed Mr. Cannon Blease. Is you ever heard of sech a thing as a lady like dat not knowing Mr. Blease?

"Now Mr. Dr. Snyder is a man dat ain't setting here 'sleep. He's a mill'onaire, kaise he run Wofford College and it must take a million dollars to do dat, it sho must. My case worker knowed him.

"De case worker calls me 'Preacher', but I ain't got up to dat yet—I ain't got dat fer. I been sold out twice in insurance. I give my last grand-baby de name 'Roosevelt', and his daddy give him 'Henry'. His Ma never give him none. Some folks loads down babies and kills dem wid names, but his ma never wanted to do dat. So us jest calls him Henry Roosevelt. Us does not drap none and us does not leave none out.

"Went to church one night and left my pocketbook in a box on my mantel. Had $120.00 in it in paper, and $8 in silver. Some niggers dat had been watching me broke down my do' dat I had locked. Dey took de $120 and left de $8. Went home and I seed dat broke do'. I went straight to my mantel and see'd what was done. Dey never bothered de books and papers in dat box. Next morning, de nigger what lived next do' to me was gone. I went to a old fortune teller, a man; he say I know dat you lost a lot. De one I thought got de money, he said, was not de right one. He say dat three hobos got it. One had red hair, one sandy hair and de other had curly hair. He say somebody done cited dem and dey sho going to be caught dis very day. He say dat dey come from Asheville. But he was wrong, kaise dey ain't never caught no three hobos dat I ever learn't about.

"One day when I was plowing, I struck de plow 'ginst something. My plow knocked off de handle. I heard money rattle. It ringed three times. I couldn't see nothing, so I called my wife and son and dey looked, but we never found but five cents. Never in my life did I hear of a bank in slavery times. Everybody buried dere money and sometimes dey forgot where dey put it. I thought dat I had run on some of dat money den, but I never found none. Lots of money buried somewhars, and folks died and never remembered whar it was.

"A nigger republican leader got kilt. I hel't de hosses fer de Ku klux. Great God-a-mighty, Dave and Dick Gist and Mr Caldwell run de sto' at de Rutherford place in dem times. Feeder of dem hosses was Edmund Chalmers. Mr. Dick say, 'Hello, Edmund, how come dem mules so po' when you got good corn everywhar—what, you stealing corn, too?' Mr. Oatzel say, 'Yes, I cotch him wid a basket on his shoulder.' 'Whar was you carrying it?' Edmund say, 'To Mr. Caldwell'. Mr. Caldwell say he ain't see'd no corn. Dey took Edmund to de jail. He had been taking corn and selling it to de carpetbaggers, and dat corn was fer de Ku Klux hosses.

"Dere was a Mr. Brown, a white man, dat come up to live in Newberry. Dey called him a refugee. Us called him Mr. 'Refugee Brown'. He was sorter destituted and not a bit up-to-date. He settled near de Gibson place. I fed de Gibson boys' fox-dogs about dat time fer dem.

"I want to git right wid you, now; so I can meet you lovely. In '73, I thought someone was shaking my house; I come out doors wid my gun; see'd white and colored coming together. Everybody was scared. All got to hollering and some prayed. I thought dat de earth gwine to be shook to pieces by morning. I thought of old Nora (Noah).

"Dem Bible folks see'd a little hand-span cloud. Nora

had done built him a house three stories high. Dat little cloud busted. Water riz in de second story of de wicked king's palace. He sont fer de northern lady. When she come a-shaking and a-twisting in de room de king fell back in his chair. He say dat he give her anything she want, all she got to do is ask fer it. She say to cut off John Wesley's head and bring it to her. De king had done got so suluctious dat he done it. Dat king and all of dem got drowned. Nora put a lot of things in de ark dat he could have left out, sech as snakes and other varments; but de ark floated off anyhow. No sir, dat wasn't de Clifton flood, dat was Nora's flood."

> Source: Sim Greeley (82), 280 Fowler's Row, Spartanburg, S.C.
> Interviewer: Caldwell Sims, Union, S.C. (8/27/37)

S-260-264-N
Project #1655
Augustus Ladson
Charleston, S.C.

No. Words: 1497

EX-SLAVE BORN DECEMBER 25, 1843

COWARD MASTER RAN OUT CIVIL WAR—LEAVING HIM

ELIJAH GREEN

"I was bo'n in Charleston at 82 King Street, December 25, 1843. The house is still there who' recent owner is Judge Whaley. My ma an' pa was Kate an' John Green. My ma had seben chillun (boys) an I am the last of 'em. Their names was: Henry, Scipio, Ellis, Nathaniel, Hobart, Mikell, an' myself.

"From the South-East of Calhoun Street, which was then Boundry Street, to the Battery was the city limit an' from the North-West of Boundry Street for sev'als miles was nothin' but fa'm land. All my brothers was fa'm han's for our master, George W. Jones. I did all the house work 'til the war w'en I was given to Mr. Wm. Jones's son, Wm. H. Jones as his "daily give servant" who' duty was to clean his boots, shoes, sword, an' make his coffee. He was Firs' Lieutenant of the South Car'lina Company Regiment. Bein' his servant, I wear all his cas' off clothes which I was glad to have. My shoes was call' brogan that has brass on the toe. W'en a slave had one of 'em you couldn't tell 'em he wasn't dress' to death.

"As the "daily give servant" of Mr. Wm. H. Jones I had to go to Virginia durin' the war. In the battle at Richmond Gen'al Lee had Gen'al Grant almos' beaten. He drive him almos' in the Potomac River, an' then take seven pieces of his artillery. W'en Gen'al Grant see how near defeat he was, he put up a white flag as a signal for time out to bury his deads. That flag stay' up for three weeks while Gen'al Grant was diggin' trenches. In the meantime he get message to President Lincoln askin' him to sen' a reinforcement of sojus. Gen'al Sherman was in charge of the regiment who sen' word to Gen'al Grant to hol' his position 'til he had captur' Columbia, Savannah, burn out Charleston while on his way with dispatch of 45,000 men. W'en Gen'al Sherman got to Virginia, the battle was renew' an' continued for seven days at the en' of which Gen'al Lee surrender' to Gen'al Grant. Durin' the seven days fight the battle got so hot 'til Mr. William Jones made his escape an' it was two days 'fore I know he was gone. One of the Gen'als sen' me home an' I got here two days 'fore Mr. William got home. He went up in the attic an' stay' there 'til the war was end'. I carry all his meals to him an' tell him all the news. Master show was a frighten' man; I was sorry for him. That battle at Richmond, Virginia was the wors' in American history.

Dr. George W. Jones, my master, ran a blockade. He had ships roamin' the sea to capture pirates ships. He had a daughter, Ellen, who was always kin' to the slaves. Master had a driver, William Jenkins, an' an' a' overseer, Henry Brown. Both was white. The driver see that the work was done by the supervision of the overseer. Master' fa'm amounted to twenty-five acres with 'bout eighteen slaves. The overseer blow the ho'n, which was a conch shell, at six in the mornin' an' every slave better answer w'en the roll was call' at seven. The slaves didn't have have to work on Sat'day.

Mr. Ryan had a private jail on Queen Street near the Planters Hotel. He was very cruel; he'd lick his slaves to death. Very seldom one of his slaves survive' a whippin'. He was the opposite to Govenor Aiken, who live' on the North-West corner of Elizabeth an' Judith Streets. He had several rice plantations, hundreds of his slaves he didn't know.

Not 'til John C. Calhoun' body was carried down Boundry Street was the name change' in his honor. He is bury in St. Phillip Church yard, 'cross the street with a laurel tree planted at his head. Four men an' me dig his grave an' I clear' the spot w'ere his monument now stan'. The monument was put up by Pat Callington, a Charleston mason. I never did like Calhoun 'cause he hated the Negro; no man was ever hated as much as him by a group of people.

The Work House (Sugar House) was on Magazine Street, built by Mr. Columbus C. Trumbone. On Charlmer Street is the slave market from which slaves was taken to Vangue Range an' auctione' off. At the foot of Lawrence Street, opposite East Bay Street, on the other side of the trolly tracks is w'ere Mr. Alonze White kept an' sell slaves from his kitchen. He was a slave-broker who had a house that exten' almos' to the train tracks which is 'bout three hundred yards goin' to the waterfront. No train or trolly tracks was there then 'cause there was only one railroad here, the Southern, an' the depot was on Ann Street w'ere the Baggin' Mill now is.

W'en slaves run away an' their masters catch them,

to the stockade they go w'ere they'd be whipp' every other week for a number of mornins. An' de for God sake don' you be cotch with pencil an' paper, dat was a major crime. You might as well had kill your master or missus.

One song I know I use to sing to the slaves w'en master went 'way, but I wouldn't be so fool as to let him hear me. What I kin 'member of it is:

> Master gone away
> But darkies stay at home,
> The year of jubilee is come
> An' freedom will begun.

A group of white men was in Doctor Wilson' drug store one day w'en I went to buy something. They commence' to ax me questions concernin' some historical happenin's an' I answer them all. So Dr. Wilson bet 'me that I couldn't tell who fired the firs' shot on Fort Sumter. I tell him I did know an' he offer's dollar if I was right. I tell him I wasn't goin' tell 'less the dollar was given to one of the men. He did so an' I told them it was Edward Ruffin who fired the firs' shot an' the dollar was mine. Anderson was determine' not to leave the fort but w'en 'bout four shells had hit the fort he was glad to be able to come out. W'en Sherman was comin' through Columbia, he fired an' a shell lodged in the South-East en' ef the State House which was forbidden to be fix'. He was comin' down Main Street w'en that happens'.

The firs' two people that was hung in Charleston was Harry an' Janie; husban' an' wife who was slaves of Mr. Christopher Black. Mr. Black had them whip' an' they planned to kill the whole fambly. They poison the breakast one morning an' if two of the fambly han' been sleep, they too would a been dead. The others die almos' instantly. An investigation was made an' the poison discovered an the two slaves hung on the big oak in the middle of Ashley Avenue.

If'en any in your owner' fambly was goin' to be married the slaves was dress' in linen clothes to witness the ceremony. Only special slaves was chosen to be at the weddin'. Slaves was alway ax how they like' the one who was comin' in the — — myself by sayin' nice things 'bout the person en hate' the person at the same time.

Slaves was always bury in the night as no one could stop to do it in the day. Ole boards was use' to make the coffin that was blackened with shoe polish.

After the war I did garden work.

Mr. Stiles Bee on James Islan' give track of lan' to the Negroes for a school jus' after the war; he put up a shed-like buildin' with a few chairs in it. It was at the place call Cut Bridge.

Henry McKinley, a Negro who ran as congressman from Charleston jus' after the war, lived on Calhoun Street. He was a mail carrier. He made an oath to Almighty God that if he was elected, he'd never betray his trus'. In one of his speeches he said: "I hope God 'ill paralize me should I do as others have done." He was elected an' never see the Congress. One white man from Orangeburg, Samuel Dibbin, bought him out. An' three weeks later McKinley took a stroke that carry him to a' early grave. James Wright, a Negro judge of Charleston in 1876 sol' out for ten thousand dollars—a dime of which he hasn't receive' yet. He 'cross the bridge an' stay in a' ole house an' die there. The Probate Judge, A. Whipper, refused to give up the books of Judge Wright to the white man he sell out to. Judge Whipper went in Beauford jail an' die there 'cause he wouldn't give up the books. Wright kept such a poor record that Judge Whipper was ashamed to have them expose', an' that's why he didn't give up the books. Henry Smalls, owner of the Smalls Lot on Comin' Street was Second Lieutenant on the Police Force. Henry Fordham was Second Assistant Lieutenant. Captain James Williams, Third Assistant Lieutenant who become Captain of the Military Department an' forme' the Carolina Light Infantry which was recogniz' 'til Ben Tillman call' them on the Green an' take their guns.

I was janitor at Benedict College in Columbia for two years an' at Clafflin in Orangeburg for twelve. The Presidents under which I worke' was: Allen Webster, grandson of the dictionary maker; J.C. Cook; an' Dr. Duntin.

Now all that is pass' an I'm livin' from han' to mouth. The banks took all my money an' I can't work. I do the collectin' for my lan'lord an' he give me a room free. If it wasn't for that I don't know what I'd do.

Source: Interview with Elijah Green, 156 Elizabeth Street, Charleston, S.C.

Project 1885-1
FOLKLORE
Spartanburg, Dist. 4
Sept. 7, 1937

Edited by:
Elmer Turnage

STORIES OF EX-SLAVES

W. M. GREEN

"Cap, I was born on de Bonner place, five miles from Gaffney. Jest about de very first recollection dat sticks wid me, is my mammy a-hiding me when de Ku Klux was riding. She heard de hosses a-trotting and she rushed us out'n our beds and took us and buried us in de fodder out in our barn, and told us to be as quiet as possible. Both my parents went and hid in de edge of de woods. De Ku Klux passed on by widout even holding up dere hosses.

"During slavery my mother went to Mississippi wid her mistress, Artimesse Smith Ross. Soon atter Freedom dey come back to Smith's Ford on de Pacolet. Steers pulled 'slides', wid de white folk belongings on de slides. We niggers went to meeting on de slides. De ends of de slides was curved upward. When we got to meeting, we went under de brush arbors. Fresh brush was kept cut so dat de sun would not shine through. Under de arbors we sat on slabs and de preacher stood on de ground. We had better meetings den dan dey have now. Everybody had better religion den dan dey does now. In dem days religion went further dan it does now. Yes sir, religion meant something den, and went somewhars. My pappy rode a ginny to preaching.

"Dere was not as much devilment as dere is now. Times was better fer niggers. One day last week I went to meeting and took dinner. We eat on a slab table and had ice tea to drink. Meas was dere drinking on de side, and all other devilment dey could carry on in sight of de church. De preacher eat wid us. Some eat out of dere buckets and would not come and be wid de crowd. Long time ago, nobody didn't act greedy like dat. Girls cut up like boys now, and nobody don't look down on dem.

"When I was a boy, girls acted like de old folks and dey did not carry on. Nobody ever heard of a girl drinking and smoking den. If a girl made a mistake in de old days she was throwed overboard. Why when I was little, us boys went in a-washing wid de girls and never thought nothing 'bout it. We was most grown befo' we know'd a thing 'bout man and woman. I was fifteen years old when I got my first shoes and dey had brass toes. We played ball wid de girls in de house, and sung songs like: 'Goosey, Goosey Gander'."

"We had wheat bread only once a week," said Jesse Stevenson who came up and entered the conversation, "and dat was on Sunday. I had a good time at Green's wedding. Green married Carrie Phillips who lived two miles above me. We boys talked to de girls in school. We was around twenty years old befo' we went to school. Of course dat was atter Freedom. De teacher would light on both of us fer talking across de books. Carrie was about a year younger dan Green. Green, tell de gentleman (interviewer) what you said when you ax'd uncle Ben fer Carrie."

"I say," said Green, "come out into de cool of de yard, please sir, if you will uncle Ben; I has a question of de utmost concern to us both to lay at your feet'. Uncle Ben say, 'Look here, young nigger, don't you know dat I ain't got no business gwine out in no night dew—what ails you nohow?' I 'lows, 'Uncle Ben, it is a great matter of life and death dat I wishes to consult wid you over'. He clear his throat and spit in de fire and say, 'Wait, I'll come if it's dat urgent.' I took him under a tree so dat no dew wouldn't drap on his head and give him a cold. I said, 'I want to marry your daughter, uncle Ben.' He say, 'Which one is dat dat you wishes, Sir?' 'De purttiest one, Carrie,' says I; 'dat is, if you ain't got no objection.'

"Befo' I axed fer Carrie I was loving two gals, but of course I drapped de other'n after uncle Ben give me a favorable answer. Me and Carrie married at Miss Twitty Thompson's house. Dat whar uncle Ben had raised Carrie. Carrie's missus give her a good wedding supper wid chicken, ham, turkey, cake and coffee, and tater salad. Seventy-five people is what Miss Twitty let Carrie ax to dat supper. All dem niggers was dere, too.

"I had on a grey suit wid big stripes in it. Carrie had on a white dress and a white veil. We used dat veil to keep de skeeters off'n our first two babies. It made de best skeeter net. We married one Sunday morning at 'leven o'clock and had dinner at twelve; give de preacher twenty-five cents. Never no one give us no presents. We stayed at my pappy's house fer years. He give us a bed, a bureau and a washstand. Carrie's folks give us de bed clothes, and dats what we started on. Jesse, tell de gentleman what you did at my wedding."

"I stood wid Green," said Jesse Stevenson, "and I had on a brown suit wid grey stripes gwine up and down it. Atter de ceremony all de gals wanted to swing me and Green, but Carrie grabbed him and shake her head and grin; so I got all de swinging."

Green said, "Me and Carrie never went no whar atter our marriage. We stayed on wid my pappy and worked. We been doing well ever since."

>Source: W. M. Green (71); Jesse Stevenson (71), Rt. 1, Gaffney, S.C.
>Interviewer: Caldwell Sims 8/23/37

Project #-1655
Phoebe Faucette
Hampton County

Approx. 390 words
FOLKLORE

ADELINE GREY 82 YEAR OLD
Ex-Slave

ADELINE GREY

Adeline Grey seemed in good health as she sat before her granddaughter's comfortable fire. She spoke quietly, with little excitement, and readily recalled events of her early childhood.

"I was a girl when freedom was declare, an' I kin remember 'bout de times. My Ma used to belong to ole man Dave Warner. I remember how she used to wash, and iron, an' cook for de white folks durin' slavery time.

"I member when de Yankees come through. I wuz right to de old boss' place. It wuz on de river side. Miss Jane Warner, she wuz de missus. De place heah now—where all de chillun raise. Mr. Rhodes got a turpentine still dere now—jes after you pass de house. Dey burn de ginhouse, de shop, de buggyhouse, de turkeyhouse an' de fowlhouse. Start to set de cornhouse afire, but my Ma say: 'Please sir, don't burn de cornhouse. Gie it to me an' my chillun.' So dey put de fire out. I member when dey started to break down de smokehouse door, an' ole Missus come out an' say: 'Please don't break de door open, I got de key.' So dey quit. I remember when dey shoot down de hog. I remember when dey shoot de two geese in de yard. Dey choked my Ma. Dey went to her an' dey say; 'Where is all de white people gold an' silver?' My Ma say she don't know. 'You does know!' dey say, an' choke her till she couldn't talk. Dey went into de company room where de ole Miss wuz stayin' an' start tearin' up de bed. Den de captain come an' de ole Miss say to him: 'Please don't let 'em tear up my bed,' an' de captain went in dere an' tell 'em 'Come out!'.

De ole Miss wasn't scared. But de young Miss May was sure scared. She was courtin' at de time. She went off an' shut herself up in a room. De ole Miss ask de captain: 'Please go in an' talk to de Miss, she so scared'. So he went in an' soon he bring her out. We chillun wasn't scared. But my brother run under de house. De soldiers went under dere a-pokin' de bayonets into de ground to try to find where de silver buried, an' dey ran 'cross him. 'What you doin' under heah?' dey say. 'I'se jes runnin' de chickens out, sir,' he say. 'Well, you kin go on out,' dey say. 'We aint gwine to hurt you.'

'I remember when dey kill de hog an' cook 'em. Cook on de fire where de little shop been. Cook 'em an' eat 'em. Why didn't dey cook 'em on de stove in de house? Didn't have no stoves. Jes had to cook on de fireplace. Had an oven to fit in de fireplace. I remember when my Ma saw de Yankees comin' dat mornin' she grab de sweet potatoes dat been in dat oven and throw 'em in de barrel of feathers dat stayed by de kitchen fireplace. Jes a barrel to hold chicken feathers when you pick 'em. Dat's all we had to eat dat day. Dem Yankees put de meat in de sack an' go on off. It was late den, 'bout dusk. I remember how de Missus bring us all 'round de fire. It was dark den.

'Well chillun,' she say, 'I is sorry to tell you, but de Yankees has carry off your Ma. I don't know if you'll ever see her any mo.' Den we chillun all start cryin.' We still a-sittin' dere when my Ma come back. She say she slip behind, an' slip behind, slip behind, an' when she come to a little pine thicket by de side of de road, she dart into it, drop de sack of meat dey had her carryin, an' start out for home. When we had all make over her, we say to her den: 'Well why didn't you bring de sack of meat 'long wid you?'

Dey took de top off ole Marse John carriage, put meat in it, an' made him pull it same as a horse. Carry him way down to Lawtonville, had to pull it through de branch an' all. Got de rock-a-way back though—an' de ole man. I remember dat well. Had to mend up de ole rock-a-way. An' it made de ole man sick. He keep on sick, sick, until he died. I remember how he'd say: 'Don't you all worry'. An' he'd go out in de orchard. Dey'd say: 'Don't bother him! Jes let him be! He want to pray!' Atter a while he died an' dey buried him. His name was John Stafford. Dey Massa wasn't dere. I guess he was off to de war.

"But after freedom was de time when dey suffered more dan before. Dese chillun don't know how dey blessed. My Ma cooked for de white folks for one year after freedom. I remember dey cook bread, an' dey ain't have nuthin' to eat on it. Was thankful for a cornbread hoecake baked in de fireplace. But dey had some things. Had buried some meat, an' some syrup. An' dey had some corn. My Ma had saved de cornhouse. De rice burn up in de ginhouse. After freedom, dey had to draw de best thread out of de old clothes an' weave it again. Ole Miss had give my Ma a good moss mattress. But de Yankees had carry dat off. Rip it up, throw out de moss, an' put meat in it. Fill it full of meat. I remember she had a red striped shawl. One of de Yankee take dat an' start to put in under his saddle for a saddle cloth. My brother go up to him an' say: 'Please sir, don't carry my Ma's shawl. Dat de only one she got.' So he give it back to him. To keep warm at night, dey had to make dere pallet down by de fire; when all wood burn out, put on another piece. Didn't have nuthin' on de bed to sleep on.

"I remember when de ole Miss used to have to make soap, out of dese red oaks. Burn de wood, an' catches de ashes. Put de ashes in a barrel wid a trough under it, an' pour de water through de ashes. If de lyewater dat come out could cut a feather, it was strong.

"Used to weave cloth after freedom. Used to give a brooch (hank) or two to weave at night. I'se sometimes thread de needle for my Ma, or pick out de seed out de cotton, an' make it into rolls to spin. Sometimes I'd work de foot pedal for my Ma. Den dey'd warp de thread. If she want to dye it, she'd dye it. She'd get indigo—you know dat bush—an' boil it. It was kinder blue. It would make good cloth. Sometimes, de cloth wuz kinder strip, one strip of white, an' one of blue. I remember how dey'd warp de thread across de yard after it wuz dyed, an' I remember seem' my Ma throw dat shuttle through an' weave dat cloth. I member when de ole Miss made my Mamma two black dresses to wear through de winter. She'd keep 'em clean; had two so she could change.

"I don't know why dey didn't burn de house. Must have been 'cause de captain wuz along. De house dere now. One of de chimney down. I don't think dey ever put it up again. Colored folks are in it now.

"I never did know my Pa. He was sold off to Texas when I was young. My mother would say, 'Well, chillun, you aint never known your Pa. Joe Smart carry him off to Texas when he went. I don't guess you'll ever see him.' My father wuz name Charles Smart. He never did come back. Joe Smart come back once, an' say dat our father is dead. He say our Pa had three horses an' he want one of them to be sent to us chillun heah; but no arrangements had been made to get it to us. You see he had chillun out dere, too.

"Atter freedom, my Ma plow many a day, same as a man, for us chillun. She work for ole man Bill Mars. Den she marry again. Part of de time dey work for Mr. Benny Lawton, de one-arm man, what lost his arm in de war. Dese chillun don't know what hard times is. Dey don't know how to preciate our blessings.

Source: Adeline Grey, 82-year old resident of Luray, S.C.

Project #1655
Everett R. Pierce
Columbia, S.C.

INTERVIEW WITH FANNIE GRIFFIN
EX-SLAVE 94 YEARS.

FANNIE GRIFFIN

"You wants me to tell you all what I 'members 'bout slavery in slavery time? Well ma'am, I was just a young gal then and I's a old woman now, nigh on to ninety-four years old; I might be forgot some things, but I'll tell you what I 'members best.

My massa, Massa Joe Beard, was a good man, but he wasn't one of de richest men. He only had six slaves, three men and three women, but he had a big plantation and would borrow slaves from his brother-in-law on de 'joining plantation, to help wid de crops.

I was de youngest slave, so Missy Grace, dats Massa Joe's wife, keep me in de house most of de time, to cook and keep de house cleaned up. I milked de cow and worked in de garden too. My massa was good to all he slaves, but Missy Grace was mean to us. She whip us a heap of times when we ain't done nothing bad to be whip for. When she go to whip me, she tie my wrists together wid a rope and put that rope thru a big staple in de ceiling and draw me up off de floor and give me a hundred lashes. I think 'bout my old mammy heap of times now and how I's seen her whipped, wid de blood dripping off of her.

All that us slaves know how to do, was to work hard. We never learn to read and write nor we never had no church to go to, only sometimes de white folks let us go to their church, but we never jine in de singing, we just set and listen to them preach and pray. De graveyard was right by de church and heap of de colored people was scared to go by it at night, they say they see ghosts and hants, and sperits but I ain't never see none, don't believe there is none. I more scared of live people than I is dead ones; dead people ain't gwine to harm you.

Our massa and missus was good to us when we was sick; they send for de doctor right off and de doctor do all he could for us, but he ain't had no kind of medicine to give us 'cepting sperits of turpentine, castor oil, and a little blue mass. They ain't had all kinds of pills and stuff then, like they has now, but I believe we ain't been sick as much then as we do now. I never heard of no consumption them days; us had pneumonia sometime tho'.

You wants to know if we had any parties for pastime? Well ma'am, not many. We never was allowed to have no parties nor dances, only from Christmas Day to New Year's eve. We had plenty good things to eat on Christmas Day and Santa Claus was good to us too. We'd have all kinds of frolics from Christmas to New Years but never was allowed to have no fun after that time.

I 'members one time I slip off from de missus and go to a dance and when I come back, de dog in de yard didn't seem to know me and he bark and wake de missus up and she whip me something awful. I sho didn't go to no more dances widout asking her. De patarollers (patrollers) would ketch you too, if you went out after dark. We most times stay at home at night and spin cloth to make our clothes. We make all our clothes, and our shoes was handmade too. We didn't have fancy clothes like de people has now. I likes it better being a slave, we got along better then, than we do now. We didn't have to pay for everything we had.

De worst time we ever had was when de Yankee men come thru. We had heard they was coming and de missus tell us to put on a big pot of peas to cook, so we put some white peas in a big pot and put a whole ham in it, so that we'd have plenty for de Yankees to eat. Then when they come, they kicked de pot over and de peas went one way and de ham another.

De Yankees 'stroyed 'most everything we had. They come in de house and told de missus to give them her money and jewels. She started crying and told them she ain't got no money or jewels, 'cepting de ring she had on her finger. They got awfully mad and started 'stroying everything. They took de cows and horses, burned de gin, de barn, and all de houses 'cept de one massa and missus was living in. They didn't leave us a thing 'cept some big hominy and two banks of sweet potatoes. We chipped up some sweet potatoes and dried them in de sun, then we parched them and ground them up and that's all we had to use for coffee. It taste pretty good too. For a good while we just live on hominy and coffee.

No ma'am, we ain't had no celebration after we was freed. We ain't know we was free 'til a good while after. We ain't know it 'til General Wheeler come thru and tell us. After that, de massa and missus let all de slaves go 'cepting me; they kept me to work in de house and de garden."

Home address:

2125 Calhoun St.
Columbia, S.C.

Project 1885-1
FOLKLORE
Spartanburg Dist. 4
June 22, 1937

Edited by:
Elmer Turnage

STORIES FROM EX-SLAVES

MADISON GRIFFIN

"I will be 85 years old dis coming August. My master said I was 14 years old de August coming after freedom.

"My master was Billy Scott who had seven or eight hundred acres of land, and 48 slaves. He wouldn't have no white overseers, but had some nigger foremen dat sometimes whipped de niggers, and de master would whip dem, too. He was a fair man, not so good and not so mean. He give us poor quarters to live in, and sometimes plenty to eat, but sometimes we went hungry. He had a big garden, plenty cows, hogs and sheep. De most we had ter eat, was corn, collards, peas, turnip-greens and home-made molasses. We had wheat bread on Sundays. It was made from flour grind at our own mill. We didn't have but one day off, that was Christmas Day and den we had to grind our axes.

"We made our clothes out of cotton and wool mixed, made dem at home wid our own cards and spinning wheels. We made our shoes out of leather tanned at home, but had to use woolen shoes after de war, which would wear out and split open in three weeks.

"My daddy was Amos Wilson and mammy was Carline Griffin. I had some brothers and sisters. When freedom come, de master come to us and told us de damn Yankees done freed us, 'what you gwinter do? If you want ter stay on wid me, I will give you work.' We stayed fer awhile.

"The patrollers caught me once when I run off. I run fast and lost my hat and dey got it. I saw some slaves sold on de block. Dey was put in a ring and sold by crying out de price. We didn't learn to read and write, not allowed to. De niggers went to de corn shuckings and was give pumpkin custards to eat and liquor. Dey wasn't allowed to dance, but sometimes we had secret dances, shut up in de house so de master couldn't hear us.

"After de war, we went hunting and fishing on Sundays. We never had Saturday afternoons off. We killed wild deer and other things. Once de master killed 14 squirrels in three quarters of hour.

"We raised our own tobacco, the master did, for home use. Most always a small patch was planted.

"De master once saw ghosts, he come from his sisters and passed de graveyard and saw 9 cows with no heads. His horse jest flew home. Most white folks didn't believe in ghosts, but dat is one time de master believed he saw some.

"I went wid de Red Shirts, belonged to de company and went to meetings wid dem. I voted fer Hampton. Befo' dat, de Ku Klux had bad niggers dodging like birds in de woods. Dey caught some and threw dem on de ground and whipped dem, but de master say he don't know nothing 'bout it as he was asleep. Dey caught a nigger preacher once and made him dance, put him in muddy water and walloped him around in de mud.

"Once seven Indians come in our neighborhood an call fer meat, meal and salt. Dere was three men and four women. Dey cooked all night, murmuring something all de time. Next morning three squirrels was found up a tree, and de Indians shot 'em down wid bow and arrow.

"One time I saw horses froze to death. Dey couldn't get dere breath, and de people took warm water and wash dere foreheads. I was a small boy den. My master had 46 guineas.

"I married Nancy Robinson who belonged to Robert Calmes. She was living at de Gillam place near Rich Hill.

"We used to ask a riddle like this: Love I stand, Love I sit, Love I hold in my right hand. What is it? It was made up when an old woman had a little dog named 'Love'. She killed it and put a part of it, after it was baked, in her stockings; part in her shoes; part in back of her dress, and part in her gloves. A nigger was going to be hung the next Friday, and told if he guess the riddle he would be turned loose. He couldn't guess it, but was turned loose anyway.

"I think Abe Lincoln might ter done good, but he had us all scared to death, took our mules and burned our places. Don't know anything about Jeff Davis. Booker Washington is all right.

"I joined de church when 28 years old, because I thought it was right. Wanted to git right and git to God's Kingdom. I think everybody ought to join de church.

"O' course I rather it not be slavery time, but I got more ter eat den dan now. Den we didn't know what ter do, but now we perish ter death."

Source: Madison Griffin (84), Whitmire, S.C.
Interviewer: G.L. Summer, Newberry, S.C. (6/18/1937)

Project 1885-1
FOLKLORE
Spartanburg, Dist. 4
June 7, 1937

Edited by:
Elmer Turnage

STORIES FROM EX-SLAVES

PEGGY GRIGSBY

"I was born in old Edgefield county, about three miles below what is now Saluda Courthouse. I was a slave of Alec Grigsby. He was a fair marster, but his wife was awful mean to us. She poked my head in a rail fence once and whipped me hard with a whip. I lived in that section until eight years ago, when I come to Newberry to live with my daughters.

"I worked hard in cotton fields, milked cows and helped about the marster's house. When the bush-whackers and patrollers come around dere, us niggers suffered lots with beatings. Some of dem was killed.

"The old folks had corn-shuckings, frolics, pender pullings, and quiltings. They had quiltings on Saturday nights, with eats and frolics. When dey danced, dey always used fiddles to make the music.

"The men folks hunted much: doves, partridges, wild turkeys, deer, squirrels and rabbits. Sometimes dey caught rabbits in wooden boxes, called 'rabbit-gums'.

It had a trap in the middle, which was set at night, with food in it, and when the rabbit bite, the tray sprung, and the opening at the front was closed so he couldn't get out.

"The marster had a big whiskey still, and sold lots of liquor to people around there."

Source: Peggy Grigsby (106), Newberry, S.C.
Interviewer: G.L. Summer, Newberry, S.C. 5/10/37.

Project #1655
W.W. Dixon
Winnsboro, S.C.

VIOLET GUNTHARPE
EX-SLAVE 82 YEARS OLD.

VIOLET GUNTHARPE

"I was born a slave in de Rocky Mount part of Fairfield County, up close to Great Falls. I hear them falls a roarin' now and I see them waters flashin' in de sunshine when I close my eyes.

My pappy name Robert and my mammy name Phyllis. They b'long to de old time 'ristocats, de Gaither family. Does you know Miss Mattie Martin, which was de secretary of Governor Ansel? Dat one of my young mistresses and another is dat pretty red headed girl in de telegraph office at Winnsboro, dat just sit dere and pass out lightnin' and 'lectricity over de wires wheresomever she take a notion. Does you know them? Well, befo' their mama marry Marster Starke Martin, her was Sally Gaither, my young missus in slavery time. Her die and go to Heaven last year, please God.

Marster Richard was a good marster to his slaves, though he took no foolishness and worked you from sun to sun. 'Spect him had 'bout ten family of slaves and 'bout fifty big and little slaves altogether on dat plantation befo' them Yankees come and make a mess out of their lives.

Honey, us wasn't ready for de big change dat come! Us had no education, no land, no mule, no cow, not a pig, nor a chicken, to set up house keeping. De birds had nests in de air, de foxes had holes in de ground, and de fishes had beds under de great falls, but us colored folks was left widout any place to lay our heads.

De Yankees sho' throwed us in de briar patch but us not bred and born dere lak de rabbit. Us born in a good log house. De cows was down dere in de canebrakes to give us milk, de hogs was fattenin' on hickory nuts, acorns, and shucked corn, to give us meat and grease; de sheep wid their wool, and de cotton in de gin house was dere to give us clothes. De horses and mules was dere to help dat corn and cotton, but when them Yankees come and take all dat away, all us had to thank them for, was a hungry belly, and freedom. Sumpin' us had no more use for then, than I have today for one of them airplanes I hears flyin' 'round de sky, right now.

Well, after ravagin' de whole country side, de army got across old Catawba and left de air full of de stink of dead carcasses and de sky black wid turkey buzzards. De white women was weepin' in hushed voices, de niggers on de place not knowin' what to do next, and de piccaninnies suckin' their thumbs for want of sumpin' to eat; mind you 'twas winter time too.

Lots of de chillun die, as did de old folks, while de rest of us scour de woods for hickory nuts, acorns, cane roots, and artichokes, and seine de river for fish. De worst nigger men and women follow de army. De balance settle down wid de white folks and simmer in their misery all thru de spring time, 'til plums, mulberries, and blackberries come, and de shad come up de Catawba River.

My mammy stay on wid de same marster 'til I was grown, dat is fifteen, and Thad got to lookin' at me, meek as a sheep and dumb as a calf. I had to ask dat nigger, right out, what his 'tentions was, befo' I get him to bleat out dat he love me. Him name Thad Guntharpe. I glance at him one day at de pigpen when I was sloppin' de hogs, I say: 'Mr. Guntharpe, you follows me night and mornin' to dis pigpen; do you happen to be in love wid one of these pigs? If so, I'd like to know which one 'tis; then sometime I come down here by myself and tell dat pig 'bout your 'fections.' Thad didn't say nothin' but just grin. Him took de slop bucket out of my hand and look at it, all 'round it, put upside down on de ground, and set me down on it; then he fall down dere on de grass by me and blubber out and warm my fingers in his hands. I just took pity on him and told him mighty plain dat he must limber up his tongue and ask sumpin', say what he mean, wantin' to visit them pigs so often. Us carry on foolishness 'bout de little boar shoat pig and de little sow pig, then I squeal in laughter over how he scrouge so close; de slop bucket tipple over and I lost my seat. Dat ever remain de happiest minute of my eighty-two years.

After us marry, us moved on de Johnson Place and Thad plow right on a farm where dere use to be a town of Grimkeville. I was lonely down dere all de time. I's halfway scared to death of de skeeters 'bout my legs in day time and old Captain Thorn's ghost in de night time. You never heard 'bout dat ghost? If you went to school to Mr. Luke Ford sure he must of tell you 'bout de time a slave boy killed his marster, old Captain Thorn. He drag and throwed his body in de river.

When they find his body they ketch John, de slave boy,

give him a trial by six white men, find him guilty and he confess. Then they took de broad axe, cut off his head, mount it on a pole and stick it up on de bank where they find old Captain Thorn. Dat pole and head stay dere 'til it rot down. Captain Thorn's ghost 'pear and disappear 'long dat river bank ever since in de night time. My pappy tell me he see it and see de boy's ghost too.

De ghost rode de minds of many colored folks. Some say dat de ghost had a heap to do wid deaths on dat river, by drowning. One sad thing happen; de ghost and de malaria run us off de river. Us moved to Marster Starke P. Martin's place. Him was a settin' at a window in de house one night and somebody crept up dere and fill his head full of buck-shot. Marster Starke was Miss Sallie's husband, and Miss Mattie and Miss May's papa. Oh, de misery of dat night to my white folks! Who did it? God knows! They sent poor Henry Nettles to de penitentiary for it, but most white folks and all de colored didn't believe he done it. White folks say a white man done it, but our color know it was de work of dat slave boy's ghost.

My white folks come here from Maryland, I heard them say. They fought in de Revolution, set up a tanyard when they got here, and then when cotton come, my marster's pappy was de fust to put up a hoss-gin and screw pit in Rocky Mount section. I glories in their blood, but dere none by de name 'round here now, 'cept colored folks.

Marster Wood you read a heap of books. Did you ever read 'bout foots of ghosts? They got foots and can jump and walk. No they don't run, why? 'Cause seem lak their foots is too big. Dat night Marster Starke Martin was killed it was a snowin'. De whole earth was covered wid a white blanket. It snowed and snowed and snowed. Us measure how big dat snow was next mornin' and how big dat ghost track. De snow was seven inches, and a little bit deep. De ghost track on top de snow big as a elephant's. Him or she or it's tracks 'pear to drap wid de snow and just rise up out de snow and disappear. De white folks say 'twas a man wid bags on his foots, but they never found de bags, so I just believe it was ghost instigate by de devil to drap down dere and make all dat misery for my white folks.

Dere's a great day a comin' when de last trumpet will sound and de devil and all de ghosts will be chained and they can't romp 'round de old river and folks houses in de night time and bring sorrow and pain in de wake of them big tracks."

United States. Work Projects Administration

Project #-1655
Gyland H. Hamlin
Charleston, S.C.

FOLKLORE

INTERVIEW WITH EX-SLAVE

JOHN HAMILTON

"Good a'ternoon, suh. Yassuh, I'ze gittin' on up in de years. I be eighty-one year ole nex' May. I name John Hamilton an' I lib at sickty-t'ree Amherst Street.

"I 'member sumptin' 'bout slabery. I wuz 'bout big as dat gal gwine dere w'en de Fed'rul war broke out," indicating a child, passing down the street who appeared to be about eight years old.

"I belong' to Maussa Seabrook, an' he lib at W'ite Point, ten mile from Adams Run. De Maussa, he been daid but he got some boys. Dem boys all scatter', dough. Yassuh, ole Maussa treat us good. I not big 'nough to wuk, I jus' a li'l boy den. My fadder name' Rhode Hamilton, an' 'e hab two acre to wuk. Dere didn't been no hoss, an' 'e grub it wid de hoe.

"Some slabes no good an' not satisfy fo' tuh wuk. Dey run 'way fum de plantation. Dere been big dawgs high as street-cyar, yassuh, high as dat street-cyar. Dey name' nigger-dawg an' dey trace nigger an' put dem nigger back to wuk. Dere been Yankee man name' Tom Cudry.

I kin sho' de house 'e been in. He say 'e tired see colored mans wuk hard an' git nuttin'. He put colored mans on banjoo (vendue) table an' 'e be free.

"I didn't be marry till I git in my t'irty year. My wife, she 'bout sickty-fibe year ole'. We got fibe chillun libbin', 'bout twelbe haid in all. Grand-chillun? 'Bout sebben haid an' one gal. Hab great grand-chillun, too.

"I ain't been know nuttin' 'bout jailhouse. Ain't see a jailhouse in my life. I hab to look all day to find one in Charleston, an' don't know where 'bouts de court-house. Ain't gwine to jailhouse. Nobody hab to 'rest me no how.

"I be a Babtis'. I babtize' in de ribber, de Edisto ribber. I tryin' git to Hebben. Hebben be glory. Yassuh, Hebben be glory. You got to lub all God's chillun to git dere. God send w'ite folks an' colored folks, an' dey mus' he'p each odder an' wuk togedder. Dey got to lib in union. Yassuh, got to lib in union to git to Hebben.

"I 'pend on de w'ite folks to he'p me. Dese pore colored folks ain't got nuttin'. Nawsuh, I ain't be too ole to wuk an' mek a honest libbin' like lot o' dem no good nigger what too stiff fo' to speak. I wuk some flower-yard fo' some w'ite folks, an' I wuk a li'l gyarden.

"Yassuh, I hol' up berry well, but I can't see at night w'en de sun go down. My sight gone back den. I got git 'long now.

"You gimme a nickel or dime? T'ank you, suh. T'ank you kin'ly."

Source: Personal interview with John Hamilton, colored, of 63 Amherst Street, Charleston, S.C.

Slave Narratives

Project #-1655
Jessie A. Butler
Charleston, S.C.

FOLKLORE

OLD SUSAN HAMLIN—EX SLAVE

(Verbatim Conversation)

SUSAN HAMLIN

Old Susan Hamlin, one hundred and four years old, was strolling down lower King St., about a mile from where she lives, when she was met by a white "friend," and the following conversation took place:

"How are you, Susan, do you remember me?"

"Yes, Ma'am, I 'member yo face, Missus, but I can't 'member yo name. I gettin' ole. Dis eye (touching the right one) leabin' me. Ole age you know. Somet'ing got tuh gie way."

"Don't you remember I came to see you one morning, and you told me all about old times?"

"Yes, Ma'am, (with enthusiasm) come tuh see me 'gain, I tell you some mo'. I like tuh talk 'bout dem days; 'taint many people left now kin tell 'bout dat time. Eberybody dead. I goes 'round tuh de ole house, an' I t'ink 'bout all dem little chillen I is nuss, (calling them by name) dey all sleep, all sleep in de groun'. Nobody lef' but ole Susan. All my fambly, de massa, de missus, all de little chillen, all sleep. Only me one lef', only ole Susan. Sometime I wonder how it is. I ober a hund'ed, I stahtin' (starting) tuh forgit de years."

"Tell me one thing, Susan, you have lived a long time, do you think the young people of today are better or worse than in the old days?"

"Well, Missus, some is wuss but not all. Some stray jus' like dey always done but dey'll come back. I stray 'way myself but dey'll come back jus' like I did. Gib um time dey come back. I git converted you know."

"Yes, you told me about that."

"Yes, Ma'am, I see de Sabior. He show me hoe He die. I nebber forget dat day. Dere He hang,—so—(with arms outstretched) an' He show me de great brightness, an' He show me de big sin on my back, black as dat cyar (car). Den I pray an' I pray, an' it fall off. Den I praise Him. Nebber since dat day is I forget what I see. When I see dat reconcile Sabior countenance,—oh!—I nebber forget. No, Ma'am. I nebber forget dat reconcile countenance. As I tell yuh, I stray 'way, but not after I see dat reconcile countenance. I pray and praise Him. Sometimes all by myself I get so happy, jes t'inkin' on Him. I cyant forget all dat He done fuh me."

"People tell me I ought not walk 'round by myself so. I tell um I don't care where I drop. I 'member when my ma was dyin' I beg um not to leabe me, she say: 'Wha' I got yuh, wha' I want tuh stay yuh fuh? I want tuh go, I want tuh see muh Jesus.' I know what she mean now. I don't care if I drop in de street, I don't care if I drop in my room. I don't care where I drop, I ready tuh go."

"All you got tuh do is libe right, yuh got tuh libe (live) de life. What is de life?—Purity.—What is Purity?—Righteousness.—What is Righteousness?—Tuh do de right t'ing.—Libe right,—pray an' praise. Beliebe on de delibrin (delivering) Sabior. Trus' Him. He lead yuh. He show yuh de way. Dat all yuh got tuh do. Beliebe—pray—praise. Ebery night befo' I lay on my bed I git on my knees an' look up tuh Him. Soon I wake in de mornin' I gibe Him t'anks. Eben sometime in de day I git on my knees an' pray. He been good to me all dese years. He aint forget me. I aint been sick for ober twenty-five years. Good t'ing too, nobody left tuh tek care of me. Dey all gone. But I don't care now, jus' so I kin see my Jesus when I gone."

"I goin' down now tuh see my people I use to cook fuh. I too ole now tuh cook. I use tuh cook fine. Come tuh see me again, missus, come tuh see de ole monkey, I tell yuh mo' 'bout dose times. You know I kin 'member dem when I been a big girl, most grown, when de bombardment come ober de city."

Source: Writer's conversation with Susan Hamlin, 17 Henrietta Street, Charleston. S.C.

United States. Work Projects Administration

Project#-1655
Jessie A. Butler
Charleston, S.C.

Approx. 1739 Words

INTERVIEW WITH EX-SLAVE

SUSAN HAMLIN

On July 6th, I interviewed Susan Hamlin, ex-slave, at 17 Henrietta street, Charleston, S. C. She was sitting just inside of the front door, on a step leading up to the porch, and upon hearing me inquire for her she assumed that I was from the Welfare office, from which she had received aid prior to its closing. I did not correct this impression, and at no time did she suspect that the object of my visit was to get the story of her experience as a slave. During our conversation she mentioned her age. "Why that's very interesting, Susan," I told her, "If you are that old you probably remember the Civil War and slavery days." "Yes Ma'am, I been a slave myself," she said, and told me the following story:

"I kin remember some things like it was yesterday, but I is 104 years old now, and age is starting to get me, I can't remember everything like I use to. I getting old, old. You know I is old when I been a grown woman when the Civil War broke out. I was hired out then, to a Mr. McDonald, who lived on Atlantic Street, and I remembers when de first shot was fired, and the shells went right over de city. I got seven dollars a month for looking after children, not taking them out, you understand, just minding them. I did not get the money, Mausa got it." "Don't you think that was fair?" I asked. "If you were fed and clothed by him, shouldn't he be paid for your work?" "Course it been fair," she answered, "I belong to him and he got to get something to take care of me."

"My name before I was married was Susan Calder, but I married a man name Hamlin. I belonged to Mr. Edward Fuller, he was president of the First National Bank. He was a good man to his people till de Lord took him. Mr. Fuller got his slaves by marriage. He married Miss Mikell, a lady what lived on Edisto Island, who was a slave owner, and we lived on Edisto on a plantation. I don't remember de name cause when Mr. Fuller got to be president of de bank we come to Charleston to live. He sell out the plantation and say them (the slaves) that want to come to Charleston with him could come and them what wants to stay can stay on the island with his wife's people. We had our choice. Some is come and same is stay, but my ma and us children come with Mr. Fuller.

We lived on St. Philip street. The house still there, good as ever, I go 'round there to see it all de time; the cistern still there too, where we used to sit 'round and drink the cold water, and eat, and talk and laugh. Mr. Fuller have lots of servants and the ones he didn't need hisself he hired out. The slaves had rooms in the back, the ones with children had two rooms and them that didn't have any children had one room, not to cook in but to sleep in. They all cooked and ate downstairs in the hall that they had for the colored people. I don't know about slavery but I know all the slavery I know about, the people was good to me. Mr. Fuller was a good man and his wife's people been grand people, all good to their slaves. Seem like Mr. Fuller just git his slaves so he could be good to dem. He made all the little colored chillen love him. If you don't believe they loved him what they all cry, and scream, and holler for when dey hear he dead? 'Oh, Mausa dead my Mausa dead, what I going to do, my Mausa dead.' Dey tell dem t'aint no use to cry, dat can't bring him back, but de chillen keep on crying. We used to call him Mausa Eddie but he named Mr. Edward Fuller, and he sure was a good man.

"A man come here about a month ago, say he from de Government, and dey send him to find out 'bout slavery. I give him most a book, and what he give me? A dime. He ask me all kind of questions. He ask me dis and he ask me dat, didn't de white people do dis and did dey do dat but Mr. Fuller was a good man, he was sure good to me and all his people, dey all like him, God bless him, he in de ground now but I ain't going to let nobody lie on him. You know he good when even the little chillen cry and holler when he dead. I tell you dey couldn't just fix us up any kind of way when we going to Sunday School. We had to be dressed nice, if you pass him and you ain't dress to suit him he send you right back and say tell your ma to see dat you dress right. Dey couldn't send you out in de cold barefoot neither. I 'member one day my ma want to send me wid some milk for her sister-in-law what live 'round de corner. I fuss cause it cold and say 'how you going to send me out wid no shoe, and it cold?' Mausa hear how I talking and turn he back and laugh, den he call to my ma to gone in de house and find shoe to put on my feet and don't let him see me barefoot again in cold weather.

When de war start going good and de shell fly over Charleston he take all us up to Aiken for protection. Talk 'bout marching through Georgia, day sure march through Aiken, soldiers was everywhere.

"My ma had six children, three boys and three girls, but I de only one left, all my white people and all de colored people gone, not a soul left but me. I ain't been sick in 25 years. I is near my church and I don't miss service any Sunday, night or morning. I kin walk wherever I please, I kin walk to de Battery if I want to. The Welfare use to help me but dey shut down now, I can't find out if dey going to open again or not. Miss (Mrs.) Buist and Miss Pringle, dey help me when I can go there but all my own dead."

"Were most of the masters kind?" I asked. "Well you know," she answered, "times den was just like dey is now, some was kind and some was mean; heaps of wickedness went on just de same as now. All my people was good people. I see some wickedness and I hear 'bout all kinds of t'ings but you don't know whether it was lie or not. Mr. Fuller been a Christian man."

"Do you think it would have been better if the Negroes had never left Africa?" was the next question I asked. "No Ma'am," (emphatically) dem heathen didn't have no religion. I tell you how I t'ink it is. The Lord made t'ree nations, the white, the red and the black, and put dem in different places on de earth where dey was to stay. Dose black ignoramuses in Africa forgot God, and didn't have no religion and God blessed and prospered the white people dat did remember him and sent dem to teach de black people even if dey have to grab dem and bring dem into bondage till dey learned some sense. The Indians forgot God and dey had to be taught better so dey land was taken away from dem. God sure bless and prosper de white people and He put de red and de black people under dem so dey could teach dem and bring dem into sense wid God. Dey had to get dere brains right, and honor God, and learn uprightness wid God cause ain't He make you, and ain't His Son redeem you and save you wid His precious blood. You kin plan all de wickedness you want and pull hard as you choose but when the Lord mek up His mind you is to change, He can change you dat quick (snapping her fingers) and easy. You got to believe on Him if it tek bondage to bring you to your knees.

You know I is got converted. I been in Big Bethel (church) on my knees praying under one of de preachers. I see a great, big, dark pack on my back, and it had me all bent over and my shoulders drawn down, all hunch up. I look up and I see de glory, I see a big beautiful light, a great light, and in de middle is de Sabior, hanging so (extending her arms) just like He died. Den I gone to praying good, and I can feel de sheckles (shackles) loose up and moving and de pack fall off. I don't know where it went to, I see de angels in de Heaven, and hear dem say 'Your sins are forgiven.' I scream and fell off so. (Swoon.) When I come to dey has laid me out straight and I know I is converted cause you can't see no such sight and go on like you is before. I know I is still a sinner but I believe in de power of God and I trust his Holy name. Den dey put me wid de seekers but I know I is already saved."

"Did they take good care of the slaves when their babies were born?" she was asked. "If you want chickens for fat (to fatten) you got to feed dem," she said with a smile, "and if you want people to work dey got to be strong, you got to feed dem and take care of dem too. If dey can't work it come out of your pocket. Lots of wickedness gone on in dem days, just as it do now, some good, some mean, black and white, it just dere nature, if dey good dey going to be kind to everybody, if dey mean dey going to be mean to everybody. Sometimes chillen was sold away from dey parents. De Mausa would come and say "Where Jennie," tell um to put clothes on dat baby, I want um. He sell de baby and de ma scream and holler, you know how dey carry on. Geneally (generally) dey sold it when de ma wasn't dere. Mr. Fuller didn't sell none of us, we stay wid our ma's till we grown. I stay wid my ma till she dead.

"You know I is mix blood, my grandfather bin a white man and my grandmother a mulatto. She been marry to a black so dat how I get fix like I is. I got both blood, so how I going to quarrel wid either side?"

> Source: Interview with *Susan Hamlin, 17 Henrietta Street.

NOTE * Susan lives with a mulatto family of the better type. The name is Hamlin not Hamilton, and her name prior to her marriage was Calder not Collins. I paid particular attention to this and had them spell the names for me. I would judge Susan to be in the late nineties but she is wonderfully well preserved. She now claims to be 104 years old.

S-260-264-N
Project #1885
Augustus Ladson
Charleston, S.C.

No. Words: 1195

EX-SLAVE 101 YEARS OF AGE

HAS NEVER SHAKEN HANDS SINCE 1863

WAS ON KNEES SCRUBBING WHEN FREEDOM GUN FIRED

SUSAN HAMILTON

'm a hund'ed an' one years old now, son. De only one livin' in my crowd from de days I wuz a slave. Mr. Fuller, my master, who was president of the Firs' National Bank, owned the fambly of us except my father. There were eight men an' women with five girls an' six boys workin' for him. Most o' them wus hired out. De house in which we stayed is still dere with de cisterns an' slave quarters. I always go to see de old home which is on St. Phillip Street.

My ma had t'ree boys an' t'ree girls who did well at their work. Hope Mikell, my eldest bredder, an' James wus de shoemaker. William Fuller, son of our master, wus de bricklayer. Margurite an' Catharine wuz de maids an' look at de children.

My pa b'long to a man on Edisto Island. Frum what he said, his master was very mean. Pa real name wus

Adam Collins but he took his master' name; he wus de coachman. Pa did supin one day an his master whipped him. De next day which wuz Monday, Pa carry him 'bout four miles frum home in de woods an' give him de same 'mount of lickin' he wus given on Sunday. He tied him to a tree an' unhitched de horse so it couldn't git tie-up an' kill a self. Pa den gone to de landin' an' catch a boat dat wus comin' to Charleston wood fa'm products. He wus permitted by his master to go to town on errands, which helped him to go on de boat without bein' question'. When he got here he gone on de water-front an' ax for a job on a ship so he could git to de North. He got de job an' sail' wood de ship. Dey search de island up an' down for him wood houndogs en w'en it wus t'ought he wus drowned, 'cause dey track him to de river, did dey give up. One of his master' friend gone to New York en went in a store w'ere Pas wus employed as a clerk. He reconize' pa is easy is pa reconize' him. He gone back home an' tell pa master who know den dat pa wusn't comin' back an' before he died he sign' papers dat pa wus free. Pa ma wus dead an' he come down to bury her by de permission of his master' son who had promised no ha'm would come to him, but dey wus fixin' plans to keep him, so he went to the Work House an' ax to be sold 'cause any slave could sell e self if e could git to de Work House. But it wus on record down dere so dey couldn't sell 'im an' told him his master' people couldn't hold him a slave.

People den use to do da same t'ings dey do now. Some marry an' some live together jus' like now. One t'ing, no minister nebber say in readin' de matrimony "let no man put asounder" 'cause a couple would be married tonight an' tomorrow one would be taken away en be sold. All slaves wus married in dere master house, in de livin' room where slaves an' dere missus an' massa wus to witness de ceremony. Brides use to wear some of de finest dress an' if dey could afford it, have de best kind of furniture. Your master nor your missus objected to good t'ings.

I'll always 'member Clory, de washer. She wus very high-tempered. She wus a mulatta with beautiful hair she could sit on; Clory didn't take foolishness frum anybody. One day our missus gone in de laundry an' find fault with de clothes. Clory didn't do a t'ing but pick her up bodily an' throw 'er out de door. Dey had to sen' fur a doctor 'cause she pregnant an' less than two hours de baby wus bo'n. Afta dat she begged to be sold fur she didn't want to kill missus, but our master ain't nebber want to sell his slaves. But dat didn't keep Clory frum gittin' a brutal whippin'. Dey whip' 'er until dere wasn't a white spot on her body. Dat wus de worst I ebber see a human bein' got such a beatin'. I t'ought she wus goin' to die, but she got well an' didn't get any better but meaner until our master decide it wus bes' to rent her out. She willingly agree' since she wusn't 'round missus. She hated an' detest' both of them an' all de fambly.

W'en any slave wus whipped all de other slaves wus made to watch. I see women hung frum de ceilin' of buildin's an' whipped with only supin tied 'round her lower part of de body, until w'en dey wus taken down, dere wusn't breath in de body. I had some terribly bad experiences.

Yankees use to come t'rough de streets, especially de Big Market, huntin' those who want to go to de "free country" as dey call' it. Men an' women wus always missin' an' nobody could give 'count of dere disappearance. De men wus train' up North fur sojus.

De white race is so brazen. Dey come here an' run de Indians frum dere own lan', but dey couldn't make dem slaves 'cause dey wouldn't stan' for it. Indians use to git up in trees an' shoot dem with poison arrow. W'en dey couldn't make dem slaves den dey gone to Africa an' bring dere black brother an' sister. Dey say 'mong themselves, "we gwine mix dem up en make ourselves king. Dats e only way we'll git even with de Indians."

All time, night an' day, you could hear men an' women screamin' to de tip of dere voices as either ma, pa, sister, or brother wus take without any warnin' an' sell. Some time mother who had only one chile wus separated fur life. People wus always dyin' frum a broken heart.

One night a couple married an' de next mornin' de boss sell de wife. De gal ma got in in de street an' cursed de white woman fur all she could find. She said: "dat damn white, pale-face bastard sell my daughter who jus' married las' night," an' other t'ings. The white 'oman treaten' her to call de police if she didn't stop, but de collud woman said: "hit me or call de police. I redder die dan to stan' dis any longer! De police took her to de work House by de white woman orders an' what became of 'er, I never hear.

W'en de war began we wus taken to Aiken, South Ca'lina w'ere we stay' until de Yankees come t'rough. We could see balls sailin' t'rough de air w'en Sherman wus comin'. Bumbs hit trees in our yard. W'en de freedom gun wus fired, I wus on my 'nees scrubbin'. Dey tell me I wus free but I didn't b'lieve it.

In de days of slavery woman wus jus' given time 'nough to deliver dere babies. Dey deliver de baby 'bout eight in de mornin' an' twelve had too be back to work.

I wus a member of Emmanuel African Methodist Episcopal Church for 67 years. Big Zion, across de street wus my church before den an' before Old Bethel w'en I lived on de other end of town.

Sence Lincoln shook hands with his assasin who at de same time shoot him, frum dat day I stop shakin' hands, even in de church, an' you know how long dat wus. I don't b'lieve in kissin' neider fur all carry dere meannesses. De Master wus betrayed by one of his bosom frien' with a kiss.

Source

Interview with (Mrs.) Susan Hamilton, 17 Henrietta Street, who claims to be
101 years of age. She has never been sick for twenty years and walks as though
just 40. She was hired out by her master for seven dollars a month which had to
be given her master.

United States. Work Projects Administration

Project #1655
Stiles M. Scruggs
Columbia, S.C.

ANSON HARP
EX-SLAVE 87 YEARS OLD.

ANSON HARP

Anson Harp, eighty-seven years old, lives out in the country on Route #3. He still works on the few acres he owns, raising vegetables for himself and a few baskets to sell. He is a gray-haired, medium sized man and his geniality is frequently noticed by white and Negro friends who know him.

"I was born in Mississippi in 1850, on a big plantation dat b'long to Master Tom Harp. I can see dat big rushin' river now, 'ceptin' the mosquitoes. My daddy and mammy b'long to Master Harp and we live in a cabin 'bout a mile from the big house of my master's home.

"One day when the slaves was choppin' cotton, a strange white man come and watch us, and in a day or two me and three other chillun was called in the yard of the big house and told we goin' to git to go wid the stranger. My daddy and mammy and the other chillun's daddy and mammy all cry when we was put in a big wagon and carried 'way to somewhere.

"We gits plenty of rations on the way and when we gits to Aiken one mornin', we was told we was close to home and soon we was on the big plantation of Master James Henry Hammond. We find other boys there, too. We go to the fields and chop cotton, after we rest up. No sah, we wasn't flogged often. One time the grown men and women was choppin' two rows to our one, and a straw-boss slave twit us and call us lazy. The white overseer, who was riding by, heard him. He shake his whip at the straw-boss and tell him: 'The young niggers not yet 'spected to make a half hand and you do pretty well to 'tend to your own knittin'.

"I been there for a pretty long time befo' I really talks to my great white master, James Henry Hammond. He not at home much, and when he was home, many big white men wid him 'most every day.

"One Saturday, we always had a half holiday on Saturday, me and my friends 'bout the same age, was playin' a game on a big lot behind the barn. We quit yellin' and playin' when we see Master Hammond and three or four white men at the barn. They was lookin' at and talkin' 'bout Master Hammond's big black stallion. Master Hammond lead him out of the stall and he stand on his hind feet.

"'Well Senator,' says one big man to Master Hammond, 'I has come a long ways to see this famous hoss. It's no wonder he was s'lected as a model for the war hoss of General Jackson. I seen his statue in Washington and Nashville.'

"'And I see him in New Orleans', says another big man, in a fine black slick suit.

"'I 'clare, Governor', says the other big man, also

dressed just lak he goin' to church, 'this grand stallion look today well as he did when I use him for my model'.

"Then they all pat the hoss's nose and stroke him down his mane, and the big buckra hoss steps, just lak the fine gentlemen he is, back to his stall, while all the big men wave him goodbye!

"No, I not take the name of Hammond after we free, 'cause too many of his slaves do. I kept the name of my old master and the one my daddy and mammy had. No, I never hear of them in Mississippi. Lak as not they was sold and taken far away, lak me.

"I was eleven in 1861, when the war start, 'cordin' to my count. Master Hammond was hardly ever at home no more. He, too, was angry at President Lincoln and I love my master, so I used to wonder what sort of man the President was. My Master Hammond sure did honor President Davis. I hear him say once, dat President Davis was a Chesterfield and dat the Lincoln fellow is coarse and heartless.

"In 1862 I was twelve years old, big for my age, and I do more than half as much work as any grown slave. At dat time we see many free niggers, and nearly all of them sorry lookin'. They eat off of slave families, when they could git it.

"I come to Columbia in 1865, after all the niggers everywhere am set free. I work for white folks 'bout town and when the Freedman's aid was set up, I goes 'long wid some new found friends to the aid headquarters, and was the last one to be heard. The others got bundles of food and I see one git a piece of money, too. When I got to the white man in charge, he eye me and zay: 'What damn rebel did you slave for?' I forgot 'bout what I am there for and I say: 'I never slave for no damn rebel. I work for Governor Hammond and he is the finest buckra that is.'

"Then the aid man say: 'Dat damn rebel Hammond and all lak him yet unhung, should be, and you wid him. Go let him feed and clothe you! When you come here again maybe you have 'nough sense to ask for favors decent.' I so mad, I hardly 'member just what happen, 'ceptin' I come 'way just lak I go, empty handed.

"I am now an old man, as you see, but I am happy to know dat the white folks has always been ready to help me make a livin'. I now own a patch of ground, where I makes a livin' on the shares. My boy, a son by my second wife, works it, and he takes care of me now. If I had been as big, and knowed as much at the start of the war as I did at the end of it, I would surely have gone to the front wid my white master."

Project 1885-1
FOLKLORE
Spartanburg Dist. 4
May 25, 1937

Edited by:
Elmer Turnage

STORIES FROM EX-SLAVES

THOMAS HARPER

"I was born in Fairfield County, S.C. near Broad River. I was de son of John and Harriet Harper. I worked in slavery time and was a slave of John Stanley who was a good man and easy to work with. He give me a good whipping once when I was a boy. We earned no money but had our place to sleep and something to eat and wear. We didn't have any gardens, but master had a big plantation and lots of slaves, and worked a garden himself. I remember he whipped mother once the last year of the war,—just about to get freedom.

"Master belonged to patrollers, and let dem come on the place and punish the slaves if needed. They whipped my sister once. He had a house to lock slaves in when dey was bad. He learned us to read and write. He had a school on de plantation for his niggers. After the days work was over, we frolicked, and Saturday afternoons we had off to do what we wanted. We had to go to the white folks church and set in back of de church. Corn shuckings, cotton picking and carding and quilting, the old folks had when dey had big times and big eats.

"Weddings and funerals of slaves were about like white folks. Some would go walking and singing to de grave in back of hearse or body. There was a conjurer in our neighborhood who could make you do what he wanted, sometimes he had folks killed. The Yankees marched through our place, stole cattle, and meat. We went behind dem and picked up lots dat dey dropped when dey left. When de war was over, de niggers was promised small farms but dey didn't get 'em.

"I have been preaching many years in colored Methodist churches. I have 7 children, 22 grand-children but no great-grand-children.

"I think Abraham Lincoln was a great man, and Jefferson Davis, too. Booker Washington was a grand educator for the colored race. Bishop S.D. Chappell, colored preacher of the A.M.E. church South, one time president of Allen University at Columbia, S.C. was a great colored man, too. He went to Nashville, Tenn. as secretary-treasurer of the Sunday School Union.

"I don't believe slavery was good—much better for all of us now.

"I joined the church when I was young, because I thought it right to be a member. I think everybody ought to join some church, and they ought to join early in life, when quite young."

Source: Rev. Thomas Harper (84), Newberry, S.C., interviewed by:

G.L. Summer, Newberry, S.C. May 21, 1937.

United States. Work Projects Administration

Project #1555
W.W. Dixon
Winnsboro, S.C.

ABE HARRIS
EX-SLAVE 74 YEARS OLD.

ABE HARRIS

Abe Harris lives about nine miles southwest of the town of Winnsboro, South Carolina. His home is a two-room frame house, with rock chimneys of rough masonry at each gable end. It is the property of Mr. Daniel Heyward. Abe is one-fourth white and this mixture shows in his features. He is still vigorous and capable of light manual labor.

"My father was Samuel Lyles. My mother's name was Phenie Lyles. My father and mother had fifteen chillun. I am de only one livin'. De last one to die was my brother, Stocklin, that tended to de flowers and gardens of people in Winnsboro for many years. He was found dead, one mornin', in de Fortune Park woods.

"My parents b'long to Captain Tom Lyles, in slavery time. Father was de hog man. He 'tended to de hogs; didn't pasture them as they do now. Marster had a drove of eighty or more in de fall of de year befo' hog killin' time. They run 'bout in de woods for acorns and hickory nuts and my father had to keep up wid them and bring them home. He pen them, feed them, and slop them at night.

"My white folks was de fust white settlers in de county. De fust one was name Ephram, so I hear them tell many times. They fought in all wars dat have been fought. My old marster, Tom, live up 'til de Civil War and although he couldn't walk, he equip and pay a man to go in his place. When Sherman's men come to de house, he was in bed wid a dislocated hip. They thought he was shammin', playin' 'possum, so to speak. One of de raiders, a Yankee, come wid a lighted torch and say: 'Unless you give me de silver, de gold, and de money, I'll burn you alive.' Him reply: 'I haven't many more years to live. Burn and be damned!' De Yankee was surprised at his bravery, ordered father to take de torch from under de bed and say: 'You 'bout de bravest man I ever see in South Carolina.'

"His wife, old Miss Mary, was sister to Congressman Joe Woodward. Deir house and plantation was out at Buckhead. I was a boy eleven years old and was in de house when he died, in 1874. He was de oldest person I ever saw, eighty-seven. He had several chillun. Thomas marry Eliza Peay, de baby of Col. Austin Peay, one of de rich race horse folks. Marse Boykin marry Miss Cora Dantzler of Orangeburg. Him went to de war. Then Nicholas, Austin, John, and Belton, all went to de Civil War. Austin was killed at second Bull Run. Marse Nicholas go to Alabama and become sheriff out dere. Marse John marry Miss Morris and was clerk of court here for twenty-eight years.

"One of Marse John's sons is Senator Lyles, de cotton buyer here in Winnsboro. De youngest boy, just a lad at freedom, marry Miss Cora Irby. Two of deir chillun marry Marse Jim and Marse Bill Mobley in Columbia. De youngest child, Miss Rebecca marry Marse DuBose Ellison in Winnsboro.

"First time I marry Emily Kinlock and had one child. Emily die. Then I marry Lizzie Brown. Us had six chillun. When Lizzie die, I marry a widow, Frances Young. Us too old to have chillun.

"I live at Rion, S.C. Just piddle 'round wid chickens and garden truck. I sells them to de stone cutters and de mill people of Winnsboro. I's past de age to work hard, and I'm mighty sorry dat our race was set free too soon."

PROJECT #1655
W.W. Dixon,
Winnsboro, S.C.

ELI HARRISON
EX-SLAVE 87 YEARS.

ELI HARRISON

Eli Harrison lives on a small ten-acre tract of land near Dutchman Creek, in Fairfield County, approximately seven miles southeast of Winnsboro. The house, which he owns, is a small shack or shanty constructed of scantlings and slabs. He lives in it alone and does his own cooking. He has been on the relief roll for the past three years, and ekes out a subsistence on the charity of the Longtown and Ridgeway people. He is small, wiry, and healthy, weighing about 110 pounds.

"I sure has had a time a finding you! I was up here to Winnsboro befo' dis Welfare Society, tryin' to git a pension and they ask me who know my age. I tell them a whole lot of people out of town knows it. Then they ask if anybody in town know my age. I gived in your name. They say they will take your affidavit for it and tell me to bring dis paper to you.

"I b'long, in slavery, to your step-mother's people, de Harrisons, in Longtown. You 'members comin' down when I was a young man and you was a boy? Don't you 'member us playin' in de sand in front of de old Harrison house? Dat house older than you and me. 'Member how I show you how to call de doodles from de sand? How was it? I just git down on my hands and knees in de sand and say: 'Doodle, doodle, doodle, doodle, come up your house is afire!' Them black little doodles would come right up out of de sand to see what gwine on up dere 'bove de sand. Mighty glad you keeps dat in your mem'ry, 'til dis blessed day.

"I b'long to old Marse Eli Harrison, de grandpa of your step-mother. I was born and raised on his Wateree River plantation. They called it Harrison Flats, 'til de Southern Power Company and de Dukes taken over de land, de river, de bull-frogs, de skeeters, whoop owls, and everything else down here. De Harrisons owned dat place befo' de Revolutionary War, they say. De skeeters run them out and de folks built a string of houses out of logs, all 'long de roadside and call it Longtown. Marse John D. tell me dat, and fust thing you know they was callin' it Longtown and dats what it's called today.

"Old Marse Eli is a quiet man but him have two brudders dat wasn't so quiet. They was Marse Aaron Burr Harrison and Marse John R. Harrison. All of them have race horses. I, bein' little, ride de horses in de races at de last. De tracks I ride on? One was up near Great Falls, 'tween old Marse Strother Fords and de Martin place. De other was out from Simpsons' Turn Out. De Hamptons used to have horses on dese tracks.

"My mistress name Mary. My young marsters name: Sylvester, Lundsford, David, and John D. They all dead but de old house is still dere on de roadside and I alone is live to tell de tale.

"Dere's one thing I wants to tell you 'bout old Marse John. Him was 'suaded by de Hamptons, to buy a big plantation in Mississippi. Him go out dere to raise cattle, race horses, cotton, sugar cane and niggers. When him die, after so long a time they take him out of his grave. De Harrisons done built a long, big, rock, family vault in de graveyard here to put all de dead of de family name in. Well, what you reckon? Why when dat coffin reach Ridgeway and they find it mighty heavy for just one man's body, they open it and find Marse John's body done turned to solid rock. What you think of dat? And what you think of dis? They put him in de vault in de summertime. Dat fall a side show was goin' on in Columbia, showin' a petrified man, you had to pay twenty-five cents to go in and see it. De show leave and go up North. 'Bout Christmas, de family go together to de vault, open it, and bless God dat rock body done got up and left dat vault. What you think 'bout dat? What people say? Some say one thing, some say another. Niggers all 'low, 'Marse John done rose from de dead.' White folks say: 'Somebody done stole dat body of Marse John and makin' a fortune out of it, in de side show line.'

"Well, I's told you 'nough for one day. I's impatient to git back down yonder to them white ladies wid dis paper, so as to speed up dat pension as fast as I used to speed up them race horses I use to ride on de old race track road from Simpson's to Columbia."

Slave Narratives

Project 1885-1
FOLKLORE
Spartanburg Dist. 4
Sept. 20, 1937

Edited by:
Elmer Turnage

REMINISCENCES

CHARLIE JEFF HARVEY

"I was born July 16, 1852 at Jeter's old mill place in Santuc township. The Neal's Shoal dam now marks the site of the old Jeter mill. My family consisted of my parents and an older brother. My mother was Mandy Clark of Union township. My grandfather Clark moved to the Jeter mill and ran it for Mr. Jeter. My father, Tom Clark, was a laborer for the Jeters and old man Tom Sims up on Broad River at what was then known as Simstown. The Tom Sims and Nat Gist families owned everything in Santuc township until their lands hit the Jimmie Jeter place.

"When I was twelve, my father went to the Confederate War. He joined the Holcombe Legion of Union County and they went immediately to Charleston. They drilled near the village of Santuc in what was then called Mulligan's Old Field, now owned by Rion Jeter. This was the only mustering ground in our part of the county. The soldiers drilled once a week, and for the 'general muster, all of the companies from Sedalia and Cross Keys come there once a month. During the summer time they had what they called general drill for a week or ten days. Of course on this occasion the soldiers camped over the field in covered wagons. Some came in buggies. Slaves, called 'wait-men' cared for the stock and did the cooking and other menial duties for their masters.

"The general store at Santuc and the store at the Cross Roads at Fish Dam did good business during the summer while the soldiers were in camp. The 'cross roads' have long been done away with at Fish Dam. The store was under a big oak in front of the house now owned and lived in by W. H. Gist. The Cross Roads were made by the Fish Dam Ferry Road and the old Ninety-Six Road. They tell me that the old Ninety-Six Road was started as an Indian trail by the Cherokee Indians, way yonder before the Revolution. I have been told that a girl named Emily Geiger rode that ninety-six miles in one day to carry a message to an American general. The message kept the general and his army from being captured by the red-coats.

"Near the Kay Jeter place just below the Ninety-six road there was a small drill ground. The place is now known as the Pittman place and is owned by the wife of Dr. J. T. Jeter of Santuc, I believe. Mr. 'Kay' would send a slave on a horse or a mule to notify the men to come and drill there. From here they went on to Mulligan's Field some five or six miles away for the big drills. As I have told you, Mulligan's Field was the big field for all that countryside. They tell me that the same drilling tactics used then and there, are the same used right down yonder at Camp Jackson.

"For about four of five years after the Confederate War, we had very little to eat. We had given everything we could to the soldiers. After the 'May Surrender' there came a big flood and washed everything away, and the crops were so promising that August. As you know, that was in '65. The rains and the high water destroyed everything. I do not believe that Broad River and the Forest and Tyger have ever been as high before or since.

"On Henderson's Island they saved no livestock at all. They just did manage to save themselves. They had a hard time getting the slaves to the mainland. Mrs. Sallie Henderson, her step-son, Jack and her son, Jim, and daughter, Lyde were in the Henderson house when the freshet came down upon them. They had to go up on the second floor of their house but the water came up there.

"Mr. Ben Hancock was the ferryman at Henderson's Ferry at this time. Now you know, Henderson's Ferry is on the Enoree just above where it empties into the Broad. Henderson's Island is in the middle of Broad River in full sight of where old Enoree goes into the channel of the Broad. Well, Mr. Hancock was the best boatman in his day. He knew about the Hendersons, so he tried to go to them but failed the first three times. The fourth time, he got to the house. When he got there, he found the whites and twenty-five slaves trapped with them.

"A barrel of flour had caught in the stairway that had washed down the river from somewhere above. This was pulled upstairs and that is what Mrs. Henderson fed her family and slaves on for about five days, or until they were rescued by Mr. Hancock. Capt. Jack blew his opossum horn every two hours throughout the day and night to let the people over on the mainland know that they were still safe.

"For the rest of that year, river folks had very little to eat until food crops were produced the next spring.

"My own father was shot down for the first time at the Second Battle of Manassas. Here he got a lick over his left eye that was about the size of a bullet; but he said that he thought the lick came from a bit of shell. They carried him to a temporary make-shift hospital that had been improvised behind the breastworks. A soldier who was recovering from a wound nursed him as best he could.

"The second time my father was wounded was in Kingston, N.C. He shot a Yankee from behind a tree and he saw the blood spurt from him as he fell. Just about that time he saw another Yankee behind a tree leveling a gun at him. Father threw up his gun but too late, the Yankee shot and tore his arm all to pieces. The bullet went through his arm and struck the corner of his mouth knocking out part of his jaw bone. Then it went under the neck vein and finally it came out on his back knocking a hole in one of his shoulder blades large enough to lay your two thumbs in. His gun stock was also cut into. He lay on the battlefield for a whole day and night; then he was carried to a house where some kind ladies acting as nurses cared for him for over four months. He was sent home and dismissed from the army just a mile below Maybinton, S.C. in Newberry County. Father was unable to do any kind of work for over two years. The war closed a year after he got home. From that time on I cared for my mother and father.

"We had moved to the plantation of Mr. Ben Maybin in Maybinton before my father was sent home wounded. Father lived until March, 1st, 1932 when he died at the ripe old age of 102. When he died we were living at one of the Jeter plantations near Kelley's Chapel, in Fish Dam township, one-half mile from Old Ninety-Six Road. Father is buried at Kelley's Chapel.

"Mr. Harvey has a bullet that Gov. Scott issued to the negroes during reconstruction times when he was governor of South Carolina under the carpetbag rule. Scott issued these bullets to the negroes to kill and plunder with. Mr. Harvey says that bullets like this one were the cause of many negroes finding their graves in the bottom of Broad River. Mr. Harvey, so it is said, is still a Ku Klux. They were the chief instruments in getting him into the County Home of Union in 1925.

"The Ku Klux made a boat twenty-five feet long to carry the negroes down the river. They would take the negroes' own guns, most of them had two guns, and tie the guns around their necks in the following manner: The barrel of one gun was tied with wire around the negro's neck, and the stock of the other gun was fastened with wire around the negro's neck. When the captain would say, 'A-M-E-N', over the side of the boat the negro went, with his guns and bullets taking him to a watery grave in the bottom of Broad River. The wooden parts of the guns would rot, and sometimes the bodies would wash down on the rocks at Neal's Shoals what was then Jeter's Old Mill. Old gun stocks have been taken from there as mementoes.

"Bill Fitzgerald was my first Ku Klux Captain. He organized the clan in Newberry. When I came to the Klan over on the Union side, Judge W. H. Wallace and Mr. Isaac McKissick were leaders.

"When we got the negroes from the county jail, the same jail that we have now, that were arrested for killing Matt Stevens, I broke the lock on the jail door. Buck Allen was the blacksmith. He held a sledge hammer under the lock while I threw a steel hammer overhanded on the lock to break it.

"I think Abe Lincoln would have done the South some good if they had let him live. He had a kind heart and knew what suffering was. Lee would have won the war if the mighty Stonewall Jackson had lived. Stonewall was ahead of them all. I had two uncles, Jipp and Charlie Clark in Stonewall's company. They would never talk much about him after his death. It hurts them too much, for Stonewall's men loved him so much. Jeff Davis was a great man, too."

Source: Mr. Charlie Jeff Harvey, Rt. 4, Box 85, Union, S.C.
Interviewer: Caldwell Sims, Union, S.C. 8/18/35.

Project #1655
W.W. Dixon
Winnsboro, S.C.

ELIZA HASTY
EX-SLAVE 85 YEARS OLD.

ELIZA HASTY

Eliza Hasty lives with her son-in-law and her daughter, Philip Moore and Daisy Moore, in an old time ante bellum home. It has two stories, eight rooms, and front and back piazzas, supported by slender white posts or columns. It is the old William Douglas homestead, now owned by John D. Mobley. He rents it to Philip Moore, a well behaved Negro citizen, who, out of respect for his mother-in-law, Eliza, supports her in the sore trials and helplessness of blindness and old age. The home is five miles southeast of Blackstock, S.C.

"Boss, you is a good lookin' man, from de sound of your voice. Blind folks has ways of findin' out things that them wid sight know nothin' 'bout and nobody can splain. De blindness sharpens de hearin', 'creases de tech, prickles de skin, quickens de taste, and gives you de nose of a setter, pointer or hound dog. Was I always blind? Jesus, no! I just got de 'fliction several years ago. I see well enough, when I was a young gal, to pick out a preacher for my fust husband. So I did! How many times I been married? Just two times; both husbands dead. Tell you 'bout them directly.

"What dat? Er ha, ha, ha, ha, er ha, ha, ha! Oh Jesus, you makes me laugh, white folks! De idea of my lossin' my sight a lookin' 'round for a third husband! You sho' is agreeable. Ain't been so tickled since de secon' time I was a widow. You know my secon' husband was bad after blind tiger liquor, and harlot eyed, brassy, hussy women.

"Well, I comes down to Winnsboro today to see, I should say to find out, 'cause you know I can't see, 'bout de pension they is givin' out to de aged and blind. My white folks say dat you wanna see me and here I is.

"Yes sir, I was born two miles south of Woodward and one mile south of old Yonguesville, on de Sterling place. I born a slave of old Marse John Sterling. Him have a head as red as a pecker-wood bird dat just de-sash-sheys 'round de top of dead trees, and make sich a rat-ta-ta-tapple after worms. His way of gittin' his meat for dinner. My mistress name Betsy. Deir fust child was Robert, dat never marry; him teach nearly every school in Fairfield County, off and on befo' he died. Then dere was young Marster Tom, small little man, dat carry his Seceeder 'ligion so far, him become 'furiated and carry dat 'ligion right up and into de Secession War. Make a good soldier, too! General Bratton call him, 'My Little Jackass of de Sharp Shooters'! Marse Tom proud of dat name, from de mouth of a great man lak General John Bratton.

"Marse Tom heard de fust gun fire at Fort Sumter, and laid down his gun, him say, under a big horse apple tree at 'Applemattox'.

"Miss Sallie, one of de chillun, marry Mr. Chris Elder, of Blackstock. Miss Hepzibah, they call her Heppie, marry a man named Boyd, in Chester County. Miss Mary

Izabella, they call her Bell, marry Marse John Douglas; they are de 'cestors of dat very angel whose house us is settin' in right dis minute. Her name is Martha but when grown-up, they sublet (meaning change) dat name to Mattie, and when her marry, her become Mrs. Thomas P. Bryson. Her is a widow, just lak I is a widow. De only difference is, I's black and her is white. Her can see well enough to run after and ketch another man, but I's blind and can't see a man, much less chase after him. So dere it is! What for you laughin' 'bout? No laughin' business wid me.

"My pappy no b'long to Marse John Sterling: him slave of de Stinsons. Have to git a pass to come to see my mammy, Mary. Him name Aleck. After de war him take de name of Alexander Roseboro. Him lak a big long name dat would make folks set up and take notice of him.

"Us live in a little log-house wid a dirt floor. Us had mighty poor beds, I tell you. Us just had planks to lay de wheat straw mattress on. Pillows? De pillows was just anything you could snatch and put under your head. Yes sir, us had plenty to eat.

"They 'struct us in de short catechism, make us go to church, and sit up in de gallery and jine in de singin' on Sundays. Us was well 'tended to when sick. Marster didn't have many slaves. 'Members only two they have, 'sides us; they was Uncle Ned and Cindy. Seem lak dere was another. Oh yes! It was Fred, a all 'round de creation boy, to do anything and everything. He was a sorta shirt-tail boy dat pestered me sometime wid goo-goo eyes, a standin' in de kitchen door, drappin' his weight from one foot to de other, a lookin' at me while I was a churnin' or washin' de dishes. Dat boy both box-ankle and knock-kneed. When you hear him comin' from de horse lot to de house, his legs talk to one another, just lak sayin': 'You let me pass dis time, I let you pass nex' time.' I let you know I had no time for dat ape! When I did git ready to marry, I fly high as a eagle and ketch a preacher of de Word! Who it was? Him was a Baptis' preacher, name Solomon Dixon. 'Spect you hear tell of him. No? Well, him b'long, in slavery time, to your Aunt Roxie's people in Liberty Hill, Kershaw County. You 'members your Aunt Roxie dat marry Marse Ed D. Mobley, her fust cousin, don't you?

"I love Solomon and went down under de water to be buried wid him in baptism, I sho' did, and I come up out of dat water to be united wid him in wedlock. When us marry, him have on a long-tail coat, salt and pepper trousers, box-toed shoes, and a red lead pencil over his ear, just as long as de one I 'spects you is writin' wid, tho' I can't see it.

"How I dressed? I 'members 'zactly. I wore a blue worsted shirt, over a red underskirt, over a white linen petticoat wid tuckers at de hem, just a little long, to show good and white 'long wid de blue of de skirt and de red of de underskirt. Dese all come up to my waist and was held together by de string dat held my bustle in place. All dis and my corset was hid by de snow white pleated pique bodice, dat drapped gracefully from my shoulders. 'Round my neck was a string of green jade beads. I wore red stockin's and my foots was stuck in soft, black, cloth, gaiter shoes.

"My go-away-hat was 'stonishment to everybody. It was made out of red plush velvet and trimmed wid white satin ribbons. In de front, a ostrich feather stood up high and two big turkey feathers flanked de sides. Oh, de treasures of memory to de blind. I's happy to sit here and talk to you 'bout dat day! I sho' is!

"Us live at Marse John Douglas for a time and dat's where my fust child was born. I name her for your Aunt Roxie, tho' I give her de full name, Roxanna Dixon. Her marry John Craig. They live on your grandpa Woodward's old Nickey place, four miles southeast of Blackstock. I had another baby and I name her Daisy. Her marry Philip Moore. I lives wid them in de old William Douglas mansion. Nearly all de white folks leavin' de country dese days and de colored folks gits de fine country houses to live in.

"Well, after de years fly by, my husband, Solomon, go to de mansion prepared for him and me in hebben. I wait a year and a day and marry William Hasty. Maybe I was a little hasty 'bout dat, but 'spects it was my fate. Him drink liquor and you know dat don't run to de still waters of peace and happiness in de home. Him love me, I no doubt dat, but he get off to de bar room at Blackstock, or de still house in bottom lands, get drunk and spend his money. De Bible say dat kind of drowsiness soon clothe a man in rags. Him dead now. God rest his soul!

"De Yankees come. They took notice of me! They was a bad lot dat disgrace Mr. Lincoln dat sent them here. They insult women both white and black, but de Lord was mindful of his own.

"I knows nothin' else to tell you, 'less you would be pleased to hear 'bout what de cyclone did to my old missus and de old Sterling house. Somewhere 'bout 1880's one of them super knockshal (equinoctial) storms come 'long, commencin' over in Alabama or Georgia, crossed de Savannah River, sweep through South Carolina, layin' trees to de ground, cuttin' a path a quarter of a mile wide, as it traveled from west to east. Every house it tech, it carry de planks and shingles and sills and joists 'way wid it. De old Sterling house was in de path. Dere was a big oak tree in de front yard. Old miss and her son, Robert, was dere and Miss Heppie, a granddaughter, was in dat house. De storm hit dat house 'bout 9 o'clock dat night and never left a bit of it, 'cept some of de bricks. Some of de logs and sills was found de nex' day over at de other side of de railroad track. Some of de planks was found six miles east, some of de shingles across Catawba River, 25 miles east, and curious to say, de wind blowed old miss against de big oak tree and kill her. It blowed Miss Heppie in de top of dat tree where she was settin' a cryin' and couldn't git down, and it never harm a hair of Marse Robert's head. Him look 'round for Miss Heppie, couldn't find her, went off to get help, and when they come back, they have to git a ladder from old Mr. Bob Mobley's house to git her down.

"Well, here comes my daughters. I hear one outside but I bet you don't hear a thing. Dats deir steps I hear. Glad for you to meet them. They is mighty fine gals, if I do have to say so. They come up wid good white folks, de Mills'. Marse Jim Mills have family prayer in de mornin' and family prayer befo' they go to bed. Dat was de fust thing wid him and de last thing wid de Mills' family. If all de families do dat way, dere would be de answer to de prayer, 'Dy kingdom come, Dy will be done, on earth, as 'tis in hebben'.

"Well, give me my stick. Here they is. I bids you goodbye and God bless you."

Reference:

Personal interview with Aunt Dolly Haynes, age 91 Arthurtown, S.C.

United States. Work Projects Administration

AUNT DOLLY HAYNES
EX-SLAVE, 91 YEARS OLD, ARTHURTOWN S.C.

DOLLY HAYNES

"I nebber wuz no rockin' chair setter. I ain't nebber had no time to set down and do nuthin'. I wuz born at Euta, South Carolina. We belong to Marse Charlie Baumer. My Ma died and lef four motherless chillun but de missus wuz mighty good to us—call us her chillun. Pa rung de bell on de plantation fur ter wake de slaves up fur to go to de fiel'. My Missus wuz blind but she wuz a mighty kin' lady. Mek de cook bring plate of vittals to see ef it wuz heavy nough for her little chillun.

"After freedom all us moved wid de Marse and Missus to Childs, South Carolina and I mar'd Paul Haynes, who belonged to old Colonel Hampton.

"Paul wanted to preach but nedder of us had no learnin' an' I say to Paul, 'Does you think you got nough learnin' to lead a flock of people? I don' wan' you to git up an' mek me shame.' I tell him to go to de Benedicts an' see what book he needs to study, come by town bring me a pair of broggans for me, 'cause I wuz a-gwine to wuk and he wuz a-gwine to school. For t'ree long years I plowed de farm an' sent Paul to de Benedicts 'til he wuz edicated. De briars cut my legs an' de breshes tore my skirt, but I tuck up de skirt an' plow right on 'til I bought my little farm. Paul bin dead now 'bout twelve years, but he preached right up to de day he died.

"I got a neffu but I lives alone, wen deys some one in de house I puts down and dey picks up—I cleans up and dey tears up. I don' owe nobody nuthin'. Wen de nurvus spells leaves me an' I feels a little strong in de legs I wuks mah garden. I loves to be doin' somethin' to keep clean, 'cause I jes ain't no rockin chair setter".

Code No.
Project, 1885-(1)
Prepared by Annie Ruth Davis
Place, Marion, S.C.
Date, November 11, 1937

No. _____
Reduced from _____ words
Rewritten by _____

LINEY HENDERSON
Ex-Slave, 70 Years

LINEY HENDERSON

"Accordin to de way dey figures up my age, dey say I 70 now en I believes dat right, too, en de government ought to give me somethin. When we was born, de white folks put us chillun age down in de Bible en I know from dat I been 19 years old de year of de shake. Cose I gets clothes give to me, but no help no more den dat en all dis here wood en coal bill put on me. No, mam, ain' got no support to help me out no time. But justice will plum de line some day. I just gwine leave it in de hands of de Lord. Ain' gwine cry over it."

"I tell you, I been wid white folks all my days en I was properly cared for long as I been in dey protection. I suffers now more den I is ever think bout would come to me. Yes, mam, I done raise over 20 head of white chillun. Dat de God truth. I been in de white folks kitchen all my days en if I feel right, I think dey ought to take of me in my old age. I don' brag on myself, but if I could work like

I used to, I wouldn' ax nothin from nobody. I had a family of white people to send for me de other week to come en live wid dem en dey would take care of me, but I never had nobody to trust aun' Sallie wid. You see, child, she such a helpless, poor creature just settin dere in dat bed all de time en can' see to do one thing widout I give her my hand. Cose de government helps aun' Sallie, but dat ain' me. En, honey, I ain' even able to stand up en iron, I has dis rheumatism so bad. It hurts me so terrible at night, I has to keep my foots out from under de cover. It a sort of burnin rheumatism like. Yes, mam, it does worry me right smart."

"Oh, my Lord, I was raise down dere to old Dr. Durant plantation. Yes, mam, dem Durants had everything right to dey hand. Never had to want for a glass of water or nothin en didn' none of Dr. Durant's colored people never had no trouble wid de law from de time de law take care to dis. I remember old Massa would always kill his plantation people a cow on de fourth of July en couldn' never count de number of hogs dey would have, dere be so many. Honey, dey would take dem hogs up dis time of de year from out de swamp en put dem in dey fattenin pen. Lord, Lord, de many a time dat I been see dem take bucket on a bucket of milk to dat pen. When my mother was dere helpin dem, dey used to been a week to a time tryin up lard en makin blood puddin en sausage en joinin up ears en things like dat. Yes, mam, all dey plantation niggers what been helpin dat day set for hog killin would eat to de white folks yard. Dey would just put two or three of dese big wash pot out in de yard en full dem up wid backbone en haslets en rice to satisfy dem hungry niggers wid en would bake de corn bread to de Missus kitchen. I mean dey would have hog killin days den, too. Would have dese long old benches settin out dere under de trees to work on—long benches, child. Some days, dey would kill 15 hogs en some days, dey would kill 20 hogs en I mean dey was hogs, not pigs. De number dey would kill would be accordin to how many hands was helpin de day dey pick to kill. You see, dey would kill dem one day en hang dem up en den dey would set de next day to cut dem up. Oh, dey would hang dem up right out to de eyes of everybody en didn' nobody never have no mind to bother nothin. My Lord, couldn' trust to do nothin like dat dese days. En dey had de nicest homemade butter en whip cream dere all de time. Seems like things was just more plentiful en dey was better in dat day en time."

"It just like I tellin you, it de way of de past, everything had to be carried out right on Dr. Durant's plantation. When freedom come here, dere couldn' no head never get dem colored people to leave from dere. Yes, mam, dey great grand-chillun dere carryin on to dis very day. Dem Durant chillun ain' never had to hunt for no hand to do somethin for dem. Yes, mam, my white folks had dey own colored people graveyard what was corn crated in en it still dere right now. When one of de colored people on de plantation would die, dey white folks would be right dere to de funeral. En it de blessed truth, old Dr. Durant had his own carpenters right dere on de plantation to make de corpse boxes en line dem en all dat en dig de graves. Dat was a day, honey, en dat a day gone from here, I say."

"I ain' never been one of dese peck abouts when I was comin on cause I didn' done nothin, but nurse de white folks chillun dat was comin up. Yes, mam, I would go all bout wid de white people. Dey never didn' leave me home. Lord, de chillun what I nurse, dey got seven en eight head of chillun of dey own now. Like I been tellin you, some of dem beg me to come en live wid dem, but my God, I can' struggle wid dem chillun no more after I done wash baby breeches all my best days, so to speak. Yes, my Lord, dem chillun would get dey 10:30 lunch in de mornin en I been get mine, too. Ain' never had to work in de field in all my life. Anybody can tell you dat what know me."

"I has a little boy stayin here wid me en aun' Sallie what was give to me. I don' never think hard of de people for not fussin bout him stayin here cause he helps me so much. No, mam, I know his mother fore she die en he been stayin wid his aun' en she chillun en dey treat him mean. He been raise to himself en he can' stand no other chillun en he come home from school one day en ax me to let him stay here wid me. No, child, he ain' no trouble cause de Lord give me dat child. He can stay out dere in dat yard right by himself en play all day fore he would ever get dirty up."

"Well, I tell you, I don' know hardly what to say bout how de world gwine dese days. I just afraid to say bout it. I know one thing, I used to live better, but President Roosevelt, seem like he tryin to do de right thing. But if I could be de whole judge of de world, I think de best thing would be for de people to be on dey knees en prayin. De people talkin bout fightin all de time en dis here talk bout fightin in de air, dat what got my goat. Might lay down at night sound en wake up in de mornin en find us all in destructiveness. I say, de Lord all what can save dis country."

Source: Liney Henderson, age 70, colored, Marion, S.C. Personal interview by Annie Ruth Davis, Nov., 1937.

Project #1655
W.W. Dixon
Winnsboro, S.C.

JIM HENRY
EX-SLAVE 77 YEARS OLD.

JIM HENRY

Jim Henry lives with his wife, Mary, in a four-room frame house, three miles southeast of Winnsboro, S.C. He owns the house and nine acres of land. He has only one arm, the other having been amputated twenty years ago. He employs a boy to plough, and he and his wife make a living on the property.

"I was born in the Bratton slave quarter, about six miles northeast of Winnsboro. I was born a slave of General John Bratton. He use to tell me I come from 'stinguished stock, dat he bought my father, James, from de Patrick Henry family in Virginia. Dat's de reason my pappy and us took dat name after freedom.

"My mother, Silva, and her mother, was bought from de Rutledge family in Charleston, by General Bratton. My grandfather, on my mother's side, was name Edward Rutledge. No, sir, I don't mean he was a white man; he just ginger-cake color, so my mother say. My pappy say his father was a full-blooded Indian, so, dat makes three bloods in my veins, white folks, Indian folks, and Negro folks. Derefore, us been thrifty like de white man, crafty like de Indians, and hard workin' like de Negroes.

"In slavery time, us lived in one of de nice log houses in de Bratton quarters. Our beds was pole beds, wid wheat straw ticks, and cotton pillows. De Brattons was always sheep raisers, and us had woolen blankets and woolen clothes in de winter. My mother was one of de seamstresses; she make clothes for de slaves. Course, I'm tellin' you what she tell me, mostly. I was too little to 'member much 'bout slavery time. All de little niggers run 'round in deir shirt-tails in summer time; never work any, just hunt for grapes, muscadines, strawberries, chinquapins, hickory nuts, calamus root, slippery elmer (elm) bark, wild cherries, mulberries, and red and black haws, and was as happy as de days was long.

"I just can 'member de Yankees. Don't 'member dat they was so bad. You know they say even de devil ain't as black as he is painted. De Yankees did take off all de mules, cows, hogs, and sheep, and ransack de smoke-house, but they never burnt a thing at our place. Folks wonder at dat. Some say it was 'cause General Bratton was a high 'gree mason.

"While Marse John, who was a Confederate General, was off in de war, us had overseers. They made mother and everybody go to do field. De little chillun was put in charge, in de daytime, wid an old 'mauma', as they called them in them days. Dere was so many, twenty-five or thirty, dat they had to be fed out of doors. At sundown they was 'sembled in a tent, and deir mammies would come and git them and take them home. Dere used to be some scrappin' over de pot liquor dat was brought out in big pans. De little chillun would scrouge around wid deir tin cups and dip into de pan for de bean, pea, or turnip pot liquor. Some funny scraps took place, wid de old mauma tryin' to separate de squallin', pushin', fightin' chillun.

"De overseers was Wade Rawls and a Mr. Timms. After freedom, us moved to Winnsboro, to Dr. Will Bratton's farm near Mt. Zion College. I went to school to Mr. Richardson and Miss Julia Fripp, white teachers employed by northern white people. I got very 'ligious 'bout dat time, but de brand got all rubbed out, when us went to work for Major Woodward. His 'ligion was to play de fiddle, go fox huntin', and ride 'round gittin' Negroes to wear a red shirt and vote de democrat ticket. I went 'long wid him and done my part. They tell a tale on Marse Tom Woodward and I 'spects it's true:

"He was runnin' for some kind of office and was goin', nex' day, up in de dark corner of Fairfield to meet people. Him hear dat a old fellow name Uriah Wright, controlled all de votes at dat box and dat he was a fox hunter to beat de band. He 'quire 'round 'bout Mr. Wright's dogs. He find out dat a dog name 'Ring Smith' was de best 'strike'. Jolly Wright was de name of de cold 'trailer', and Molly Clowney was de fastest dog of de pack. Marse Tom got all dis well in his mind, and nex' day rode up to old Mr. Wright's, 'bout dinner time.

"De old man had just come in from de field. Marse Tom rode up to de gate and say; 'Is dis Dr. Wright?' De old man say: 'Dat's what de people call me 'round here.' Marse Tom say: 'My name is Woodward. I am on my first political legs, and am goin' 'round to see and be seen, if not by everybody, certainly by de most prominent and 'fluential citizens of each section.' Then de old man say: 'Git down. Git down. You are a monstrous likely man. I'll take you in to see Pinky, my wife, and we'll see what she has to say 'bout it.'

"Marse Tom got down off his horse and was a goin' to de house talkin' all de time 'bout crops. Spyin' de dogs lyin' 'round in de shade, him say: 'Dr. Wright, I am a 'culiar man. I love de ladies and admire them much but, if you'll pardon my weakness, a fine hound dog comes nearer perfection, in my eye, than anything our Father in heaven ever made to live on this green earth!'

"'And what do you know 'bout hounds?' Old man Uriah asked, turnin' from de house and followin' Marse Tom to where de dogs was. Marse Tom set down. De whole pack come to where he was, sniffed and smelt him, and wag deir tails in a friendly way. Marse Tom say: 'What is de name of dis dog? Ring Smith, did you say, Doctor? An uncommon fine dog he seems to me. If dere be any truth in signs, he oughta be a good strike.' De old man reply: 'Good strike, did you say? If dere was 5,000 dogs here, I would bet a million dollars dat Ring Smith would open three miles ahead of the best in de bunch. And you might go befo' a trial justice and swear it was a fox, when he opened on de trail.'

"Marse Tom nex' examined de pale black and tan dog, which was Jolly Wright, de coldest trailer. Feelin' his nose and eyein' him all over, he say at last: 'Dr. Wright, I think dis is one of de most remarkable dogs I has ever seen. I would say he is de coldest trailer of your pack?'

"'Coldest, did you say? Why he can smell them after they have been along three or four weeks.' Molly Clowney was nex' picked out by Marse Tom, and come in for his turn. 'Here ought to be de apple of your eyes, Dr. Wright,' say Marse Tom, 'for if I know anything 'bout dogs, this is the swiftest animal dat ever run on four feet. Tell me now, honor bright, can't she out run anything in these parts?'

"'Run, did you say? No. She can't run a bit. But dere ain't a crow nor a turkey buzzard, dat ever crossed de dark corner, dat can hold a candle to her flyin'. I've seen her run under them and outrun deir shadows many times. Dinner is 'bout ready, and I want you to meet Pinky.'

"Marse Tom was took in de house and de old man led him 'round like a fine horse at a show or fair. 'Why, Pinky, he is smart; got more sense than all de candidates put together. He is kin to old preacher Billy Woodward, de smartest man, I heard my daddy say, in Europe, Asia, Africa, North America, or South America.' They say Marse Tom promised befo' he left to pass a bill dat no fence was to be higher than five rails, to suit fox hunters. Then de old man tell Miss Pinky to bring his fiddle, and he played 'De Devil's Dream'. When he finished, Marse Tom grab de fiddle and played: 'Hell Broke Loose In Georgia', wid such power and skill dat de old man, Uriah, hugged Miss Pinky and cut de 'Pigeon Wing' all over de floor. Marse Tom, they say, carry every vote at dat dark corner box.

"I fall in love with Mary Hall. Got her, slick as a fox. Us had ten chillun. Eight is livin'. Robert is at de Winnsboro Cotton Mills. Ed in de same place. Estelle marry a Ford, and has some land near Winnsboro. Maggie marry a Pickett. Her husband took her to Washington. John Wesley is at Greensboro. Florence marry a Barber and lives in Winston Salem, N.C. Charley is in Winnsboro. Corinne marry a McDuff and is in Winnsboro.

"Mighty glad to talk to you, and will come some day and try to bring you a 'possum. You say you would like to have one 'bout Thanksgivin' Day?"

Project 1885-1
FOLKLORE
Spartanburg Dist. 4
June 1, 1937

Edited by:
Elmer Turnage

STORIES FROM EX-SLAVES

ZACK HERNDON

"Yas Sir, my ole Marster had lots o' land, a big plantation down at Lockhart whar I was born, called de Herndon Plantation. Den he live in a big house jes' outside o' Union, called 'Herndon Terrace', and 'sides dat, he was de biggest lawyer dat was in Union.

"Furs' 'membrance was at de age o' three when as yet I couldn't walk none. My mother cooked some gingerbread. She told de chilluns to go down a hill and git her some oak bark. De furs' one back wid de bark 'ud git de furs' gingerbread cake dat was done. My sister sot me down, a sliding down de side o' her laag, atter she had carried me wid her down de side o' de hill. Dem big chaps started to fooling time away. I grab up some bark in my hand and went toddling and a crawling up to de house. My mother seed me a crawling and toddling, and she took de bark out'n my hand and let me pull up to de do'. She cook de gingerbread, and when de other chilluns got back, I was a setting up eating de furs' cake.

"She put gingerbread dough in a round oven dat had

laags on hit. It looked like a skillet, but it never had no handle. It had a lid to go on de top wid a groove to hold live coals. Live coals went under it, too. Mother wanted oak chips and bark, 'cause dey made sech good hot coals and clean ashes.

"Pots biled in de back o' de chimney, a hanging from a pot rack over de blazing fire. It had pot hooks to git it down.

"Bread was cooked in a baker like de ginger cake was. Dey roasted both kinds o' 'taters in de ashes and made corn bread in de ashes and called it ash cake, den.

"Us lived in a one-room log house. Fer de larger families, dey had two rooms wid de fire place in de middle o' de room. Our'n was at de end by de winder. It had white or red oak, or pine shingles to kivver de roof wid. O' course de shingles was hand made, never know'd how to make no other'n.

"All beds was corded. Along side de railings, dar was holes bored to draw de ropes through, as dese was what dey used in dem days instead o' slats. Ropes could be stretched to make de bed lay good. Us never had a chair in de house. My paw made benches fer us to set by de fire on. Marse Zack let de overseer git planks fer us. My paw was called Lyles Herndon. We had a large plank table dat paw made. Never had no mirrows. Went to de spring to see ourselfs on a Sunday morning. Never had no sech things as dressers in dem days. All us had, was a table, benches and beds. And my paw made dem. Had plenty wood fer fire and pine knots fer lights when de fire git low or stop blazing.

"Us had tallow candles. Why ev'ybody know'd how to make taller candles in dem days, dat wudd'n nothing out de ordinary. All you had to do, was to kill a beef and take de taller from his tripe and kidneys. See, it de fat you gits and boil it out. Stew it down jes' as folks does hog lard dese days. De candle moulds was made out'n tin. Fer de wicks, all de wrapping string was saved up, and dar wasn't much wrapping string in dem times. Put de string right down de middle o' de mould and pour de hot taller all around it. De string will be de wick fer de candle. Den de moulds was laid in raal cold water so dat de taller shrink when it harden, and dis 'low de candle to drap easy from de mould and not break up. Why, it's jes' as easy to make taller candles as it is to fall off'n a log.

"Firs' lamp dat I ever seed was a tin lamp. Dat was at Dr. Bates' place in Santuc. Him and his brother, Fair, lived together. It was a little table lamp wid a handle and a flat wick. He had it in his house. I was Dr. Bates' house-boy.

"My son tuck me back to Union last year, 1936, I 'members. Nothing didn't look natual 'cept de jail. Ev'ything else look strange. Didn't see nobody I knowed, not narry living soul. Marse big white house, wid dem kallems (columns) still setting dar; but de front all growed up in pine trees. When I slave time darkey, dat front had flowers and figgers (statues), setting all along de drive from de road to de big house. T'aint like dat now.

"Atter Mr. Herndon died, I was sold at de sale at Lockhart, to Dr. Tom Bates from Santuc. He bought me fer $1800 so as dey allus told me. Marse Zack had a hund'ed slaves on dat plantation. Stout, healthy ones, brung from $1,000 on up to $2,000 a head. When I was a young kid, I heard dat he was offered $800 fer me, but he never tuck it. Dis de onliest time dat I was ever sold. Marse Zack never bred no slaves, but us heard o' sech afar off. He let his darkies marry when dey wanted to. He was a good man and he allus 'lowed de slaves to marry as dey pleased, 'cause he lowed dat God never intent fer no souls to be bred as if dey was cattle, and he never practice no sech.

"I is old and I does not realize who Marse Zack's overseer was, kaise dat been a long while. I was Dr. Bates' house-boy. I allus heard dat Dr. Bates bought my maw fer $1,500, at de same time he bought me. He give $2,000 fer my paw. My brother, Jim, was bought fer $1,800. Adolphus, 'bout fifteen years old, sold fer 'bout $1,400; and my onliest sister, Matilda, was bought fer a maid gal, but I cannot recollect fer what price. She was purty good size gal den. All o' dem is dead now but me, even all my white folks is done gone. I sees a lonely time now, but my daughter treat me kind. I live wid her now.

"Dr. Bates' brother, Fair, was single man dat live in de house wid Dr. Bates fer thirteen years. I lived in slavery fer over twenty-one years. Yas, I's twenty-one when Freedom come; and den Dr. Bates up and marry Mr. Henry Sartor's daughter, Miss Ma'y. Don't know how long she live, but she up and tuck and died; den he pop up and marry her sister, Anne. It was already done Freedom when he marry de furs' time. When he married de second time, Mr. Fair, up and went over to de Keenan place to live. He never did marry, hisself, 'though.

"As house-boy dar, I mind de flies from de table and tote dishes to and fro from de kitchen. Kitchen fer ways off from de house. James Bates, his cook. Sometime I help wash de dishes. Marse never had no big house, kaise he was late marrying. Dar wasn't no company in dem days, neither.

"Rations was give out ev'y week from de smokehouse. Twenty-five or thirty hogs was killed at de time. Lots o' sheep and goats was also killed. All our meat was raised, and us wore wooden-bottom shoes. Raised all de wheat and corn. Hogs, cows, goats and sheep jes' run wild on Tinker and Brushy Fork Creeks. On Sat'day us git one peck meal; three pounds o' meat and one-half gallon black molasses fer a person; and dat's lot mo' dan dey gits in dese days and times. Sunday morning, us git two, or maybe three pounds o' flour. Didn't know nothing 'bout no fat-back in dem times. Had sassafras and sage teas and 'dinty' tea (dinty tea is made from a wild S.C. weed).

"Marse's coachman called Tom 'Cuff', kaise he bought from old Dr. Culp. He driv two black hosses to de carriage. Marse's saddle hoss was kinder reddish. Gen'ally he do his practice on hossback. He good doctor, and carry his medicine in saddle bags. It was leather and fall on each side o' de hoss's side. When you put something in it, you have to keep it balanced. Don't never see no saddle bags; neither does you see no doctors gwine round on no hosses dese days.

"Never seed no ice in dem days 'cep in winter. Summer time, things was kept in de milk-house. Well water was changed ev'y day to keep things cool. Ev'ybody drink milk in de summer, and leave off hot tea, and de white folks only drink coffee fer dere breakfast. T'other times dey also drink milk. It bees better fer your health all de time.

"At de mouth o' Brushy Fork and Tinker Creek whar dey goes together dar is a large pond o' water. Us n'used to fish in dat pond. One day, me and Matilda tuck off a-fishing. I fell in dat pond, and when I riz up, a raft o' brush held my head under dat water and I couldn't git out no ways. 'Tilda sees my dangerment, and she jump in dat deep water and pull me from under dat raff. She couldn't swim but us both got out. Can't think no mo' today."

Source: Zack Herndon, Grenard St., Gaffney, S.C. (col. 93)
Interviewer: Caldwell Sims, Union, S.C. 5/11/37

Project #1655
Stiles M. Scruggs
Columbia S.C.

LAVINIA HEYWARD'S STORY
OF SLAVERY AND RECONSTRUCTION.

LAVINIA HEYWARD

Lavinia Heyward, a Negro woman 67 years old, living at 515 Marion Street, Columbia, S.C., is a daughter of ex-slaves. Her parents were Peter Jones and Rachel Bryant Jones. They married in Columbia, soon after they were freed, in 1865. Lavinia reviews her mother's experiences with a famous South Carolina family, before and after bondage, and takes a glance at Columbia's progress in the past half century.

"Sho' I's been here 67 years, and I's seen a stragglin' town of 10,000 grow from poverty to de present great city and riches. Shucks, I 'spects if you was to set me down at Broad River bridge and tell me to go home, I might git lost tryin' to find my way to where I has lived for many years. Durin' my time I's sho' seen dis city sad and glad, and I's happy to say dat it seem to be feelin' a right smart lak itself now.

"My mammy, and her daddy and mammy, was bought from de Bryants at Beaufort by de Rhett family, when my mammy was a little pickaninny. She not able to tell nothin' 'bout her 'speriences with de Bryants, but she sho' recall a lot of things after she jine de Rhetts. She live with them 'til she was just turnin' twelve years old, then she come to Columbia as a slave of Master John T. Rhett. He move here, as a refugee, in 1862. Master Rhett was not healthy 'nough to go to war but some of his folks go.

"One of Master Rhett's brothers, who was too old to go to war, march 'way to fight Yankees at Honey Hill. De Yankee fleet send an army in boats to cut de Charleston and Savannah Railroad, and de Confederates meet them at Honey Hill, half way 'tween Beaufort and Savannah. In a bloody battle dere de Confederates won. Master Rhett, of Beaufort was wounded dere, and his brother, John, leave Columbia and go dere to see him while he was in bed, battlin' for life.

"My mammy never work in de field at Beaufort, nor after she come to Columbia. She was kep' on duty in de big house and learned to sew and make garments, quilts, and things. She also learn to read, write, and cipher, and she could sing many of de church songs them days. She play with de white chillun dat come to see de Rhetts in Beaufort and in Columbia. She tell me 'bout things in Beaufort, where de Rhetts live then.

"She say de Rhetts has been buckra since de time when Colonel William Rhett go out in his battle ships to chase and kill pirates, in de days when Carolina was ruled by de King of England. She say they own many big plantations in Beaufort County and raise big crops of rice and sea island cotton. She say de sea island cotton was so costly that it was handpicked by slaves and placed in hundred pounds sacks. Then it was shipped to France and de growers reap a rich harvest.

"Mammy tell us chillun dat de Rhetts sho' was de 'big folks' of South Carolina, and I reckons dat's so, 'cause de books, swords, guns, windlasses and things lak dat, in a room at de John T. Rhett home, show what they has been doin' for several hundred years.

"Oh yes, you wants to know where 'bouts John T. Rhett live in Columbia? He live at de house now number 1420 Washington Street, right 'cross de street from where de parsonage of the Washington Street Methodist Church now stands. I go dere with Mammy, often, and play 'round de yard. Mammy always work dere as long as she able to serve a-tall. She take sick and die in 1883.

"Master John T. Rhett was mayor of de city three times, in 1882, 1884 and in 1886. I knows well, 'cause he see to it dat us chillun go to school, 'long 'bout then, and not a one of us has been unable to read, write, and cipher since. He see dat we gits chances to become useful citizens, and his very name is sweet to me since he died.

"You ask if I knows R. Goodwin Rhett of Charleston? I sho' does; I has talked with him and he ask me many questions. He was born in Columbia but move to Charleston many years ago and, lak the buckra dat he is, he climb to de top as de mayor of Charleston, big banker, and president of de Chamber of Commerce of de United States. So you see, my mammy was lucky in livin' with such a fine family.

"You asks if my man (husband) has come down from de Heyward family of de Combahee River slaves? No. He come from de North and he say dere was Heywards up dere, both white and black. He got that name in de North. He has been a carpenter, hired by de month, at de State

Hospital for many years, and we bought dis two-story home by de sweat of our brow. We lives, and has always lived, as my mammy tell us to. And we git 'long pretty well by trustin' in God and doin' our best."

Project #-1655
Mrs. Chlotilde R. Martin
Beaufort County

Approx. 530 Words
FOLKLORE

Stories from Ex-slaves
Lucretia Heyward
Ex-slave Age - 96

LUCRETIA HEYWARD

W'en gun fust shoot on Hilton Head Islandt, I been 22 year old. Muh Pa name Tony MacKnight and he b'long to Mr. Stephen Elliott. My Ma name Venus MacKnight and she b'long to Mr. Joe Eddings, who had uh plantation on Parri (Parris) Islandt. De overseer been Edward Blunt. He been poor white trash, but he wuk haa'd and save he money and buy slave. He buy my Ma and bring she to Beaufort to wuk in he house by de Baptist chu'ch. I been born den. I hab seven brudder name Jacob, Tony, Robert, Moses—I can't 'member de odders, it been so long ago. I hab one sister Eliza—she die de odder day.

W'en I been little gal, I wuk in de house. Wuk all day. I polish knife and fork, mek bed, sweep floor, nebber hab time for play game. W'en I git bigger, dey send me to school to Miss Crocker to learn to be seamstruss.

W'en I small, I sleep on floor in Miss Blunt room. I eat food left ober from table. Dey nebber learn me to read and write. I ain't hab time for sech t'ing. I go to chu'ch in white Baptis' chu'ch. Nigger hab for sit up stair, white folks sit down stair. If nigger git sick, dey send for doctor to 'tend um. Mr. Blunt nebber lick me, but Miss Blunt cut my back w'en I don't do to suit her. Nigger git back cut w'en dey don't do wuk or w'en dey fight. Dey hab uh jail in town, run by Mr. McGraw. If nigger be too bad, run street and t'ing, he git in jail and Mr. McGraw lick um. I been lock in jail one time. Dey hang me up by wrist and beat me twenty-five lick wid uh cowhide. I forgit w'at I don't to git dat.

W'en Yankee been come de Blunts leab Beaufort, and I walk out house and go back to Parri Islandt. De Yankee tell we to go en Buckra corn house and git w'at we want for eat. Den I come back to Beaufort and go to wuk in cotton house (gin.) De Yankee pay we for wuk and I tek my money and buy twenty acre ob land on Parri Islandt. I ain't had dat land now 'cause de Government tek em for he self and mek me move. (This was when the Government bought Parris Island for a naval station.)

I been hab two husband. De fust name Sephus Brown. How I 'member w'en he die, it been de year ob de ninety-tree storm. My odder husband been Cupid Heyward—he daid (dead) too.

I hear tell ob de Ku Klux, but I nebber shum (see them). I don't know nuting 'bout no night rider.

See um sell slabe? I see um. Dey put um on banjo table and sell um just lak chicken. Nigger ain't no more den chicken and animal, enty? (isn't it so?)

Abraham Lincoln? Sho' I 'members him. He de one

w'at gib us freedom, enty? He come to Beaufort. He come 'fo de war. He sho been one fine man. He come to Beaufort on uh ship and go all 'round here, but I nebber shum.

Jefferson Davis? No I nebber hear ob him. Booker T. Washington. I 'members him. I hear him mek speech in Beaufort. It been uh beautiful speech. Dat been one smaa't colored man.

W'at I t'ink 'bout slabery? Huh—nigger git back cut in slabery time, enty?

Does I hate Mr. Blunt? No, I ain't hate um. He poor white trash but he daid now. He hab he self to look out for, enty? He wuk, he sabe he money for buy slabe and land. He git some slabe, but he nebber git any land—de war cum.

United States. Work Projects Administration

Slave Narratives

Project #-1655
Mrs. Genevieve W. Chandler
Murrells Inlet, S.C.
Georgetown County

FOLKLORE

MARIAH HEYWOOD

Aunt Mariah Heywood, born in 1855, was 'Allston labor' on Waccamaw Neck. Given as a bridal present to 'Miss Susan Alston by her father, Mr. Duncan Alston of Midway Plantation Waccamaw, Aunt Mariah has for the last fifty years lived much in the past when 'I wuz raise on the cream of the earth' and her head is just a little higher and her backbone just a little stiffer than that of the average colored person because of pride—family pride—in her people—her white people. And as one can readily see from her testimony, her chief cause for her pardonable snobbery seems to be that her Massa was the last man to surrender and "swear gainst his swear."

Her sons, one of whom is a preacher in the Methodist Conference and 'one a zorter—a locust' and her youngest son John (who got all the credrick) have built her a comfortable house (painted a bilious yaller) which she keeps clean and sweet with flowers in the front yard—two treasured plants having been sent by her brother (born after mancipations) clean from Pittsburgh.

The fact that she was raised by aristocrats shows plainly in her dealing with both races and she is a leader in church activities and her opinion valued when a vote is taken about school matters.

Being the oldest 'communion steward' she is affectionately spoken of as 'THE MOTHER OF HEAVEN'S GATE'—the Methodist church founded in Murrells Inlet community by colored leaders shortly after Mancipation.

"Aunt Mariah, you home?"

"Missus, what you brought me?"

"— — — — — —

"I too thank you."

(Soon she began to reminisce)

"You could hear 'em over there slamming and banging. The Yankee tear up the Dr. Flagg house but they didn't come Sunnyside. Bright day too! Old man Thomas Stuart lead 'em to Hermitage. Had team they take from Mr. Betts and team they take from Dr. Arthur to Woodland. Free everywhere else and we wasn't free Sunnyside till June third or second. Sunday we got our freedom. Bright day too. Our colored people fare just like the white; wearing, eating, drinking. I wuz raise on the cream of earth.

"They wuz glad. Sign a contract for your boss you would work the same and get pay the end of the year-and tend you when you sick all the same." (The same medical attention to be given that was given before 'Freedom') "Big guns shooting! House jar to Sunnyside and one day water shake out the glass! Miss Susan take her spyglass and stand behind one them big posses (posts) and spy them big boats shooting. And boss say, 'Don't get in front of them posses-they might shoot you!'

"Yankee come to Mrs. Belin and Parson Betts. And they tell Mrs. Belin, they want her to know no more slave holding and she thank 'em and she say, HE people wuz always free! Grandma Harriet, (Harriet Mortor wuz her title but that time they always gone by they Master title). Joe Heywood wuz Joe Belin—he was Parson Belin man—he take the Heywood title after mancipation. Poinsette (Uncle Fred) ALWAYS carry that title. That day, all the right hand servant always take they Massa title. When the big gun shooting, old people in the yard, 'Tank God! Massa, HE COMING!' (Referring to 'Freedom') 'HE COMING!' (Guns gone just like thunders roll now!) Chillun say, "What coming? What coming? What coming, Grandma?"

'You all will know! You all will know!'

"Massa live 'Wee ha kum' for years. We are fifty-five (55) chillun. Mary Rutledge Allston and I one year chillun." (She and Mary R. Allston born same year.) "My missus have four chillun—Mary Rutledge, Susan Bethune, Marsa Pink and Marse Fanuel. (Benjamine Nathaniel!)

"Four years of the war been hold prayer-meeting." (Praying for 'freedom'). Lock me up in house. Me, I been PREsent to Miss Minna—'Miss Mary! We, us lock up! My brother and I listen! (Two brother mancipation chillun. Smart Robert Brockington and Harrison Franklin Brockington in Pittsburgh. I nuss (nurse) him—jess like you hold that book.) Old people used to go to Richmond

Hill, Laurel Hill and Wachesaw have these little prayer-meeting. All bout in people house. Hold the four year of the war. Great many time the chicken crow for day. Hear the key. We say 'Yeddy!' Change clothes. Gone on in the house. Get that eight, seven o'clock breakfast.'

"Parson Glennie (Rector All Saints, Waverly lived at Rectory there and did wonderful work teaching and preaching to slaves as well as whites—preaching at beautiful St. Mary's chapel, built by Plowden Weston at Hagley for the slaves of materials from England—baptismal font from this chapel now in Camden Episcopal church and stained glass also removed before chapel burned some few years ago. At this period—prior to mancipation Waccamaw slaves were usually educated in the faith of their masters—the Episcopal.) Parson Glennie come once a month to Sunnyside. Parson Glennie read, sing, pray. Tell us obey Miss Minna. (I wuz little highest.) Two of us 55 chillun! We'd fight. She knock me. I knock back! Wouldn't take a knock! She say, 'I tell Parson Glennie! Lord won't bless you! You bad.' I say, 'You knock me, I knock you!'

"Have a play-house. Charlie buy from Mott. Used to summer it at Magnolia. Row from Bull Creek once a month to Chapel. (10 miles or more) Put them All Saints eleven o'clock service. Four best men his rowsmen. Fuss (first) year war we tuh Bull Creek. Nobody go (to All Saints) but Missus and Massa and the four rowsmen.

"Flat going from Midway to Cheraw. Best rice on flat. (Couldn't grind corn) Kill chicken. Gone to protect from Yankees—to hide! When they come (to Cheraw). Sherman coming from MONDAY till SATDY! Come on RAIL! Said 'twas a shocking sight! When Sherman army enter Cheraw, town full of sojers. Take way from white people and give horses colored people! Didn't kill none the horses. (On Sunnyside on Waccamaw) Cheraw Yankee kill horses! (Indeed—YES! It is history in Marlboro, near Cheraw they were killed and thrown in the wells to pollute the water.)"

"Mr. Charley horse, couldn't nobody ride but him! Father-in-law (Mr. Duncan to Midway) had a pair of grey—BUCK and SMILER. Driver, Tom Carr. Come in carriage every month to Sunnyside. Get the family. Go and spend ten days—Midway! Family wuz MYSELF, MISS MINNA, and the three and the Massa and Miss Susan. Mary Huger one my Missus sister. One marry a Huger to Charleston.

"Major Charles say he'd die in Sunnyside yard fore he'd go there (Georgetown) and take off his hat and 'swear gainst my swear.' He'd die in Sunnyside yard. My Massa, Major Charles Alston, was the last one to gone to Georgetown and gone under that flag! He was Charles Jr., but after Confederick war he was Major Charles! Major Charles the last man off Waccamaw gone under the flag! At Georgetown. Went down in row-boat. My fadder gone and tell old man Tom Nesbitt to have his boat and four of his best mens. Got to go off a piece! Pa gone. Have boat ready. Ma got up. Cook a traveling lunch for 'em. Fore day! Blue uniform. Yellow streak down side—just like this streak in my dress. Yellow bar!" (Most of 'em had to rob dead yankees or go naked) "LAST GENTLEMAN GONE UNDER THE FLAG!

"Walking up and down the piazza! Say, Can I go to town and swear gainst my slave?" Can I? Up and down!

"I hear bout them slave try to run way. Aunt Tella Kinloch eye shot out. Marsh (baby) cry! Mother say take her apron and stuff the child mouth. Blockade (patrollers) wuz hiding. Shot in range of that sound. Row! Row! Row! Put everything in jail! All in jail! Mr. McCuskey tell us! He wuz one of the men help lynch. I got married 1873. They wuz talking bout the time (war) "Mr. McCuskey told us Nemo Ralston was one. Say he never see a fatter man. Fat in there in shield! Like a fattening hog! (They running way from Oregon—Dr. McGill place). Say they put four horses to him—one to every limb. Stretch 'em. And cut horses and each horse carry a piece! Mr. McCuskey was one help lynch Nemo.

"Uncle William Heywood didn't birth till after mancipation. Not a thing to do with slavery time! But I know when the big gun shooting to free me! Yankee come and free Waccamaw! No slave hold. Whole neck free but us! Last people free on 'Neck.' MY MAJOR last one to went under flag to Georgetown! Old man Moses Gibson and Peter Brockington build Sunnyside kitchen.

"I wuz birth November 5th, 1855. Mr. Buck say, 'Aunt Mariah, know your birth?'

"'Yes, sir!'

"'Aunt Mariah, you too old to work! You born 1800, go on home raise your chicken!'"

Aunt Mariah Heywood
Age—82
Murrells Inlet, S.C.

Project 1885-1
FOLK LORE
Spartanburg, S.C.
May 10, 1937

Edited by:
Elmer Turnage

SLAVE STORIES

JERRY HILL

Living with his married daughter is an old negro slave by the name of Jerry Hill. He was born Jan. 12, 1852. He and his mother were owned by Jim Fernandes who had a plantation between Union and Jonesville, S.C. His father was a slave owned by another white man on an adjoining plantation. "Uncle" Jerry was nine years old when the war began, and thirteen when he was set free. He was born near Rocky Creek which ran into Fairforest Creek. He was always treated kindly by his master. He was taught to plow and work on the farm, which he did regularly; though he always took his time and would not let anybody hurry him. He said that he had always taken his time to do his farm work, so got along fine with all for whom he worked. He says that he always had plenty to eat; yet most of the "niggers" had to eat Ash-bread. This is corn-bread which is cooked in hot ashes raked from the fireplace. Once a week he was given biscuits, though this was a luxury to colored folks. He said, that when a slave had to have a whipping, he was taken to a whipping post in Jonesville. A bull-whip was used for the punishment and it brought the blood from the bare back of the man or woman being whipped. One day a grown slave was given 150 lashes with the bull-whip, for teaching the young boys to gamble. He saw this punishment administered. He had climbed a tree where he could get a better view. He said that several slaves were being whipped that day for various things, and there were several men standing around watching the whipping. He said that he was laughing at the victim, when some by-stander looked up and saw him; "that boy needs 150 lashes, too," he said. "He is laughing at the punishment being given." So his master told the by-stander to get the boy and give him the lashing if he thought he needed it. When he was led up to the whipping post, some man there shook his head at the by-stander; so the boy did not get whipped. Jerry says that the sister of Jim Fernandas used to carry a bull-whip around her neck when she walked out on the farm, and would apply it herself to any slave she thought needed it.

"When the Yankee soldiers came," he said, "my master had to hide out for awhile, as he had gotten into some trouble with them at Union. They would search the house occasionaly and then go into the woods looking for him. One day the soldiers caught him down on the branch and killed him. As the Yankee soldiers would come to the plantation, they would leave their worn-out horses and take our good ones. They also stole meat, hams, sugar etc.; but they were pretty quiet most of the time. One of our neighbors caught a Yankee stealing his horse and killed him right there. His name was Bill Isom. All his family is now dead. The soldiers would slip around and steal a good horse and ride it off. We would never see that horse again. After we were told by my master that we were now free and could go to work whereever we chose, my mother hired me out to a man and I stayed with him two years. It was pretty hard to make a living after we were free, but I worked hard and always got on."

Source: Jerry Hill, 265 Highland St., Spartanburg, S.C. Interviewed
by: F.S. DuPre, Spartanburg Office, Dist. 4.

United States. Work Projects Administration

Project #-1655
Martha S. Pinckney
Charleston, S.C.

FOLKLORE

JANE HOLLINS
AGE 97

JANE HOLLINS

Jane was found in the sunshine on her piazza, busily occupied, as she always would be. With her full cotton skirt she brushed off the hard-wood bench, and asked the writer to have a seat; this being declined, she said,

"Then I'll sit, because I'm old and get tired.

"Now what you want with old Jane? From old Mausa time you can get my age—you can 'pute it up. (compute) I was 95 June before this last June gone. I got a son 70 what lives in the country—he pay my rent. I dunno how many children I had; my son July Ladson lives here with me—he gone out now. One son is gone off somewhere in the world; he's married and has a family—I dunno where he is—somewhere in the world!"—spreading, out her arms.

"I come from Eutawville and Belvidere and Belmont. My Master?—Charles Sinkler, Belvidere Plantation, (a few miles from Eutawville) Mausa went to Eutaw for

Miss—I remember all two place, Belvidere and Eutaw. We live at Belvidere. My master house been beautiful—'e dey yet! (in her deep feeling and excitement she lapsed into Gullah). That was the plantation where we lived—and, the beautiful steps went up at the back to the 'pantry and to the side was the smoke house', she jumped up and illustrated—'the smoke come up from here, and the meat was hangin' all here', she showed vital interest in everything she told, and was absorbed in her subject, as when we relate experiences which we have loved.

"You know what 'Daily Gift'?—I was Daily Gift—Mausa give me to Miss Margaret, his daughter, when she was married to Mr. Gaillard—I give to Miss Margaret—I never was sold." She repeated twice, and was very proud of it that she was a "Free Gift". "I never was sold, and my Mama never was sold." (Faithful servants remained for generations in one family, inherited and willed like other valued property)

"What I do?—I milk cows", and she illustrated. "I do outside work wid de hoe—plant corn, potato, peas, rice!" She beamed with pride and pleasure as she told of each thing she could do—"Help fix the hogs, you know, make lard and cracklings to put in bread. When dinner time they blow the big conk and everybody come for dinner. I not the cook. The cook, Delia, stout round, (illustrated) she do cook! We jus' make out now with dese vittles.

"We went to church all de time—an' I sing an' shout in de Heavenly land! De church been on de plantation. Mausa had a white minister for us. His name Mr. Quinbey. I believe in God. Heaven a restin' place—there we is all one spirit—the spirit go about jus' how we go about here."

"Do they come back? Did you ever see one?" she was asked.

"I hear 'bout dat," she frowned, "but I never see um. My mama, Eve, died after freedom. My mama gone—she never come back—my children never come back to me any time. I dont know how many of my children dead. My daughters, dey lookin' to themselves."

"I come to Charleston long after Freedom. I remember all two place—Belvidere and Eutawville. Belmont I cant forget—de name Gaillard I cant forget, cause I was 'Free Gift.' Dese time aint like de times way back dere."

"I been a mid-wife here 60 years. My name writ right down dere and you can find it. No longer than this mornin' I burn up some papers. I aint have any remembrance any more." Here she went in to the house and got some sheets of paper.—"I want to be truthful to you, dese was my nursery book."

"I'm too old to sing.—I did know spirituals but cant remember them—I tell you dese things, then they go out of my remembering."

"My sister been seamstress in de house—her name Rachel—I do de pointing I can work at anything—after supper, before dark come, do cutting out for next days work."

"I cut out a suit for my master," she said proudly—"pants, and a waistcoat—you know?" Then she remembered suddenly that she could spin—card the cotton and spin it into yarn—"'I glad I can remember things I do in those days—.'"

Her farewell benediction was: "I trust de Lord will carry you whereever you want to go!"

Source: Jane Hollins, age 97, the Lane at 50 Ashe St, Charleston, S.C.

Project #1655
W. W. Dixon
Winnsboro, S.C.

CORNELIUS HOLMES
EX-SLAVE 82 YEARS OLD.

CORNELIUS HOLMES

Cornelius Holmes lives with his wife, Nancy, in a two-room annex to the house that his son, David, occupies. It is on the old Harden place, nine miles northwest of Winnsboro, S.C. The land and the house belong to Mr. John Means Harden, a resident of Winnsboro. Cornelius is intelligent, courteous in manner, tidy in appearance, and polite. His occupation is that of basket-making, in which he is an adept. He picks up a little money by repairing chairs and putting split-bottoms in them.

"I was born in de town of Edgefield, South Carolina, November 29th, 1855, 'cordin' to de Bible, and was a slave of Marse Preston Brooks. Dat name seem to make you set up and take notice of me.

"How come I a slave of Marse Preston? Well, it was dis way. My grands b'long to de Means family of Fairfield County, 'round old Buckhead section. My grandpap, Wash, tell me Marse Preston come dere visitin' de Harpers, 'nother buckra family dat live further toward de Broad River side of de county. When he git up dere, it come over his 'membrance dat de Meanses was some punkins too, as well as him and de Harpers. Maybe he done heard 'bout Miss Martha, how her could ride a horse and dance a cotillion in Columbia, when Marse John Hugh was de governor. Well, de part goes, he comes over dere but didn't do lak they does now, bust right in and 'clare his 'fections to de gal. Him fust, solemn lak, ask to see de marster and ask him if he object to him pursuing Miss Martha, in de light of becomin' his son-in-law? Then, when dat was settled, Marse Preston and Miss Martha gallop and race all 'round de country but de hosses was always neck and neck. Dat fall, dat race ended in a tie. Dat what Grandpap Wash tell me.

"After they marry, my mother, Scylla, was give to Miss Martha and 'company her to Edgefield. Dere she marry de carriage driver, Hillard, who was my pappy. I was born in a room 'joinin' de kitchen and a part of de big kitchen. De plantation was out in de country. I never was dere, so I can't tell you nothin' 'bout dat. De fact is, I was just a small boy and most I know, comes from mother and grandpap. They 'low Marse Preston was in Washington most of de time. One day he marched right in de Senate, wid his gold head cane, and beat a Senator 'til him fainted, 'bout sumpin' dat Senator say 'bout him old kinsman, Senator Butler. Dat turn de world up side down. Talk 'bout 'peachin' Marse Preston. Marse Preston resign and come home. De town of Edgefield, de county of Edgefield, de state of South Carolina, and Miss Martha, rise to vindicate Marse Preston and 'lect him back to Washington.

"Marse Preston go back and stay dere 'til he die, in 1859. His body was brought back to Edgefield. De nex' year de war come on. I's too young to 'member much 'bout it but my pappy die while it was goin' on. Him have three chillun by mother: Me, Audie, and Nancy. They is dead now but I 'members them crawlin' 'round on de plank floor in de winter time and in de sand in de summer time.

"I never worked in slavery time. Us eat from de dairy and de kitchen, just what mistress and her chillun eat. One thing I lak then was 'matoes. They wasn't big 'matoes lak they is now. They was 'bout de size of marbles. Us cooked them wid sugar and they was mighty good dat way.

"My mistress had chillun by Marse Preston. Sho' I recollect them. Dere was Preston; de last I hear of him, him livin' in Tennessee. Then dere was Miss Mary; her marry Mr. George Addison of Edgefield. Miss Carrie; her marry Marse Capers Byrd. De youngest, Miss Martha, marry Col. McBee of Greenville, S.C.

"Does I 'members 'bout de Yankees? Not much. I 'members more 'bout Wheeler's men. They come and take nearly everything, wid de excuse dat de Yankees was not far behind and when they come, they would take all, so they just as well take most of what was in sight.

"When freedom come, my pappy was dead. Mother brought me back to Fairfield County and give me to my grandpap, Washington Holmes. Us live on 'Possum Branch; now own by Mr. Jim Young. I stay dere 'til I 'come twenty-one. Then I marry Maggie Gladden, 'cause I love her. Us had four chillun, in de twenty years her live. Henry is in Philadephia. David, de oldest, is fifty years old, livin' out in de county from Winnsboro. Lula died, unmarried. Carrie lives here, in Winnsboro; her husband is Arthur Rosboro, dat you white folks all know so well. When Maggie die, I marry Nancy Holmes, a widow. Us have had no chillun.

"Now you is finished wid me and you wants me to relax, you say, and talk to you freely 'bout de past and slavery, de present and social conditions, and de risin' generation and de future? Well, dat is a heap of territory. Now let's think. You see I got a heap a white blood in me, and a heap of de Negro too. Slavery did de white race a whole lot a good but it wasn't lastin' good. It did de Negro good, dat will be lastin' good forever. De Negro women protected de pure white woman from enticement and seduction of de white man in slavery time. My grandpap say he never heard of a bad white woman befo' freedom. I leave it wid you if dere's any dese times? Dat was worth more to de South, my grandpap say, dis santification of de white women, than all de cotton and corn dat de Negroes ever makes, in all de years of slavery times.

"Now it was de finest thing could have happen for de Negro, to have been snatched out of Africa and brought here in touch wid civilization and Christianity. It will work out untold benefit to de race. 'Bout social conditions? De Bible say, 'De poor you will have wid you always.' Tho' de slave question am settled, de race question will be wid us always, 'til Jesus come de second time. It's in our politics, in our justice courts, on our highways, on our side walks, in our manners, in our 'ligion, and in our thoughts, all de day and every day.

"De good Marster pity both sides. In de end, will it be settle by hate or by de policy of, love your neighbor, as you do yourself? Who knows? Dere's not much promise at de 'mediate moment of de risin' generation, of either side, and I means no disrespect to you. My grandpap say no race can rise higher than its women. De future of de Negro race, depends on its mothers. I leave you to answer de last half of de question."

United States. Work Projects Administration

Slave Narratives

Project #-1655
Mrs. Genevieve W. Chandler
Murrells Inlet, S.C.
Georgetown County

FOLKLORE

UNCLE BEN HORRY

Uncle Ben lives in his own cabin with his second wife, Stella. Formerly almost inaccessible, the new Coastal Highway has put Uncle Ben and Aunt Stella in the world. The rural electricity program has current right at their door. Aunt Stella was asked 'Why don't you have lights, Aunt Stella?' and she replied, 'White folks run me if I do that!' So you see the old couple still live with many old and odd beliefs one being that the white man only is entitled to the good things—the better things. Like most old ex-slaves in South Carolina low country, they love and revere the names and memories of their old masters.

"Right now, I oldest one from Longwood to Prospect—see dere? (Pointing to forest wall—great pines and live-oaks in front of the cabin)—Look! I know when he cleared and plant! Josh Ward have potato there. I have manure and plant tater. I been here, daughter!" (He pronounces it 'Dater' with a short 'a')

(Aside: "Stella, mind now! Don't quarrel me to-night! What you do?"

Aunt Stella: The second wife—some years his junior—probably 65—"I do nuff!")

"Got to go up there and cook supper to the Schoolfield house." (This was Uncle Ben's announcement as he crawled into the car with a bucket in which were his shoes. He was walking down the Coastal Highway and not staying where he belonged—on the shoulder!) "Got to cook crab and ister (oyster). Ain't got much to cook. They don't eat much. Got a gal there to fry fish. They give me recommend for cook. Been get the sea foods for 'em for five year. Iron oven the way we raise." (Aside to his wife) "Stella, if that man come there, see that sack there? Tell that man I put fire there. Gie 'em fork and knife. Tell 'em eat all he want!" (Uncle Ben arranges oyster roasts.)

"That man to Schoolfield house want me to stay and sleep wid 'em. All women gone. Tell me keep the man and lock up the house when he gone. I tell 'em too much o' tief!"

Lillie: "Aunt Stella, ain't you fraid when Uncle Ben stay out all night?"

Uncle Ben: "Stella keep pot o' water boil and tief come she trow 'em!"

Visitor: "Uncle Ben tell Lillie bout your father and the whiskey jug."

Uncle Ben: "You see, to Brookgreen we nuster plant rice and my fadder had the barn key. He kinder boss man. He nuster (used to) take me and go out woods night time." (Aside to mother of child at pump—"Take care dat child!")

"Fadder take me out woods night time (What you say, Primus?) and I hold storch (torch) for him see for trash (thrash) out rice what he take out the barn. Rice been money dem time you know. And he take he rice and gone on down to town for get he liquor. And he come from town wid whiskey. Boss find it out. Five or six chillun and always give us rations. Broke that jug and when they call his name (put rations in pile you know—pile for every one been in fambly) when they call my fadder name but a piece o' broken jug there is discourage him from whiskey—. He come from town and been drop the jug and it break up. And Boss know. Far as I can remember he keep give 'em that broken jug bout a year. You see he sponsible for key. Seem like I member right where we go beat that rice. Pine tree saw off and chip out make as good a mortar as that one I got. Dan'l, Summer, Define! Define the oldest brother my fadder have. Young Missus Bess, Florence, Georgia, Alice. Those boys the musicianer—go round play for the girl."

Aunt Stella: Interrupting, "You orter be carry money with you. Get the meat. I ain't going no whey (where)."

Lillie: To Primus who has walked up. "Handful back yet?" (Handful his wife's basket name.)

Primus: "No. This man bacco barn burn up."

Lillie: "What?"

Primus: "Mr. Len barn. Must'er been asleep!"

Lillie: "Rich most cure all his'n. Taint mine! Rich tease me. He say, 'MY bacco; YOUR kitchen!'"

Lillie: "What you all think bout that tale the Elder tell Sunday bout his Great Uncle and the snakes!"

Stella: (To Uncle Ben) "What you tink bout it? You tink a man truss to go in cypress hollow wid rattle-snake?"

Uncle Ben: "Let me see how was it!" (Deep thought as he rubbed his face in his palm; smile as recollection came) "On Rutledge Plantation a man wouldn't take no beating. Found a large hollow cypress tree been rotten out long years. Gone in. Lie down sleep. Fore day wake up! Feel something crawl over him. Nother one crow like game chicken!" (Negroes all say rattlers crow!) "Smell him. Crawl over him. Crawl out. Get out."

Stella: "Revents had it wuz a man in a cypress tree and seven—how much wuz it? Twelve? These twelve monster snake crawl over him. If you move, he strike."

Uncle Ben: "Right there where Dr. Ward stay had a big old stable—see these two hole in my jaw. Had a stable high as that tree. Big Jersey bull gone in there eating that straw like we thrashing. Big rattle-snake pop 'um. Fell dead."

"How does we mark shoat? Under-bit; upper-bit. Swallow fork in the right year! And a square crop in the left!

"How much been task? A quarter (acre) if you mashing ground. Ten compass digging ground. Cutting rice one half acre a day." (awful job.)

Stella: "Plow; harrow 'em."

Ben: "Ain't you mash 'em?"

Stella: "Mash a bed a day three task deep."

Ben: "Mashing raw ground half acre—some quarter. Mash 'em—take hoe full up them hole, level dem, chop dem big sod!"

Stella: (age 65) "You got a mis-sheen (machine). Ox pull dat mis-sheen!"

Ben: "Dat mis-sheen come in YOU day, darling! My day I trenching hoe trench dat! I done dat, Stella. You come on sow in trench lak (like) dey sow turnip. YOU day got mis-sheen! Ox pull 'em. Great I AM! Missus, fifteen to old islant (island), twenty silver islant, (I been Silver Islant. Cross old islant go Silver islant.) Josh Ward one some four or five hundred acre. Something been here, darling! Something been here! Left Brookgreen go Watsaw; left Watsaw gone Longwood. Plant ALL DEM plantation. I work there. Cut rice there. Cutting rice task been half acre a day.

"Squirrel creek? Cedar tree and cypress hang low. Squirrel love dem ball. Tree work up wid dem. Good place for go shoot squirrel. Give 'em name Squirrel Creek.

"Bury live? I did hear some talk o' that. I didn't know whether they bury 'em to scay 'em (scare 'em) or what. I DID hear tell bout it. I most know that man name. Some these white people that day something! They either manage you or kill you."

Lillie: (To Primus who was a listener to Uncle Ben standing propped by a post of the porch where Uncle Ben, Aunt Stella, and the white visitor sat)

"Prime! Why you keep that church door lock Sunday and not let the Missus out?"

Primus: (Grinning—and he hadn't grinned Sunday but steadfastly shook his head when, after a three hour service, guests thought it time to go) "Second man next to me, Asham, Secretary, tell me keep door shet through sacrament.

Ben: (Who is quite deaf—ignoring interruption—when asked about Oregon Plantation which was owned by a family who, from all accounts, had a cruel overseer.)

"I didn't have to much to do to Oregon in them dark days. If I go from Brookgreen, I go Cap'n Josh git my mittment. Anybody bother me I say, 'I not a run-way nigger! I got mittment!'

"Very FUSS girl—FUSS one I go with name wuz Teena. How many girl? Great God! I tell you! FUSS one Teena; next Candis. Candis best looking but Teena duh largest! Go there every Sunday after school. (Oatland Plantation—blong to Marse Benjamine Allston.) Stay till sunset. Got to have paper. Got to carry you paper. Dem patroller put you cross a log! Beat you to death. I see them beat Ben Sharp. Beat 'em till Ben kin hardly git cross fence. Jump over fence give 'em last chop! Patroll jess like road men now! (Stella! That man ain't coming! I got to go! Got to cook my supper. Cook dem crab—) Blood! Christ! Yes, man. Listen me. Lemme tell you what I see wid my eye now! (here he pried both eyes wide with his ten fingers) If I much of age reckon they have to kill me! I see gash SO LONG (measuring on fore-finger) in my Mama—my own Mama! (aside to Lillie) I shame fore Miss Jinny! If one them driver want you (want big frame gal like you Lillie!) they give you task you CAN'T DO. You getting this beating not for you task—for you flesh!"

Lillie: "That why nation get mix up so!" (Races)

Ben: "Susan wuz a house woman, to buckra woman like a you to Miss Jin. (Susan worked in the house—no field hand—like Lillie works for Miss Jin) To my knowing she had three white chillun. Not WANT 'em. HAB 'em. Boy (you know 'em Lill) near bout clean as them boy of Missus! Tief chillun show up so! Woman over-power! My mother nuss (nurse.) Get up so high—natural nuss for white people.

"Place they call duh 'Bull Pen.' In 'Bull Pen' thing they call 'PONY'. Got to go on there—on the 'PONY.'

Lillie: "RIDE you on it, Uncle Ben?"

Ben: "Ain't going ride you on 'PONY'; going RIDE YOU! I stay there look wid DESE HERE (eyes)! Want you to know one thing—MY OWN DADDY DERE couldn't move! Couldn't venture dat ober-sheer! (Colored overseer) Everybody can't go to boss folks! (Meaning only house servants could contact Missus and Massa). Some kin talk it to Miss Bess. Everybody don't see Miss Bess. Kin see the blood of dat ober-sheer fuss year atter Freedom; and he blood there today! Atter Freedom mens come from French Broad and you know the colored people—we go there whey (where) they music. Agrippa—daddy name Parrish—Redmond one he child outside. (Outside chillun are those not born to a man's legal wife) He say, to gal, 'Go that barn!' YOU GO. You could yeddy him SLAP cross dat creek! When fowl crow (daylight) and you yeddy him SQUALL, you best git to flat! I stand dere and my Daddy HAVE to stand dere and see! Josh Ward from French Broad—hundred mile away. (Boss Massa 'summering it' in mountains) and negro over seer—just fresh out of Africa TURNED LOOSE. White obersheer a little different for one reason! White obersheer want to hold his job. (On Waccamaw—and same true of all south as all know—white overseers worst kind of 'White trash'—respected less by negroes than by whites) Nigger obersheer don't care too much. He know he going stay on plantation anyhow.

"Now, dater, I tell you bout the loom and weaving next time!"

And we left Uncle Ben Horry—age 87
Murrells Inlet, S.C.
August 1937.

to go on 'to the Schoolfield house and cook supper for a house-party. This week he stepped up to Con-o-way. Says he had to walk it twice a week—formed the habit when he was on old river Steamer Burroughs and had to walk up to Conway Monday and back home Saturday. About thirty miles (or more from his place) to Conway. At 87 he still takes this little exercise almost weekly. Having such a struggle holding on to his land. All the lawyers saying 'sign here' and trying to rob him! Poor Uncle Ben needs desperately a Massa to help him out with his land. Not many Uncle Ben's left to be robbed—

(told that the cruel negro overseer was shot down after Freedom—blood still on ground (according to Uncle Ben) because he led Yankees to where silver, etc., was buried. Have heard story from other old livers.)

United States. Work Projects Administration

Project # 2570
Mrs. Genevieve W. Chandler,
Murrell's Inlet, S.C.
Georgetown county.

Ex Slave Story.

UNCLE BEN HORRY

Uncle Ben and his wife, aunt Stella, live in their two-room, white-washed cabin that sits sideways to the King's Highway, which Uncle Ben always calls 'the King Road,' near Murell's Inlet, S.C. Paving and straightening this old King's Road, now US 17, has put the two old people in the world. Around the cabin lie the fourteen and three quarter acres that were paid for by Uncle Ben and his father, six or eight acres cleared, the rest woodland. Uncle Ben earns a living by gathering oysters from the Inlet's waters, opening and roasting the oysters for white visitors. Uncle Ben is a great walker. He walks to Conway, the county seat of Horry (Murrell's Inlet is situated on the line between Horry and Georgetown counties), a distance of approximately thirty miles depending on whether one sticks to the paved highway or takes short cuts through the woods, in preference to riding. One day he had walked to Conway and back by eleven o'clock in the morning. Uncle Ben's scrappy conversation will tell how he earns his bread, fears and fights 'the Law', provides for Stella's future, and works for and honors white folks. Brookgreen, which he mentions as the plantation on which he was born and raised, is an open-air museum, donated to South Carolina by A.M. Huntingdon, and visited by thousands of tourists. (See US17, Tour 1).

"I the oldest liver left on Waccamaw Neck that belong to Brookgreen, Prospect, (now Arcadia), Longwood, Alderly Plantations. I been here! I seen things! I tell you. Thousand of them things happen but I try to forget 'em. Looker!" He pointed to what appeared to be primeval forest in front of his battered little porch. "That woods you see been Colonel Josh Ward's taters patch. Right to Brookgreen Plantation where I born. My father Duffine (Divine) Horry and my brother is Richard Horry. Dan'l and Summer two both my uncle. You can put it down they were Colonel Ward's musicianer. Make music for his dater (daughter) and the white folks to dance. Great fiddlers, drummers. Each one could play fiddle, beat drum, blow fife. All three were treat with the same education. You know, when you going to do anything for them big people you got to do it right. Before time (formerly) they danced different. Before strange city people fetched different steps here. But, then, they could use they feet all right!

"My father fore he dead been the head man for old Colonel Josh Ward. Lived to Brookgreen. They say Colonel Ward the biggest rice man been on Waccamaw. He start that big gold rice in the country. He the head rice Cap'n in dem time. My father the head man, he tote the barn key. Rice been money dem day and time. My father love he liquor. That take money. He ain't have money but he have the rice barn key and rice been money! So my father gone in woods (he have a head, my father!), take a old stump, have 'em hollow out. Now he (the stump) same as mortar to the barn yard. And my father keep a pestle hide handy. Hide two pestle! Them pestle make outer heart pine. When that pestle been miss (missed), I wuzn't know nothing! The way I knows my age, when the slavery time war come I been old enough to go in the woods with my father and hold a lightard (lightwood) torch for him to see to pestle off that golden rice he been tote out the barn and hide. That rice he been take to town Sat'd'y when the Colonel and my father go to get provision like sugar, coffee, pepper and salt. With the money he get when he sell that rice, he buy liquor. He been hide that sack o' rice fore day clean (daylight) in the prow of the boat and cover with a thing like an old coat. I members one day when he come back from town he make a miss (step) when he onloading and fell and broke he jug! The Big Boss see; he smell; and he see WHY my father make that miss step; he already sample that liquor! But the Boss ain't say too much. Sat'd'y time come to ration off. Every head on the Plantation to Brookgreen line up at smoke-house to draw he share of meat and rice and grits and meal. (This was fore my father been pint (appointed) head man. This when they had a tight colored man in that place by name Fraser. They say Fraser come straight from Africa). Well, Sat'd'y when time come to give my father he share of rations, the headman reach down in the corner and pull out a piece of that broke whiskey jug and put on top my father rations where all could see! Colonel Ward cause that to be done to broke him off from that whiskey jug. My father was a steady liquor man till then and the Boss broke him off.

"Slavery going in. I members Marse Josh and Miss Bess had come from French Broad (Springs) where they summered it. They brought a great deal of this cloth they call blue drilling to make a suit for every boy big enough to wear a suit of clothes and a pair of shoes for every one. I thought that the happiest 'set up' I had in boyhood. Blue drilling pants and coat and shoe. And Sund'y come we have to go to the Big House for Marse Josh to see how the clothes fit. And him and Miss Bess make us run races to see who run the fastest. That the happiest time I members when I wuz a boy to Brookgreen.

"Two Yankee gun boats come up Waccamaw river! Come by us Plantation. One stop to Sandy Island, Montarena landing. One gone Watsaw (Wachesaw landing). Old Marse Josh and all the white buckra gone to Marlboro county to hide from Yankee. Gon up Waccamaw river and up Pee Dee river, to Marlboro county, in a boat by name Pilot Boy. Take Colonel Ward and all the Cap'n to hide from gun boat till peace declare. I think Pilot Boy been a rear-wheeler. Most boats like the Old Planter been side wheeler.

"They say the Yankee broke in all the rice barn on Sandy Island and share the rice out to colored people. The big mill to Laurel Hill been burn right den. That the biggest rice mill on Waccamaw river. Twuzn't the Yankee burn dem mill. Dese white mens have a idea the Yankee mean to burn dese mill so they set 'em afire before the Yankee come. Nothing left to Laurel Hill today but the rice mill tower. That old brick tower going to BE there. Fire can't harm 'em.

"The worst thing I members was the colored oberseer. He was the one straight from Africa. He the boss over all the mens and womens and if omans don't do all he say, he lay task on 'em they ain't able to do. My mother won't do all he say. When he say, 'You go barn and stay till I come,' she ain't do dem. So he have it in for my mother and lay task on 'em she ain't able for do. Then for punishment my mother is take to the barn and strapped down on thing called the Pony. Hands spread like this and strapped to the floor and all two both she feet been tie like this. And she been give twenty five to fifty lashes till the blood flow. And my father and me stand right there and look and ain't able to lift a hand! Blood on floor in that rice barn when barn tear down by Huntingdon (A.M. Huntingdon). If Marse Josh been know 'bout that obersheer, the oberseer can't do 'em; but just the house servant get Marse Josh' and Miss Bess' ear. Them things different when my father been make the head man. What I tell you happen fore Freedom, when I just can remember.

"Father dead just before my mother. They stayed right to Brookgreen Plantation and dead there after they free. And all they chillun do the same, till the Old Colonel sell the plantation out. Where we going to? Ain't we got house and rations there?

"How many chillun I got? Lemme see. Lemme see how many head of chillun. You, Stella! Help me now! Don't let me tell the Missis wrong. Charles Henry, thirty eight, dere in New York. Ben Horry—I gie' 'em directly!" (Lifting cap and scratching high forehead and gray wool). "Twenty four. I going to give you all I got! All I know about! Bill Horry, that's a boy, he twenty. Dinah, that's a gal, twenty five. Christine, she bout twenty. Mary Horry, I would say fifteen. When the last war come, the last war deputize them boy and take 'em way up North and the gals follow, trail 'em on to New York. That the war when you can't get no sugar and have to put candy in your coffee.

"How old I is?" Slowly and deliberately "December 13th., 1852. Eighty five years or more. When my mother dead to Brookgreen I would say I 'bout thirty three year old.

"After Freedom, from my behavior wid my former owner, I wuz pinted (appointed) head man on Brookgreen Plantation. By that put drop in my hand (getting the drop on others). When kennel been dug out (canal dug) from the Oaks Plantation to Dr. Wardie Flagg house, I wuz pint (appointed) head man. Take that down, Missis. Kennel (canal) cut 1877. Near as I kin, I must task it on the kennel (canal) and turn in every man's work to Big Boss. That kennel (canal) bigger than one Mr. Huntingdon dig right now with machine.

"Missus, slavery time people done something."

Uncle Gabe Lance, born on Sandy Island the first year of the Civil War, a visitor at Uncle Ben's: "Yes sir. All them rice field been nothing but swamp. Slavery people cut kennel (canal) and dig ditch through the raw swamp. All these fields been thick woods. Ditching man task was ten compass."

Uncle Ben continues:

"Storm? Ain't I tell you I BEEN here? Yes, sir. More than one storm I live through! Been through the Flagg storm. Been turn over twice outside there in the sea. One time been have the seine. Been rough. Have weather. And the breakers take the boat. I swim till I get the rope hold. Two men on the shore have the rope end of the seine rope and I hold to that and that how I save THAT time.

"Member another time. Had a boat full of people

this last go 'round. Wuz Miss Mary, he aunty and the lawyer. I take them fishing outside in oshun. Been in the Inlet mouth. Come half way to Drunken Jack Island. Breaker start to lick in the boat! I start to bail! Have a maters (tomatoes) can for bail with. And that been danjus (dangerous); have too much women in there; dey couldn't swim like a man. And it happen by accident, when the boat swamp and full with water, our FEET TOUCH BOTTOM. When he (the boat) turn over, I didn't aim to do no thing but swim for myself. Wasn't able to help nobody. But here out feet touch bottom. Only an accident from God!

"One time again I swamp outside, 'tween Georgetown and Charleston. Try to bail. Swim with one hand, hold boat with the other. Roughest time I ever see 'cause it been cold wedder (weather). Old before-time yawl boat, carry eight oar, four to each side. Young man then; 1877. After the wedder (weather) surrender, we we gone back in dere and find cork going up and down and save us net and all!

"When the Flagg storm been, 1893, I working for Ravanel and Holmes. I was taken up in that storm in a steamer boat. Leave Charleston generally about five in morning. That trip never reach Georgetown till nine that night. Meet a man on that trip got he wife hug to mast in a little kinder life boat. Had he two chillun; rope wrap 'em to that mast. Save man and wife and chillun and gone back and save he trunk. After that they quit call me 'Ben'; they call me 'Rooster'.

"After Flagg storm, Colonel Ward take me and Peter Carr, us two and ah horse, take that shore (follow the ocean shore line) to Little River. Search for all them what been drowned. Find a trunk to Myrtle Beach. Have all kinder thing in 'em; comb for you hair, thing you put on you wrist. Find dead horse, cow, ox, turkey, fowl—everything. Gracious God! Don't want to see no more thing like that! But no dead body find on beach outside Flagg family. Find two of them chillun way down to Dick Pond what drownded to Magnolia Beach; find them in a distance apart from here to that house. Couldn't 'dentify wedder Miss or who. All that family drown out because they wouldn't go to this lady house on higher ground. Wouldn't let none of the rest go. Servant all drown! Betsy, Kit, Mom Adele! Couldn't 'dentify who lost from who save till next morning. Find old Doctor body by he vest stick out of the mud; fetch Doctor body to shore and he watch still aticking. Dr. Wardie Flagg been save hanging to a beach cedar. When that tornado come, my house wash down off he blocks. Didn't broke up.

"Religion! Reckon Stella got the morest of dat. I sometimes a little quick. Stella, she holds one course. I like good song. One I like best?"

> 'Try us, Oh Lord,
> And search the ground
> Of every sinful heart! (Uncle Ben stopped to think).
> What 'eer of sin
> In us be found
> Oh, bid it all depart!'

"Reason I choose that for a favorite hymn, I was to Brookgreen doing some work for Dr. Wardie Flagg and I had to climb as high as that live oak tree, and I fell high as that tree! I lay there till I doze off in sleep. And I tell you what happen to me curious. While I was sleep I seen two milk white chickens. You know what them two white fowl do? They gone and sit on my mother dresser right before the glass and sing that song. Them COULD sing! And it seem like a woman open a vial and pour something on me. My spiritual mother (in dem day every member in the church have what they call a spiritual mother) say, 'That not natural fowl. That sent you for a token.' Since that time I serve the choir five or six years and no song seem strange to me since that day. God ain't ax about you color; God ax about you heart.

"Make my living with the ister (oyster). Before time (formerly) I get seventy five cents a bushel; now I satisfy with fifty cents. Tide going out, I go out in a boat with the tide; tide bring me in with sometimes ten, sometimes fifteen or twenty bushels. I make white folks a roast; white folks come to Uncle Ben from all over the country—Florence, Dillon, Mullins—every kind of place. Same price roast or raw, fifty cents a bushel.

"I bout to quit up with sell. All the lawyer. Turn all my papers over to Mr. Burris. I got too much of paper in that Con-o-way. Court House. Got more paper in there than the house worth! Have to step to Con-o-way all the time. Struggle and starve myself out for these fifteen acres. Thirty miles to Con-o-way. Thirty miles back by the course I travels. All them tricky mens try to go and get old Ben's land sign to 'em. That's the mainest thing take me to Con-o-way every week. They all talk so sugar mouth till my name down; then when my name write is another thing. When I in too much trouble, I just has to step up to Con-o-way and see Mr. Burris. He's a good man.

"They try to mix old Ben up in this whiskey business. It look too brutish to me.

"Missis, I want to tell you all I kin but the old man punish with this bone felom (felon). Worse'n I ever been punish in all my eighty five year. Crab bite 'em and ister (oyster) cut 'em (hand). Woman die and bury Sunday have hand just like this. If you say so, I'll go to doctor. Don't want no blood poison. He (bone felon) did act like he trying to dry up. I tie pea leaf on 'em. Can't put my hand to my head."

The next day Uncle Ben was found with the doctor's white bandage very muddy. Uncle Ben had gotten out of bed to go get oysters and even the bone felon did not stop him. Uncle Ben is still hale and hearty, having triumphed over the bone felon, and is one of the noted characters of that region.

Project #-1655
Mrs. Genevieve W. Chandler
Murrells Inlet, S.C.
Georgetown County

FOLKLORE

UNCLE BEN HORRY (REB'S TIME NIGGER—OVER 80)
(UNCLE BEN AND VISITORS)

BEN HORRY

Uncle Ben: (To white children) "Go on see if you can find one or two plum on duh tree. I been want to go to town wid you—dat all right daughter. (He pronounces it Dater—long Italian 'A') Chillun, ain't find duh plum, enty? Dem Sandy Island people come and clean the tree. Too sorry wonneh ain't get them plum!

"Stella gone in creek fishing. Him and Lula gone—Lula McCoy. You say me?" (To neighbor walking up) "Four men been here load they car up wid hand. How come you ain't gone to the bacco?" (To work in the tobacco fields in truck sent to find hands)

Pauline Pyatt: "If they ain't pay my price, I ain't going leave home. I ain't gone for 75¢ a day. Feenie Deas gone yestiddy."

Uncle Ben: "Near bout blind. Couldn't see out no eye nor nare (neither) one o' my eye. Doctor put sumptin in 'em do me too much o' good. How I is? Fall out? Deth come I fix! Don't know bout you!"

Pauline: "I fix!"

Mary Gary: "You fix, Uncle Ben?"

Uncle Ben: "I gwine fix!"

Pauline: "You ain't fix?"

Uncle Ben: "I fix all right! I going fudder dan duh grave!"

Pauline: "I been Tarbox." (To Mr. Tarbox)

Uncle Ben: "Down by Gallie?" (Gallie's house)

Pauline: "I ain't see nobody. What you see?"

Uncle Ben: "Ain't see nobody tall—tall—."

Pauline: "Alice! I see Alice!"

Uncle Ben: "Ain't see nobody else?"

Pauline: "Nobody else!"

Uncle Ben: "Nobody else?"

Pauline: "Nobody else. She by herself!"

Uncle Ben Reminisces

"Fore freedom? Fore freedom? Well now, fore freedom we were treated by our former owners I will say good—cording to situation of time. Every year when Massa and Missus gone mountains, they call up obersheer (overseer) and say, 'Don't treat them anyway severe.

Don't beat them. Don't maul them.' (Mr. Heminingway been severe.)

"Anybody steal rice and they beat them, Miss Bessie cry and say, 'Let 'em have rice! My rice—my nigger!'

"Brookgreen and Springfield every Sunday morning, every gal and the young one must dress up and go to the yard and Miss Bessis give 'em candy. Don't want too much o' beating. Glad to see young women dance. But some cruel to the colored. Some on 'Prospect,'—'Hermitage'—and 'Woodland' treat all right.

"I know the Yankee boat come to Inlet and went to Oaks sea-shore with load of cotton. Band of our sojer gone—(Rebs—'OUR sojer!), and Yankee sojer come off in a yawl boat and our sojer caught two of them men and they hang that man to Oaks sea-shore. And when the Yankee find out—do my Lord! A stir been! A stir here! Shell clean to Sandy Island! Knock hole through the sick-house (at Brookgreen!) Pump! Well, ain't it? Brick work pump. Well. Handle. You turn! Turn. One bucket gone up; one gone down. Ward take care of his nigger, sho! Best man own slave! Ward and Ploughdon sho treat they nigger right! Live 'Laurel Hill.'

"Ward had on Prospect and Brookgreen. You know what I see? Right there to Oaks sea-sho after them people done that murdering with that man? Take all the slave, get on flat and gone out way of shell. Gone sand hole. Take all the people from Brookgreen and Springfield—and carry dem to Marlboro. Boat tow flat. Carmichael came through and established the freedom through here. They come back from Marlboro where they refugee to and Maham Ward come back on the flat. And this Ward, share out the rice—broke open barn. We people? Anything like a silver, bury right there in that garden! Right to Brookgreen garden, what Hontington got now. All Ward thing bury there. Them old time people kill you—you meddle them thing. Cry out, 'Massa Ting!' You better let 'em stay there!

"After Freedom Miss Bessie gone to she house in Charston—Rutledge Street Charston. And you could see way out in ocean.

"My fadder—him and Uncle Dan'l and Uncle Summer uster been fiddler. Gone all round when the white people gone to Prospect to ball and sich as that. Dem white people didn't treat you so brutish! Dem obersheer!" (Aside) "Wonder Christ sake why Lula stay out that creek so long!"

Pauline: "Fine season for corn!"

Ben: "Sho is!"

(Uncle Ben keeps a little grocery and fruit for sell. Customer comes)

"Missus, Take twenty cent out a dollar."

Pauline: "My grand-mother in that storm. They leave that Thursday. I been to Oaks. When Flagg storm wuz. Richmond come off Magnolia beach to Oaks Plantation and get the washing—the missus clean clothes. Had to swim the horse off the beach to get the clothes. I been on the beach Thursday—and cousin Joshuaway. Pony Myers daughter born in Brookgreen street day of storm. Pony Myers wife name Adele. Marse Arthur had one little twin. Joshua Stuart and Ben find dem to the end of Myrtle

Beach. Arthur twin baby—bout that high—little walking chillun. Look how curious thing is! Them two chillun drown and find to the foot of Myrtle Beach! (fifteen or twenty miles north). Find Tom Duncan mother. Find Francis mother—Francis Gadsden. Doctor Ward pa—find him by duh vest. Vest sticking out duh mud. Watch going. My grand-mother was keep a walking from door to door.

"Find a mer-maid and kept to Magnolia." (Pauline said, 'mere-maid') "Doctor Ward and dem shut 'em up a month. Mer-maid. Had a storm ball. Keep a turning round. Keep a telling him (Dr. Arthur) storm coming. He wouldn't b'lieve 'em. (Barometer—called by Uncle Isaac's wife, gatekeeper at Brookgreen, chronometer.) He wouldn't b'lieve. And a cussing man! All the time cuss! Mere-maid got a forked tail just like shark. From here down (illustrating by pantomine) all blue scale like a cat-fish. Pretty people! Pretty a white woman as you ever lay your eye on."

Ben: "Pretty, enty?"

Pauline: "Dem stay in sea. Dey walk—slide long on tail." (twisting from her waist to illustrate.) Pretty. From they waist down to tail blue scale. You got a bathing house on beach. Leave bread in there. They sho eat bread.

"Marse Allard say top of the barn fly off. Cat jump and on it! And horse too. And he jump too and tide bring 'em to Brookgreen.

"Joshuaway Stuart been plantation carpenter. He made one box for the twin what drown and Colonel Mortimer bring one from Georgetown."

(Aunt Stella and Lula arriving from fishing trip)

"What ketch?"

Lula: "Get some catty!" (cat-fish) "Mary, you dress down!"

Mary: "I gwine ketch me a fellow! (Looking in bucket) Gosh! Did got a good mess!"

Lula: "Little fellow."

Mary: "Rather eat them than large one."

Pauline: "What yinnah nuse for bait?"

Lula: "Swimp."

Pauline: "How you catch 'em?"

Lula: "Take a crocus and dip 'em up."

Pauline: "I gwine try to-morrow."

Lula: "To-morrow been Sundy! How old I is? Have to put a guess on 'em. Bout fifty I guess. Flagg storm? That big one? When the storm wuz, I wuz seven year old."

(Discuss Reb time and Flagg storm.)

Pauline: "Yes. Wind bring young Allard in to Uncle Joshuaway Stuart field right down there where Cindy Poinsett now. Joshuaway been Cindy Pa.

"Doctor Ward shut that mere-maid up. He been in that! When that storm wuz, he wuzn't old. I go there now and talk bout that storm and he eye get full o' water. Looker his Papa clothes. Got 'em all pack in trunk. I never shee 'um court myself. Every time I shee 'um with a crowd o' man.

"Long as he have mere-maid shut up, it rain! People gone there to look at 'em. Long as keep 'em shut up it rain. That time rain thirty days. That just fore Flagg storm." (Looking toward creek) "Yonder Stella, wonneh, now!"

(Uncle Ben gave each white child a little cake—then gave, from his hand, hunks of corn bread to each colored woman.)

Conversation taken down on Uncle Ben Horry's porch where he sat awaiting the return of Aunt Stella who had gone 'in the creek' to 'catch a mess o' fish.' Murrells Inlet, S.C. June 15, 1937.

United States. Work Projects Administration

Project 1655
Genevieve W. Chandler
Georgetown County, S.C.

FOLKLORE

(VERBATIM)
MISS GEORGIE AT WOODLAND
EX-SLAVE STORY

UNCLE BEN HORRY

"He was a full-blooded man—the Cap'n. Didn't disgrace. He put goat on Goat Island. Money was bury to Goat Island. People after people been sent. I dinnah know wedder they find or no.

"Mack McCosky was sent by the State to fetch molasses, meal and hominy and goat on Goat Island. He can't tell you! People can't know sumpin when they ain't born!

"After de war 'e come back and take into big drinkin' and was 'em (waste them) till 'e fall tru. He been fell tru wid his money (lost his property). Didn't bury so destent (decent).

"We smaller one didn't have chance to go to war. My Daddy have for go. Have to go ditch and all and tend his subshun. His subshun was waste and steal. Paris! He the man control all the Buckra ting. And, by God, he go and show Yankee all dem ting! Ole Miss git order to have him kill and don't harm none! She ain't one to see him tru all that thousand head o' nigger for get 'em.

"They come have big dinner. Cap'n come from Muldro. (Marlboro). Drum beatin' little one dancin'. Gone back to Muldro. (Maham Ward and these udder come from Muldro.) And they leave ting in Uncle William Gaillard hand. And he carry on till everting surrender. And then the Cap'n come home from Muldro and they try give you sumpin to make start on like cow and ting. They ain't treat you like a beast. Ain't take no advance o' you. What the Cap'n do he do for you good. I b'long Dr. Ward. I entitle to bring him two string o' bird. Rice bird come like jest as tick as dat (thick as that) Sometimes a bushel one shot.

"They put you in the flat and put you over there. When they tink Yankee comin' you take to Sandhole Crick for hide. Mr. Carmichael sent by the state. Go to Brookgreen, Longwood, Watsaw. Tell everting surrender. Go to any located place. He's a Gineral. Go open the barn door and give us all us need. He better to we nigger boy dan he Daddy been! Wouldn't beat you 'thout the lil' boy really fightin'.

"Time o' the war the colored people hear 'bout Yankee. Not a one eber understand to run way and go to Yankee boat from WE plantation. These Yankee people wuz walkin' 'bout on the beach. And while they come in to the hill, the Reb have a battery to Laurel Hill and they cut off them Yankee from the ocean. These they cut off they carry dem to Brookgreen barn. Hang one colored man and one white man to Oaks Seashore. White man musser be Sergeant or big Cap'n. Just as soon as the sun go down you see a big streak come over and they BUSS (bust) Duds. Woman in the street killed. (Street of negro Quarters—Brookgreen) Blacksmith killed. Cut off he brudder-in-law (Judy's) and kill Judy. Dem shell go clean to Sandy Island. Pump make out o' brick to Brookgreen. Dat boy (shell) come and hit the pump. De horn blow and they make for flat and gwine on to Sandhole down that black crick. There a man for dat—dat flat. Get everbody line up. Ain't gone there for PLAY. Gone for wuk (work). I was big 'nouf to do diss—go wid my fadder and hold light.

"It this way. You ain't LOW to eat the whole rice you kin make money outer. Beat dat rice. But my Daddy been a great whiskey man. Liquor. Didn't have 'em less he go to town. Money scase. ('E wuz a kind of musicianer for the Ward fambly). But he break he jug. He break he whiskey jug. En when de obersheer (overseer) git out de ration and gib'em to mah Ma and us chillun he hand mah Pa a piece o' dem break jug! That keep him in mind o' that whiskey jug.

"Yankee come here and butt us colored people. I 'member we youngun's just could 'tote up dem gold pitcher and bury dem in the garden. Not far from the flowers tank. Tank have on 'em a woman head (Flowers' tank was a fountain). All the master fine ting way down there bury! De Ward didn't loss nothin'. They move us out the plantation. Col. Ward took 'em in a flat to Mulbro.

"Dr. Heriot after the war took into big drinkin'. Didn't bury so decent. Fell tru wid all he money. Not bury so decent."

Source: Told by Uncle Ben Horry, Age 88, April 1938,

United States. Work Projects Administration

Murrells Inlet, S.C.

Project #1655
Everett R. Pierce
Columbia, S.C.

INTERVIEW WITH EX-SLAVE
MARGARET HUGHES, 82 YEARS.

MARGARET HUGHES

"Missy, I likes to talk to de white folks, I gits awful lonesome for my massa and missus, and de white folks I used to be wid. Yes'm, I was born out here 'bout ten miles from Columbia, at a little place called Nipper Hill. My massa was named Daniel Finley, and my missus was named Elizabeth, but we called her Missy Betsy. My massa had a big plantation and a heap of slaves; he had so many he couldn't keep us faces in his mind. One day he see some of us over on another plantation, and he ask us who we b'long to, and we tell him, and he just smile and say he couldn't 'member all of us. De massa and de missus was so good to us 'til de slaves on other plantations was jealous; they call us free niggers befo' we was freed.

The grown-up slaves had to work in de field all day and then at night they spin cloth and make their clothes. We had one shoemaker what didn't do nothing else much 'cept make shoes for all of us. I was too young to do much work, so the missus mostly keep me in de house to nurse de chillun. When de chillun go to school, she make me go 'long wid them for to look after them and tote their books. I stayed wid them all day and brought their books home in de evening.

I got in trouble one day while I was at de school house; I was a right bad little gal, anyway. I got mad wid one of de little white chillun 'cause she talk mean to Sissy, dat's one of my missus little girls, and I took her books and put them in a bucket of water. The teacher punish me, and told my missus I couldn't come back to de school house, 'less she teach me how to behave more better. I was right good after that, 'cause I was scared of whippings. My missus had three chillun: Mary, we call her Sissy 'cause she de oldest, then Sally and Willie. I slept in de big house and play wid de white chillun. When de white folks went off in de carriage they always let me go too; I set up in de seat wid de driver. They had awful pretty horses to drive.

Massa Daniel had a overseer, named Jake Graddick. He kept de slaves at work and looked after de crops. He woke de slaves every morning by blowing a big cow horn, and called them to dinner the same way. We went to work at sunrise, had two hours for dinner, and stopped work at sundown.

The slaves had plenty to eat, and had their own gardens. I helped work de gardens. My old daddy worked in de garden and made chairs for de slaves, besides working in de fields.

My massa never whip de slaves very much, but he do sometime. Once I saw my poor old daddy in chains. They chained his feet together, and his hands too, and carry him off to whip him, 'cause he wouldn't tell who stole a trunk that was missing. He couldn't tell though, 'cause he didn't know, but they thought he did.

No ma'am missy, us slaves never had no church to go to. We was allowed to go to de white folks' church though. There was a low partition in de church wid a little gate in it; we set on one side of it, and de white folks on de other. We listen to de preaching and sung de songs right 'long wid de white folks. Us never had no baptizings though. I learned a heap of things in Sunday School.

Talking 'bout patrollers, I was awful scared of them. We had to have a pass from our massa to go from one plantation to another, and if we went without a pad the patrollers would ketch us and whip us. I never did get ketched though. De only time de massa ever let us ride de horses was when he want us to carry a message from one plantation to another.

Yes ma'am, 'bout these weddings you asked me 'bout; well, we had a big time when any of de slaves got married. De massa and de missus let them get married in de big house, and then we had a big dance at one of de slave house. De white folks furnish all kinds of good things to eat, and de colored peoples furnish de music for de dance. My mammy's brother been one of de best fiddlers there was; he teach de other niggers how to play.

The best times we had was 'long in summer time, 'tending them Camp Meetings. We had good men to preach de service, and then all of us women got together and spread a big picnic dinner, that we'd brought from home in baskets, and we sure had a good time. Sometime some of them eat so much they get sick. We ain't had so much sickness 'long them times though, not like we do now. Us used to wear garlic and asafetida 'round our neck to keep off diseases; never had many neither. We was vaccinated to keep from ketching smallpox.

Well little missy, I done told you just 'bout all I 'members 'cept 'bout de Yankees. When I used to hear de older niggers talking 'bout de Yankees coming, I was scared, 'cause I thought it was some kind of animal they was talking 'bout. My old aunty was glad to hear 'bout de Yankees coming. She just set and talk 'bout what a good time we was going to have after de Yankees come. She'd say; 'Child we going to have such a good time a settin' at de white folks table, a eating off de white folks table, and a rocking in de big rocking chair.'

Something awful happen to one of de slaves though, when de Yankees did come. One of de young gals tell de Yankees where de missus had her silver, money and jewelry hid, and they got it all. What you think happened to de poor gal? She'd done wrong I know, but I hated to see her suffer so awful for it. After de Yankees had gone, de missus and massa had de poor gal hung 'til she die. It was something awful to see. De Yankees took everything we had 'cept a little food, hardly 'nough to keep us alive.

When de slaves were freed de most of them didn't had nowhere to go, so we just stayed on wid de massa and missus and they was good to us as long as we stayed wid them. I wishes sometime I was a slave again, 'cause I likes being a slave, didn't have nothing to worry 'bout then."

Home address
3105 Asylum Road.

Code No.
Project, 1885-(1)
Prepared by Annie Ruth Davis
Place, Marion, S.C.
Date, May 18, 1937

No. _____
Reduced from _____ words
Rewritten by

_____

MOM HESTER HUNTER
Ex-Slave, 85 years.

HESTER HUNTER

"Well, bless ye little heart, honey, ye say ye is wan' me to tell ye 'bout how de people lived way back dere in slavery time. Honey, I dunno wha' to tell ye cause I ain' never been treated no ways but good in me life by my Missus. I tell dese chillun here dat dey ain' never see no sech time uz dere been den. My Missus been marry Massa John Bethea en dey is raise dey flock up dere to de crossroads next Latta. Dat whey I been raise. Honey, my Missus see to it she self dat we look a'ter in de right way. Ain' never been made to do no work much den. Jes played dere in de back yard wid me dolls aw de time I wanna. Honey, I dunno nuthin to tell ye cause I is lib lak uh lamb in dem days."

"I wus born on de 25th uv December, right on de big Chrissmus day, dere on Massa John plantation en I was 14 year old when freedom declare. I is 85 year old now en, honey, me health jes uz good now uz ever it wuz. My Missus take sech good care uv us aw de time en see a'ter us she self when we sick en I is take sech good care uv me self a'ter I leab dere dat I 'spect to be here long time from now. Ain' know no ailment tall. Coase de rheumatism is worry me right smart on uh night. Honey, dis rheumatism ain' been cause from no bad teeth. I is hab eve'y tooth in me head wha' I hab when I wuz 7 year old en dey jes uz good uz dey was den. It jes dis way, jes uz long uz I is workin', I feels mighty smart, mighty smart, child!"

"I 'clare to goodness white folks come down here jes to hear me talk. Honey, I is wish I could stay wid yunnah aw de day. I could tell yunnah aw 'bout dem days cause I ain' know nuthin but big living den. I tell me grandchillun dat dem times 'ud be uh show for dem now. My Massa had uh big plantation, honey, uh big plantation! Right in de center wuz me Missus house en den dere wuz two long row uv we house to de right dere on de place close to de big house. I 'members when de plantation hand wha' work in de field been come to de house in de middle uv de day to ge' dey dinner, I been lub to stand 'round de big pot en watch em when dey ge' dey sumptin to eat. Yas'um, dey is cook aw de food for de field hand in de same big ole black pot out in de yard. Yas'um, dey is put aw de victual in one pot. Dey'ud go to de smokehouse en cut off uh whole half uh side uv bacon en drap it right in dat pot. Dat been flavor de pot jes right cause in dem days, us ration been season wid meat. Honey, dere 'ud be 'bout thirty uv dem hand wha' had to eat out dat pot. Dere been uh shelter built over de pot to keep de rain out en den dere was uh big scaffold aw 'round de pot whey de put de pans when dey dish de victual up. De field hands 'ud come dere en ge' dey pan uv ration offen dis scaffold."

"Now de chillun on de plantation ain' been 'low to eat outer dat pot wid de field hand. My auntie cook us victuals right dere in de kitchen on de Missus fireplace an we eat right dere outer us own separate pan. My Missus see she self dat we been fed right en she see dat de food been cook done, cook done, honey, en been seasoned right aw de time. My Missus ain' never stand fa me to go widout me meat fa break'ast. Al'ays had hominy en milk en meat fa me break'ast en when supper time come, dey is al'ays gi'e us uh big bowl uv corn bread en milk. Folks ain' eat den lak dey does nowadays. Dey been eat more meat den en it ain' hu't dem lak it hu'ts em now. Honey, peoples ain' lib peaceful lak dey been lib den. Den peoples ain' cook dey food done lak de food been cook den. My auntie cook aw de bread right dere in de kitchen on de fireplace. I is hab some uv dem spider right here in de yard now. (She showed us two iron spiders about 8 inches deep with three legs. One was being used in the yard as a drinking place for the chickens and the other was carelessly thrown just under the edge of her house.) When I come 'way from my Missus plantation, I been take care uv wha' I bring 'way wid me. Dere uh ole loom dere in de house right now. I 'members how I use 'er lub to lie down on de Missus floor under de loom en watch my auntie when she wuz spinning dere."

"Dey'ud hab gray sheep en white sheep den en dey'ud make sech nice cloth. Yas'um, dey'ud dye de cloth right dere on de plantation. I 'member aw 'bout dat. De Missus hab uh big patch uv indigo dat dey growed right dere en dey'ud gather it en boil it in de pot en den dey'ud take de cloth dat my auntie is help weave an put it in dat pot en dye it jes uz pretty. My Missus see to it she self dat de plantation peoples clothes been make right en dat we is hab nice clean place to sleep. De Missus never 'low none uv us to lay down in rags. She see 'bout aw dis she self. I know my Missus gone to Hebbun, honey, en I hope she restin' dere."

Source: Mom Hester Hunter, age 85, colored. (Personal interview, Marion, S.C., May 1937.)

Code No.
Project, 1885-(1)
Prepared by Annie Ruth Davis
Place, Marion, S.C.
Date, October 15, 1937

No. _____
Reduced from _____ words
Rewritten by

MOM HESTER HUNTER
Ex-Slave, 85 Years

MOM HESTER HUNTER

"Yes, mam, I remember all bout slavery time just as good as I know you dis mornin. Remember de first time dem Yankees come dere, I was settin down in de chimney corner en my mammy was givin me my breakfast. Remember I been settin dere wid my milk en my bowl of hominy en I hear my old grandmammy come a runnin in from out de yard en say all de sky was blue as indigo wid de Yankees comin right dere over de hill den. Say she see more Yankees den could ever cover up all de premises bout dere. Den I hear my Missus scream en come a runnin wid a lapful of silver en tell my grandmammy to hurry en sew dat up in de feather bed cause dem Yankees was mighty apt to destroy all dey valuables. Old Missus tell all de colored people to get away, get away en take care of demselves en tell we chillun to get back to de chimney corner cause she couldn' protect us noways no longer. Yes, honey, I was a little child settin dere in dat chimney corner listenin to all dat scamperin bout en I remember dat day just as good as it had been dis day right here."

"Oh, my God, dem Yankees never bring nothin but trouble en destructiveness when dey come here, child. I remember I hear tell dat my old stepfather been gone to de mill to grind some corn en when he was comin down de road, two big Yankees jump out de bushes side de road en tell him stop dere. He say dey tell him if he want to save his neck, he better get off dat ox right den en get away from dere. He say he been so scared he make for de woods fast as he could get dere en tell dat he lay down wid knots under his head many a night fore he would venture to come out from dat woods. Never hear tell of his ox en corn no more neither. Oh, honey, my old Missus was a dear old soul en didn' none of her colored people have no mind to want to leave dere no time."

"We chillun never didn' know nothin bout no hard times in dat day en time. Seems like de Lord had just open up en fix de way for us to have everything we want. Oh, honey, we chillun never been harness up in no little bit of place to play like dese chillun bout here dese days. We had all de big fields en de pretty woods to wander round en bout en make us playhouse in. Seems like de Lord had made de little streams just right for we chillun to play in en all kind of de prettiest flowers to come up right down side de paths us little feet had made dere, but dat wasn' nothin. Dere was flowers scatter bout everywhe' you look in de woods en all kind of birds en squirrels en rabbits en honey, dey was live play things. Dat how-come we been so satisfy. I here to tell you my old Missus was a dear old soul en we chillun sho had a fine time comin up. She didn' never have her niggers cut up en slashed up no time. She was good to us en we stuck to her."

"In de mornin bout dis time, me en my Missus would take a walk in de woods down by de creek. I remember I would be dere wid my mammy en old Missus would say, 'Judy, whe' Hester? I want her to take a walk wid me dis mornin.' I been bout five or six years old den en I would get tired. I say, 'Mittie, I tired, I tired.' She say, 'Well, set down en rest awhile.' I remember dere been a big old sweet gum tree settin dere side de creek dat had a place hollow out in it dat looked just like a chair been made dere. Old Missus would set down dere en take me right down side her en stay dere till we was rested. I go wid her one day when de creek been rise way up high en dere been a heap of water in de road. I say, 'Mittie, I scared, I scared.' She tell me dere couldn' nothin hurt me en I remember we went on en see a big black fish just a jumpin in de road. Old Missus say, 'Hester, catch him, catch him.' I say, 'Mittie, I can', I can', I scared.' I recollects she caught dat fish en tied it wid her garter en let me drag it home en tell my mammy cook it for my supper. Honey, dat been a day. Never couldn' forget bout dat."

"I remember me en my old Missus went to de graveyard one mornin en we found a runaway nigger hidin in a house dat was standin in de graveyard. Dat was an old, old slavery time house to de graveyard en people would go dere en hide. It was just like dis, honey, generally people in de country be scared of a graveyard en wouldn' nobody go dere to hunt dem. I remember just as good when he see us, he squatted down right low. I say, 'Mittie, looka, looka, I scared.' Den she say, 'Hester, I notice de clouds are growin more en more gray en I fear we better be gettin back home. I never like for a rain to catch us away from home.' I know Missus say dat to make me think she wasn' scared, but I never had no mind to tell her I know what been de matter dat she want to hurry home. Yes'um, dat old house in de graveyard was one of dem kind dat been settin high off de ground. Dat de kind of house dey cook underneath in slavery time. Cose it was closed up when dey had de kitchen down dere. No, mam, Massa never didn' go to walk wid old Missus. He was seein over all de plantation en Missus didn have but one son, little John O. Bethea, en he was gone off to school. No, child, old Missus wouldn' never allow nobody to go wid her but just me."

"You see, it was like dis, my old Missus been name Sara Davis fore she marry Massa John Bethea en my mammy en grandmammy had come up wid her in de country en dat how-come dere been such a feelin twixt dem. Yes, mam, I love my old Missus better den I ever love honey en flour bread cause she was a dear old soul. You see, she was always lookin to me to do somethin for her. Say I was her favorite child to pick up things bout de house en yard for her. She always had my mammy preserve me en Bob as her favorite house chillun. She wouldn' never allow none of dem other nigger chillun to come nowhe' round whe' she was cause dem what went bout de Missus never didn' stay to de nigger quarter no time. My grandmammy, she had to get all dem other plantation chillun together en see dat dey do what de Missus look for dem to do."

"My God, child, people never know nothin but to go to church on de big Sunday in dat day en time. No, mam, dey know dat been dey Massa rule en didn' nobody have no mind to question nothin bout it. My old Missus was a dear old soul en she would see to it dat all her niggers wash en iron en cook on Saturday cause she never allow no work gwine on round whe' she was when Sunday come, be dat she know bout it. I remember my old Massa en Missus used to ride to church in dey big black carriage en dey always would carry me en Bob right dere in de carriage wid dem somehow another. Stuff us down 'tween de seats somewhe'. I recollects just as bright as de stars be shinin old Missus would carry me en Bob to de same little seats we been sit in every Sunday en den she en old Massa would go to dey certain pew in de front part of de church. Oh, honey, dat was a day for dem niggers to walk de road to church. Dat was a picnic for dem. Oh, dey never had to walk but bout four miles. Why, darlin, I used to walk fourteen miles to church every Sunday en didn' think nothin bout it. I think dat was de finest thing I know for me en my grandfather to walk 14 miles to church over dere on de hill every Sunday. I remember we would set out bout time de sun would be risin. Yes, mam, we would carry our dinner wid us cause we know we would be till night gettin back home again. It just like I been tell you, de peoples sho cook dey dinner for Sunday on Saturday in dat day en time. Dat been a mighty good thing, child, been a mighty good thing. Honey, it been de rule to follow what de Bible say do in dat day en time en now it seem like de rule must be, do like you see de other fellow is doin. Yes, mam, if you ain' been to church in dat day en time, you sho had to report how-come you ain' been dere."

"I tell you, child, I been here. If I live to see de Christmas day, I'll be past 85 years old. I ain' been up town in God knows when en I wants to go so bad back to see my white folks. Dem Evans chillun, dey comes to see me often. Dat child had took dat trip round de world en she come right back en tell me all bout it. Well, bless my heart, she done gone en get married last Sunday en I never know bout it. She tell me she was gwine marry one of dese days, but I never know. I hope dat man will take care of her en be good to my baby. I hope her older days won' be her worser days."

"Yes, mam, I remember just as good as it was yesterday what dey say when freedom come here. Oh, I hates to think bout dat day till dis one. Remember dey call all de niggers up to de yard en I hear old Missus say, 'You don' no more belong to me. You can go if you want to en if you want to, you can stay.' I say, 'Yes, mam, I do want to stay, I ain' gwine leave you.' Dat was my white mammy en I stay dere long as she live too. Didn' want no better livin den I was gettin right dere. It been a Paradise, be dat what I calls it."

Source: Hester Hunter, ex-slave, 85 years, Marion, S.C. Personal interview by Annie Ruth Davis, Oct., 1937.

Code No.
Project, 1885-(1)
Prepared by Annie Ruth Davis
Place, Marion, S.C.
Date, October 26, 1937

No. _____
Reduced from _____ words
Rewritten by

───────────

MOM HESTER HUNTER
Ex-Slave, 85 Years

HESTER HUNTER

"Bless my soul, honey, I tell you I been here a time. Been here a day. I tell dese chillun here de other week dere ain' no need for me to be frettin bout nothin no more cause my time bout out. I got my ducks en my chickens en my chair right dere in de yard en I stays out dere wid dem all de day till sundown. You see, I have such a hurtin in my back en such a drawin in my knees en seems like de sun does just help me along to bear de pain, but honey, I been walkin a long time. I remember I been a little child in de bed listenin on en I hear my aunt come in one day en say, 'Ma, I hear boss talkin bout dey gwine free de niggers.' Ma say, 'I don' have no mind for nothin like dat. I gwine be gone en you gwine be gone too fore den.' Child, I sho been here a time. Remember dey been four years buildin dem embankments en dey been four years fightin. Yes, mam, I been through a day since I come here."

"Honey, I was a hustlier when I was a young woman en dat de reason my chillun had such good schoolin. If it had been left to my husband, dey wouldn' been know A from B. I think bout how my old Massa used to try to learn me to spell en dat how-come I had such a feelin for my chillun to get some learnin. My daughter, she taught 20 years in dat school right over dere en when she see dat I wasn' able to carry on no longer, she throwed up her hands one day en say she wasn' gwine teach school no more. Tell Bill en dem chillun dat she was gwine stay here home en keep me from fallin in de pots. Den she put out de word dat she would do a washin for dis one en a washin for dat one en honey, I see her dere washin so hard sometimes, I have a feelin dat I would rather she be out en gone from here. Seems like it does hurt me so to see her wastin away like dat after I been worry so to give her such a good school learnin."

"I tell you when I come up, it de Lord's truth, I ain' know nothin but a decent livin all de time. My old Missus was a dear old soul en I been raise dat way. I hear talk bout how some of de white folks would bout torture dey niggers to death sometimes, but never didn' see my white folks allow nothin like dat. Dey would whip dey niggers dat runaway en stay in de woods, but not so worser. No, mam, my Missus wouldn' allow no slashin round bout whe' she was. I remember my boss had one of my old Missus niggers up dere in de yard one mornin en say he was gwine whip him en my Missus say, 'John O., you let my nigger alone.' You see, my Missus had her niggers en den old Boss had his niggers cause when old Missus been marry Massa John O. Bethea, she had brought here share of niggers from whe' she was raise in de country. It been like dis, old Missus father had scratch de pen for everyone of his chillun to have so many niggers apiece for dey portion of his property so long as dey would look after dem en treat dem good. Den if dere been talk dat dem chillun never do what he say do, dey was to take dem niggers right back to dey old Massa home. But, child, dey never didn' take no niggers away from my old Missus cause she sho took care of dem. Stuck to her niggers till she died."

"I remember just as good dere been two long row of nigger house up in de quarter en de Bethea niggers been stay in de row on one side en de Davis niggers been stay in de row on de other side. En, honey, dere been so much difference in de row on dis side en de row on dat side. My God, child, you could go through dere en spot de Sara Davis niggers from de Bethea niggers time you see dem. Won' no trouble no time. All old Missus niggers had dey bresh (brush) pile side dey house to sun dey beds on en dry dey washin cause my Missus would see to it herself dat dey never kept no nasty livin. We was raise decent, honey, en dat how-come me en my chillun is dat way to dis very day. Dere dat child in de house now, she does put fresh sheet on all us bed every week just like dey was white people bed. You see, if you raise dat way, you ain' gwine never be no ther way. Yes, mam, my old Missus sho took time to learn her niggers right. Honey, both dese hands here was raise not to steal. I been cook for heap of dese white folks bout here dat been left everything right wide open wid me en ain' nobody never hear none of dem complain bout losin nothin to dis day. No, mam, ain' nobody never didn' turn no key on me. I remember, if my old Missus would hear talk dat we been bother somethin dat didn' belong to us, she would whip us en say, 'I'm not mad, but you chillun have got to grow up some day en you might have to suffer worse den dis if you don' learn better while you young."

"Yes, mam, dat been a day. Dem niggers what been bred on Massa John C. Bethea's plantation never know nothin but big livin in dat day en time. Remember all bout dem days. Recollect dat dey would give all dey colored people so much of flour for dey Sunday eatin en den dey had a certain woman on de place to cook all de other ration for de niggers in one big pot out in old Massa's yard. All de niggers would go dere to de pot on Sunday en get dey eatin like turnips en collards en meat en carry it to dey house en make dey own bread. Den in de week time, dey would come out de field at 12 o'clock en stand round de pot en eat dey pan of ration en den dey would go back in de field en work. When dey would come home at night, dere would be enough cook up for dem to carry home to last till de next day dinner. Didn' eat no breakfast no time. Had meat en greens en corn bread en dumplings to eat mostly en won' no end to milk. Got plenty of dat en dey was sho glad to get it. Cose dem what been stay to de white folks house would eat to de Missus kitchen. En, my Lord, child, my white folks had de prettiest kind of rice dat dey made right dere on dey own plantation. Had plenty rice to last dem from one year to de other just like dey had dey hominy. Den old Massa had a big fish pond en in de summer time when it would get too hot to work, he would allow all his plantation niggers to catch all de pikes en jacks dey wanted en salt dem down in barrels for de winter. Didn' allow nobody to go nowhe' bout dat fish pond but us niggers. En another thing, dey wouldn' cure dey meat wid nothin but dis here green hickory wood en I speak bout what I been know, dere ain' never been nothin could touch de taste of dem hams en shoulder meat. Oo—oo—oo, honey, dey would make de finest kind of sausages in dem days. I tell my chillun I just bout turn against dese sausage de people make bout here dese days."

"Yes, mam, I been hearin bout dat thing call conjurin all my days, ever since I been in dis world, but I ain' never put no faith in nothin like dat. I say, I don' want no hand but what God give me. I remember I got de sore eyes one time en a woman come to me en say, 'Miss Hester, dere a woman in dis town poison you.' Tell me dey put somethin on de rag I had wipe my eyes wid. I tell her she was wastin her speech cause I know I never had nothin to worry bout. It de blessed truth I'm tellin you, dere some of dese people right bout here now got dese transfer driver gwine down in de country to get people to do somethin for dem all de time. Honey, if some people in dis town had dis rheumatism I got, dey would swear somebody do somethin to dem. Oh, my God, dere so much devilment gwine on in de world dese days. I sho has faith in God en I reckon dat how-come I gets along so good."

"Oh, de people, dey is awful worser den what dey used to be. I know by my comin on dat dey awful worser. De little tots bout here dese days know things de older people used to be de only ones dat know bout. Yes, mam, I sets down en prays when others sleep en I say, 'Lord, what gwine happen? Look like de young people on de straight road to hell gettin in so much devilment. When I was comin up, I didn' have nothin to grieve over, but seem like dere somethin all de time dese days. I does worry bout it so much sometimes, child, I goes along just a whistlin, 'Lord, I wish I had went fore I had so much to grieve over.'

United States. Work Projects Administration

Source: Hester Hunter, age 85, Marion, S.C.
Personal interview by Annie Ruth Davis, October, 1937.

Slave Narratives

www.ingramcontent.com/pod-product-compliance
Lightning Source LLC
Chambersburg PA
CBHW071646160426
43195CB00012B/1373